SHAMANISM AND THE ANCIENT MIND

A Cognitive Approach to Archaeology

JAMES L. PEARSON

ALTAMIRA PRESS
A Division of Rowman & Littlefield Publishers, Inc.
Walnut Creek • Lanham • New York • Oxford

ALTAMIRA PRESS
A Division of Rowman & Littlefield Publishers, Inc.
1630 North Main Street, #367
Walnut Creek, CA 94596
www.altamirapress.com

Rowman & Littlefield Publishers, Inc.
4720 Boston Way
Lanham, MD 20706

12 Hid's Copse Road
Cumnor Hill, Oxford OX2 9JJ, England

British Library Cataloguing in Publication Information Available

Library of Congress Cataloging-in-Publication Data

Pearson, James L., 1938–
  Shamanism and the ancient mind : a cognitive approach to archaeology / James L. Pearson.
    p. cm. — (Archaeology of religon)
  Includes bibliographical references and index.
  ISBN 0-7591-0155-8 (cloth : alk. paper) — ISBN 0-7591-0156-6 (pbk. : alk. paper)
  1. Archaeology—Methodology. 2. Cognition and culture. 3. Archaeology and religion.
  4. Ethnoarchaeology. 5. Shamanism—History 6. Civilization, Ancient—Psychological
  aspects. 7. Rock paintings. 8. Prehistoric peoples—Religion. 9. Prehistoric
  peoples—Psychology. I. Title. II. Series.

  CC175 .P43 2002
  930.1'01—dc21

Printed in the United States of America

∞™ The paper used in this publication meets the minimum requirements of American National Standard for Information Sciences—Permanence of Paper for Printed Library Materials, ANSI/NISO Z39.48-1992.

CONTENTS

Foreword

A RCHAEOLOGISTS STUDY ANCIENT BEHAVIOR and long-vanished human
societies over a canvas of two and a half million years. We converse with
material "voices" from the past—with stone artifacts and potsherds, ru-
ined buildings, broken animal bones and minute seeds—durable legacies of long-
forgotten human behavior, made and used by ancient cultures. Our finds tell
tales, but these narratives are necessarily incomplete, describing for the most part
only the business of daily life. The real storytellers are long silent. The beliefs,
myths, and rituals that were an integral part of their vanished world have died
with them. Only their artifacts, and sometimes their art, remain to give us insights into the spiritual worlds of our remote ancestors. We should not be surprised that, since the very early days of archaeology, researchers have grappled
with fundamental questions: How can archaeologists use science to recover the
symbolic worlds of the past and the mythic and ritual settings that defined them?
How can we bridge the gap between the tangible and the intangible, move from
the material to the spiritual? We are only beginning to grapple with the dimensions of this most fundamental of archaeological problems.

The theoretical debates have raged fast and furiously since the 1960s, when
Lewis Binford and others developed processual archaeology as a new and scientific
way of explaining the past. This "New Archaeology," with its emphasis on cultural systems and ecology, turned out to be less new than originally claimed.
Processualism is still alive and well. So is "postprocessual archaeology," a bewil-
dering array of competing theoretical approaches concerned with studying the ancient intangible, arguments often remarkable more for their oratory than for their
intellectual substance. The theoretical clouds have cleared somewhat in recent
years with the emergence of what is loosely called "cognitive archaeology" or the

"archaeology of mind." This approach combines the rigor of scientific archaeology with data from ethnographic, historical, and other sources to peer cautiously into the realm of the intangible. Such research will never be easy, for, as archaeologists Kent Flannery and Joyce Marcus (1993) have reminded us, it is but a short "bungee-jump" from the realm of science to that of ungoverned speculation. That we can now take cognitive archaeology seriously is in large part due to remarkable, even revolutionary, advances in the study of prehistoric rock art over the past quarter century.

Credit for this revolution (it is nothing less) belongs to many scholars, but in particular to Wilhelm Bleek, a late-nineteenth-century German linguist, and to David Lewis-Williams, an expert on San rock art from southern Africa. Bleek recorded the oral traditions of San prisoners in Cape Town more than a century ago; their myths and tales encompassed the meaning of some of their rock art. His research notes were rediscovered by Lewis-Williams in the 1970s and found to be an extraordinary source for attempting a comprehensive analysis of the meaning of prehistoric rock art. In his many writings, Lewis-Williams has drawn attention to the vital role of shamans and of altered states of consciousness in interpreting ancient rock art. His research has received international acclaim and has been used to offer new perspectives on Upper Paleolithic art. His ideas have also influenced studies of Native American rock art in western North America and elsewhere, using the ethnographic work of anthropologists John P. Harrington and Julian Steward, among others. For the first time, rock art specialists like David Whitley have been able to place shamans and altered states of consciousness at the very core of rock art studies in North America.

Much of this important research has been piecemeal, conducted on a small scale and with minimal budgets. The time is long overdue for a step back from the basic data, for a synthesis of what we know—and do not know—about the role of shamanism, hallucinogenic drugs, and altered states of consciousness as part of a cognitive approach to archaeology. Jim Pearson now provides us with such an overview. He gives us a valuable critical synthesis of theoretical approaches to cognitive archaeology and reminds us that a large part of the archaeological record results from human cognition. Ideology, cosmology, and beliefs played critical roles in shaping human societies of every kind over long periods of time. He argues for more detailed studies of hallucinogens in ancient societies, a point also made by the religious studies scholar Lawrence Sullivan (1988) in his groundbreaking study of Latin American religions, *Icanchu's Drum*. We cannot afford to dismiss hallucinogens as "noxious weeds," nor can we ignore the extraordinary ethnographic records of shamans and their activities preserved in unpublished archives and in obscure, long-forgotten literature. Pearson makes a strong plea for a multidisciplinary approach, incorporating not only archaeology, anthropology, and other more obvious sources, but also the startling finds of neuroscientists, who are publishing remarkable data on the effects of trance on the human brain.

Pearson puts us on notice that there is far more to the study of the past than merely what he calls "good dirt archaeology" and the study of ethnographic records. He shows us that we have only begun to understand the rich record of the past preserved in rock art and in the archaeological record as a whole. His book reminds me of a memorable comment by the Australian historian Inga Clendinnen, author of a notable book on the Aztecs. She likened our search for the intangible to Ahab's quest for the great white whale: "We will never catch him . . . it is our limitations of thought, of understanding, of imagination we test as we quarter these strange waters. And then we think we see a darkening in the deeper water, a sudden surge, the roll of a fluke—and then the heart-lifting glimpse of the great white shape, its whiteness throwing back its own particular light, there on the glimmering horizon" (1991, 275).

Pearson shows us that we do indeed have occasional glimpses of the intangible. But he is right—we have hardly begun. He throws down a powerful intellectual gauntlet for the future. This is an important book that should be on every aspiring archaeologist's bookshelf.

Brian Fagan
University of California, Santa Barbara

Archaeology's Final Frontier I

THE RENOWNED ASTRONOMER EDWIN HUBBLE first detected the existence of galaxies in our universe in the 1920s, and scientists have been trying to trace the evolution of these remarkable star clusters ever since. Now, after decades of looking far into the dimly lit reaches of space and even deeper into the murky past, researchers are finally getting a better glimpse of galaxies in the making. The trickle of data that distant galaxy hunters once collected has turned into a veritable flood. Because of important technological breakthroughs, such as the opening of the giant Keck telescope on Hawaii's Mauna Kea, the improved capabilities of the Hubble Space Telescope, and new innovations in telescopic detectors, astronomers have located hundreds of young galaxies, and more are being discovered every week. As a result, the early cosmos has become much more familiar, and advances in infrared telescopes promise to push our cosmic vision even farther into the distant past.

Astrophysicist Craig Hogan believes that astronomy is now experiencing its third truly great moment of the last one hundred years. The first occurred during the 1920s when Hubble, peering through the largest telescope of the time—the 100-inch reflector atop Mount Wilson in southern California—recognized that our Milky Way galaxy was not alone. The second revolution came in the 1960s, when astronomers began to probe the heavens at nonvisible parts of the electromagnetic spectrum. Radio telescopes helped astronomers locate quasars, and they in turn provided the first clues that the early universe was quite different from our own galactic neighborhood. The new instruments that began to come on line in the early 1990s gave astronomers another option. For the first time, they were able to look for far more subtle evidence of an alternative scenario—the notion that galaxies were born over many billions of years rather than all at once (Bartusiak 1997).

All well and good, but what does this have to do with archaeology? These seem to be distinctly different disciplines; most people think of astronomy as a truly "hard" science where many of the significant advances are driven by technological innovation. Although archaeologists have recently tried to become more "scientific," archaeology is not considered one of the natural sciences—it is usually more closely associated with history, ethnography, or cultural anthropology. Archaeologists are also noted for borrowing and modifying theories from other disciplines such as biology, sociology, or geology, rather than creating theoretical positions of their own (Yoffee and Sherratt 1993). Nevertheless, the differences between these two fields may not be as great as they appear. By way of illustration, consider the following example of the way some astronomers conceptualize their work.

For ten days in December 1995, the rejuvenated Hubble Space Telescope trained its eye on one small portion of the sky while it took a series of 342 time-exposure photographs. These pictures were combined and computer-enhanced to produce the most penetrating images ever recorded in astronomy—the Hubble Deep Field. Robert Williams, the director of the Space Telescope Science Institute, remarking on the significance of this phenomenon, said, "It's an archaeological dig that allows us to see some 2,000 galaxies at different stages of development" (Bartusiak 1997).

Some archaeologists might be intrigued by the idea that astronomers think of their work as an "archaeological dig." Others would probably consider it an inappropriate analogy since archaeology, by definition, studies "extinct human societies using the material remains of their behavior" (Fagan 1991, 524). Looking at distant galaxies that were formed billions of years ago certainly has little do with the material remains of past human societies, but this way of thinking misses the point. Understanding how galaxies were created is just as important to astronomers as deciphering the origin of species to biologists or the study of culture change to archaeologists. All are attempting to comprehend and interpret events that occurred over time and long ago, and there are parallels between developments in astronomy and archaeology.

American archaeology has, like astronomy, witnessed considerable change during the past hundred years. Some would suggest that it, too, experienced at least three significant episodes over that time. The first change occurred in the 1920s, when the majority of archaeological research was directed toward locating, excavating, recording, and describing findings at individual sites. With these data at hand, researchers tried to develop chronological sequences and establish broader outlines of regional prehistories. Beginning in the 1960s, Lewis Binford (1962, 1964, 1965) melded earlier lines of archaeological thought with a concern for a scientific methodology and field research designs, and thereby set the guidelines for an approach that would come to be known as the "New Archaeology." Based on the work of W. W. Taylor, Albert Spaulding, Julian Steward, and Leslie White, among others, Binford and his colleagues extended the existing goals of archaeology beyond typology and stratigraphy. In the 1980s, the appearance of the post-processualist paradigm presented another set of options, and archaeology has not been quite the same since.

Technological innovation is clearly an important element in astronomy. We should not, however, lose sight of the fact that astronomers—since they cannot touch the things that their instruments reveal—must rely on theories to interpret their data. As Michael Hawkins puts it, "Astronomy is a science based on appearances. Nobody has ever touched a distant star; what we know is what we see" (Hawkins 1997, 4). Hawkins suggests that the problem for the astronomer is much like that of an airline passenger on a night flight trying to deduce the nature of the world solely from the glow of cities passing below: "The idea that underlying these islands of light and the dark voids between them was a globe of almost unimaginable mass would require an inspired leap of imagination." Science is our tool for tackling such problems, but science is a very human—and thus fallible—process (Hawkins 1997). Archaeologists also try to coax interpretations from very fragmentary evidence. They constantly search for theoretical approaches and methodological tools that will help make their job easier. This is not an easy task when we consider that this "science" is just as human and fallible as astronomy.

Astronomers have recently accumulated so much data that they are now finding it difficult to keep up; with the flood of new information, old ideas about how galaxies evolved are toppling. Particularly imperiled is the idea that virtually all galaxies came into existence at exactly the same moment, sending out a collective burst of light like some great fireworks display. Astronomers embraced this explanation because it was the simplest and seemed to fit the available data. In the 1950s and 1960s, all galaxies as far back as astronomers could see (which was not very far) looked pretty much like our own. Now, however, astronomers believe that galaxies condensed out of a primordial ocean of hydrogen and helium not all at once but continuously and vigorously, like a raging fire, over a period of billions of years.

It would be difficult to count the number of times during the past several decades that archaeologists seized upon an explanation of culture change or some other aspect of prehistory because it appeared to be the simplest or seemed to fit the available data. (This was during a time when, in an attempt to become more scientific, they also embraced the strict hypothesis-testing approach of the hard sciences.) As more data became available, some old ideas were overturned. With new information and different ways of interpreting the data, many archaeologists believe they, too, can look for far more subtle evidence of alternative scenarios to explain the past.

For those theorists in astronomy who endured the lean years of scant data, the debate is quite invigorating, but precisely what they are seeing at the edge of the universe is still open for discussion. They concede that the mystery of galaxy formation would be solved immediately if astronomers could follow a particular galaxy through time. They also realize this is not possible. "We can't use a telescope as a time machine . . . we're either here or there," says astrophysicist Simon White, "We can't wait around for any individual galaxy to evolve" (Bartusiak 1997, 60). However, by adding more "snapshots" to their cosmic album they can forge a link between one epoch and the next. In this respect, archaeologists have the advantage. They work with material remains that are, for the most part, palpable and relatively close at hand, and the time scales are considerably more finite. They *can* use archaeology as a time machine to forge connections between different periods in prehistory.

David Koo, at the University of California at Santa Cruz, suggests that astronomers have been "feeling" various parts of the cosmos, in the sense that various astronomical techniques pick out different types of objects. Koo does not believe this presents an obstacle to legitimate interpretation: "If you insist on taking the view that galaxies evolved in only one way, then you end up with a dilemma. . . . I believe the universe can accommodate a richness of diversity" (Bartusiak 1997, 63). If astronomers can think in these terms, archaeologists should be willing to accept a similar richness of diversity in their universe and to consider a variety of theoretical as well as methodological approaches.

There are indications that this has already taken place. During the 1970s, a number of archaeologists began to realize that there was much more diversity in prehistoric cultures than could be accounted for by general evolutionary schemes like those of Sahlins and Service, or even by Julian Steward's multilineal evolutionism (Trigger 1989, 329). There is a growing willingness to admit that human behavior is shaped by a variety of different factors and that at least some forms of behavior may not be recorded in an unambiguous fashion in the material remains of the past. Archaeology, as the record of different cultures that are in turn the product of individual actions, will inevitably be viewed from a variety of theoretical perspectives by observers with a diverse range of interests. As more data become available, including theoretical and technical advances from other disciplines, archaeologists can reformulate their theories and use this new knowledge to interpret the past from a different point of view.

In the broadest sense, this book deals with the way in which these new perspectives and tools are being applied to the practice of archaeology at the beginning of a new millennium. More specifically, it has to do with a particular brand of archaeology that is one of the products of the latest upheaval within the discipline—the archaeology of the mind. Here we will look more carefully at the cognitive sphere, a realm that is finally being recognized as a legitimate area of study.

In the following chapters, I will review the development of cognitive archaeology over the past several years and try to assess whether the current methods and theory of this approach can be effectively used to interpret the material record. I will begin by tracing the theoretical and methodological trends that have prevailed in American archaeology since the early part of the twentieth century; a review of more recent movements that have led to a cognitive approach will follow. This review will include a discussion of the processual versus postprocessual debate, the emergence of ideas about the importance of individual actors and ideology, and the perceived need to explore the workings of the human mind.

I will examine the end product of this process—the components that define the current cognitive approach as well as the prevailing theory and method. I will also discuss the principle tenets, how and why they were developed, and the way that cognitive archaeology works within a postmodern philosophy of science; consider the concept of culture from a cognitive perspective and explore new and innovative ways of interpreting the ethnographic record; and review refinements in the use of analogical inference, the development of a neuropsychological model, advances in neuroscience, and the way in which all of these are employed in cognitive research.

Since cognitive archaeologists believe that one of the best applications of this approach is through rock art studies (e.g., Earle 1994; Whitley and Loendorf 1994), I will examine the evolution of rock art research in both the Old and New Worlds, from the earliest discoveries to the most recent interpretations and show how the use of a cognitive approach to the rock art of two continents led to the realization that shamanism was deeply implicated in the creation of much of this art. I will also review the various components of the phenomenon of shamanism on a worldwide scale and examine the ways that shamanistic beliefs and practices are reflected in the material record. The final chapter comprises an evaluation of various interpretations and competing hypotheses concerning the creation of the rock art as well as an assessment of whether, simply put, cognitive archaeology works and whether it affords us a rational, defensible means of accessing the minds of ancient people, thereby providing a route to a better understanding of the prehistoric past.

Antecedents to Cognitive Archaeology

2

F ROM ITS EARLIEST DAYS, archaeology has been concerned with classification, with time, with how assemblages come about, with relating long-dormant artifacts to the living people who made them, with the discrepancies between fragmentary evidence and complicated wholes (Chippindale 1993, 33). A brief assessment of the ways that archaeologists pursued these concerns over the past hundred years is relevant to the current discussion. It will show how and why they shifted from the descriptive methodology that was so prevalent early in the twentieth century to a decidedly different approach by the beginning of the new millennium.

The Early Years

The traditional practice of archaeology, which was geared toward describing and ordering artifacts in chronological sequences, using careful stratigraphic excavation, stylistic seriation and, eventually, dendrochronology and radiocarbon dating, evolved because of a heightened awareness of the complexity of the material record (Trigger 1989, 186). As early as 1913, the American ethnologist Berthold Laufer correctly observed that the most serious shortcoming of American archaeology was its lack of chronological control (Laufer 1913, 577), a problem that a number of archaeologists had already recognized and begun to remedy. Although, for the first time, researchers realized that culture change was clearly evident in the archaeological record, the principal product in the decades after 1914 was a series of regional chronologies. With the advent of a cultural-historical approach, these archaeologists were encouraged to excavate sites primarily to recover samples of artifacts that could be used to elaborate trait lists and to define cultures (Trigger 1989, 204).

In the mid-1920s, Alfred Kidder (1924) created the first cultural-historical synthesis for the archaeology of the American Southwest. In this scheme, cultural areas were defined as geographic units that had similar languages, subsistence patterns, and material remains. Stylistic similarities within each of these culture areas were used to establish local "traditions" over time and regional "horizons" across space (Earle and Preucel 1987, 503). What other archaeologists found most interesting about Kidder's work, however, was his chronology, which was based on extensive stratigraphic excavation.

During the depression years of the 1930s, government relief agencies, working through universities, museums, park services, and other institutions made large amounts of money available for archaeological research. As a result, entire sites were excavated, especially in areas that were to be flooded by construction of hydroelectric dams (Willey and Sabloff 1980, 115, 127).

Cultural-historical archaeologists continued to focus on prehistoric cultures during the 1940s and 1950s, trying to explain the archaeological record in greater and more specific detail than they had done in the past. There was very little interest in culture *per se*, although widely recognized classificatory components (such as phases, aspects, or foci) were characterized as cultural units. All prehistoric cultures in North America were thought to be extremely conservative, with change being routinely attributed to external factors that were frequently subsumed under the general processes of diffusion and migration (Watson 1995, 684). A number of scholars began to realize, however, that these descriptive procedures could not adequately explain how prehistoric cultures functioned or how they changed over time. In due course, American archaeologists adopted a new approach to the study of prehistory that was based on a systematic understanding of human behavior.

This so-called functionalist perspective had its beginnings in the United States in the late 1800s. A widespread interest in how various artifacts were manufactured and used continued into the twentieth century, and the large horizontal excavations of the depression years helped rekindle this concern for a functional analysis of archaeological data. Now, however, instead of directing their attention primarily to artifacts, researchers focused on site features, house patterns, village plans, and the relationship of the distribution of material remains. Scholars initially justified this work as a way of expanding trait lists, but eventually it stimulated an interest in examining how people lived in prehistoric times. Nevertheless, in spite of the increasing variety of data, many of the reports written in the 1930s and 1940s continued to emphasize trait lists in an ethnographic or pseudoethnographic format instead of viewing material culture as evidence of human behavior. This type of classificatory orientation tended to suppress interest in other explanations of the archaeological record (Trigger 1989, 272–74).

A growing minority of archaeologists became dissatisfied with this approach and began to look for a functional explanation within the framework of a broader view of culture. They also became more interested in the interpretations proposed by Childe, Clark, and other European archaeologists who provided theoretical as well as practical evidence that it might be possible to study nonmaterial aspects of human behavior. The notion that archaeological remains could be investigated from a functional point of view led many archaeologists to renew their ties with ethnologists. Several researchers (Martin, Lloyd, and Spoehr 1938; Martin and Rinaldo 1939; Strong 1936; Waring and Holder 1945; Wedel 1941) used functional explanations to identify sociopolitical or religious aspects of the material record. While these and other studies were quite disparate and provisional, there were enough of them by 1943 to be recognized as the beginning of a trend in American archaeology—one that J. W. Bennett (1943) labeled as a "functional" or "sociological" approach to archaeological explanation. These studies, in conjunction with Kluckhohn's (1940) advocacy of a "scientific" approach, prepared the way for Walter Taylor's (1948) controversial work that examined some of the differences between traditional cultural-historical archaeology and the new functional interests.

Taylor devoted much of his effort to a detailed review of the shortcomings of the work of American archaeologists. In his critique he showed that their cultural-chronological objectives had hampered and limited their investigations of the archaeological record (Trigger 1989, 276). Taylor argued that Kidder's work provided very little information about issues like settlement, craft specialization, urbanism, or diet. To remedy these defects he proposed a "conjunctive" approach that combined context and functionalism to reconstruct process (Earle and Preucel 1987, 503). Taylor advocated detailed intrasite studies that paid careful attention to all artifacts and features and the way they were interrelated. He tried to avoid the difficulties archaeologists appeared to have with the concept of material culture by following Kroeber and other Boasian anthropologists in characterizing culture as a mental construct and viewing material remains as *products* of culture rather than culture itself (Osgood 1951). He concluded that, even though culture was ideational and therefore did not survive in the archaeological record, many elements of culture other than the knowledge that went into the manufacture of artifacts were reflected archaeologically. Taylor's work was significant because it urged archaeologists to recover and analyze the archaeological data in far greater detail than they had ever done before. The result was reinforcement of a trend, already under way in American archaeology, that favored more functional interpretations (Trigger 1989, 279).

Following World War II, the increasing awareness of the importance of an ecological perspective, based mainly on the works of Julian Steward and Grahame

Clark, stimulated major research programs that involved interdisciplinary teams in which archaeologists and natural science specialists worked together to analyze archaeological data. Steward was one of the first scholars to adopt a specifically materialist perspective of human behavior, greatly enhancing an awareness of the influence that ecological factors had in shaping prehistoric sociocultural systems. Steward also played a role in the development of settlement archaeology, a trend that became especially significant during the 1950s, with researchers undertaking settlement-pattern studies that examined how prehistoric populations adapted on a regional basis.

The first explicit research of this sort was Gordon Willey's (1953) analysis of several archaeological sites within the Virú Valley of Peru. These studies investigated the correlation between population growth, economic change, and social evolution (Earle and Preucel 1987, 503). Although it was Steward who persuaded Willey to conduct a settlement-pattern survey as a part of the project (Willey 1974, 153), Willey's interpretation of the data collected during this survey was an important departure from Steward's ecological approach (1974, 1). While Willey did not deny that ecological factors were important in shaping settlement patterns, he did observe that the archaeological record also revealed many other components of a social or cultural nature. He would not accept the contention that these elements were simply a reflection of some general pattern of ecological adaptation.

Willey recognized the potential usefulness of settlement-pattern data for the systematic study of the economic, social, and political organization of ancient societies. His work was thus a valuable pioneering effort in the use of archaeological evidence for interpreting long-term social change. A growing number of American archaeologists also began to view settlement patterns as an important source of information for the examination of demographic trends and the social, political, and religious institutions of prehistoric societies (Trigger 1989, 282–84).

The Rise of Processualism

Settlement archaeology tended to encourage a more holistic study of prehistoric cultures at specific points in time and of the way these cultures changed. This concern about changes in structural and functional relations over time marked the beginning of a processual—as opposed to a synchronically functional—study of ancient societies. Functional and processual approaches stimulated a new interest in the way in which prehistoric cultures operated and changed. They eventually replaced the increasingly sterile preoccupation with ethnicity that had become so much a part of the cultural-historical approach. American archaeologists also renewed and strengthened their long-established ties with anthropologists as they searched for ethnographic parallels and theoretical concepts that would help them to analyze and interpret their data from a functional or processual point of view (Trigger 1989, 288).

Because of their growing interest in functionalist and processualist explanations of the archaeological record, many American archaeologists were more receptive to neoevolutionary concepts that emphasized regularities in culture. The leading advocates of this neoevolutionism in the 1950s were Julian Steward (1955) and Leslie White (1949, 1959). White advocated a form of technological determinism, whereas Steward championed an alternative multilineal, ecological, and more empirical approach to the study of cultural evolution. Researchers noted that many of the key variables that White and Steward proposed as major causes of culture change were quite easily accessible for archaeological study.

In 1959 Joseph Caldwell published an article in *Science*, titled "The New American Archaeology," in which he referred to the growing interest in ecology and settlement patterns as evidence of a new concern with cultural process. Caldwell adopted the neoevolutionary position, which held that not all cultural facts are equally important in effecting change. He also suggested that the primary goal of archaeologists should be to explain changes in ancient societies in terms of cultural processes. Caldwell's paper revealed that, during the decade following the publication of Taylor's work, the idea of looking for processual change within cultural systems had achieved a higher level of importance. While developments within archaeology (particularly studies having to do with ecology and settlement patterns) encouraged this perspective, it was also aided by the growing popularity of neoevolutionary anthropology, with its emphasis on cultural regularities.

Although the fundamental elements of processualism were the collective creation of a large number of American archaeologists during the 1950s, one name stands above the rest—Lewis Binford, its original champion and promoter. In a series of articles published during the 1960s, Binford (1962, 1964, 1965) merged earlier lines of thinking with a concern for scientific methods and field research designs and set the guidelines for the New Archaeology. In an effort to expand the goals of archaeology, Binford and his disciples developed a vehicle that could, to their way of thinking, more carefully examine cultural processes and provide a viable means of searching for culture change in prehistory.

Binford believed that the goal of archaeology was the same as that traditionally assigned to anthropology—to explain the full range of similarities and differences in cultural behavior. He argued that there were strong regularities in human behavior and that there was very little difference between explaining a single instance of social change and a whole class of similar changes. Thus his primary concern had to do with cultural similarities rather than differences (Trigger 1989, 296). Like his professor, Leslie White, Binford characterized culture as "mankind's extrasomatic means of adaptation" (Binford 1962; White 1959, 8).

Changes in almost all aspects of cultural systems were thought to be adaptive responses to alterations in the natural environment or in adjacent and competing cultural systems. This approach essentially ruled out human inventiveness and innovation as independent elements capable of producing major change within cultural traditions. Binford had little interest in the meanings that archaeological remains might once have had for their makers and paid no serious attention to ideational issues, regarding them as "epiphenomena," at best (Watson 1995, 686).

One of Binford's principle contributions at this time was his insistence that any correlations used to infer human behavior from archaeological data had to be based on the demonstration of a constant articulation of specific variables in a system. His followers believed that a rigorous application of this positivist view—the notion that explanation and prediction are equivalent and that both rest upon the demonstration of a constant articulation of variables—could effectively eliminate subjective components and establish a basis for an objective, scientific interpretation of the archaeological data. To reach this level of rigor, archaeologists had to adhere to deductive canons that utilized well-established correlations, as outlined by Carl Hempel (1962, 1965) in his covering-law model of explanation. Unfortunately, an extension of the covering-law method to the explanation of cultural change tended to exclude consideration of all situations except those that demonstrated notable regularity (Trigger 1989, 301) and deflected archaeological interest from significant aspects of cultural change that did not display such regularities.

Thus the New Archaeologists embraced various forms of ecological and demographic determinism that situated the primary factors responsible for change outside the culture system. They viewed humans as passive victims of forces that were mostly beyond their comprehension and control. Any aspects of human behavior that involved religion or belief systems, aesthetics, ideology, or scientific knowledge received little or no consideration. This ecosystem approach treated entire populations and whole behavioral systems as units of analysis to show how groups of people adapted to their environments. Because of Binford's influence, the New Archaeology became materialist, functionalist, and evolutionist in its orientation, overtly anthropological and scientific in its aspirations (Watson 1995, 686).

This way of thinking was evident in much of the research conducted during the 1970s. Cultural ecology and cultural materialism provided theoretical bases for studies of agricultural intensification and population trends—areas considered to be the most significant for successful research. Archaeological data were used to construct regional cultural histories, with a heavy emphasis on population growth in relation to limited resources.

Convinced that cultural systems exhibited a high degree of uniformity and that it was possible to account for this uniformity by identifying all of the ecological constraints that shaped human behavior, archaeologists adopted techniques that worked most effectively when applied to those aspects of culture that are subject to the greatest restraint. While these methods provided a better understanding of prehistory, many archaeologists became increasingly aware that recourse to environmental adaptation and technological and evolutionary positions seemed to fall short in explaining the archaeological record.

Dissension in the Ranks

During the 1970s, a growing number of researchers began to see more diversity in ancient cultures than could be accounted for by general evolutionary schemes, like those of Sahlins and Service, or even by Steward's multilineal evolution. It also became increasingly evident that neoevolutionism had restricted a variety of questions about the past that archaeologists were prepared to consider important (Leach 1973). This perception was due in part to empirical problems in the field data uncovered during these ecologically oriented projects.

Researchers in Mesopotamia, for example, found that the complex interaction between political, social, and economic factors had more to do with culture change than did irrigation and population dynamics (Demarest 1989, 93). Similar problems were evident in the New World. Richard Blanton (1976) argued that neither the timing nor scale of demographic pressures and economic factors could fully explain the major political changes in the Valley of Mexico. He also concluded that population pressure and agricultural intensification were not primary components in the rise of urbanism at Monte Alban in the Valley of Oaxaca (Blanton 1978). It appears that those hypotheses that mechanically linked early political systems to demographic pressures and economic responses failed to fit the form or timing of early state formation.

Reacting to these findings, researchers began to consider new theories that incorporated an interest in human actors and ideology as major components in an evolutionary explanation. Even conservative field archaeologists like Gordon Willey (who was more inclined than most to relegate such things as ideology to an epiphenomenal position) came to the realization that "[a]s we examine the record for evidence of population growth, subsistence resources, warfare and trade . . . there are indications that idea systems played an important part throughout the course of Maya development" (Willey 1977, 416).

Some of the best examples came from areas of the New World where the materialist, ecosystemic interpretative approaches were inadequate. Marcus, for instance, noted that "[t]he familiar variables of agricultural intensification, population growth, warfare, and interregional trade are by themselves insufficient to explain the diversity of Mesoamerican cultures. We must recognize that human behavior is shaped by diverse factors, and at least some forms of behavior may not be recorded in an unambiguous fashion in the archaeological record" (Marcus 1983, 360). Arthur Demarest argued that the unequal distribution of power in more complex societies could often result in the dominance of interests of specific individuals or small groups of elites, even though such interests might be maladaptive for the society as a whole. He emphasized that the central cult of the Mexica State was politically manipulated to overturn the existing social order. This stratagem for controlling the state religion by elite interest groups resulted in ideological revisions that became a force for expansionism (Demarest 1989).

Other researchers reiterated and expanded this type of analysis. Maya scholars showed that religion and rituals were one of the primary elements in the initial formation of distinctive state institutions. The transformation of existing religious cults played a crucial role in the early development of the Maya State. Maya kings held more influence through their role in ritual than through economic or coercive power (e.g., Freidel and Schele 1988; Schele and Freidel 1990). For the Maya, Aztec, and Inca, ideology was a source of power that could be either legitimating or used by individuals or institutions as a disruptive or revisionary force (Demarest 1989, 98).

By the 1980s, a number of archaeologists, including some who had played an instrumental role in establishing the New Archaeology, were questioning their basic assumptions about human behavior and the way the material record should be interpreted. They rejected the materialist-adaptationist approach and began to explore a broader range of theoretical positions, expanding the scope of archaeological concerns beyond the habitual social, ecological, and political interests of processual archaeology to engage religious beliefs, ethnicity, gender, and a variety of other subjective states that most processualists considered taboo or dismissed as wholly epiphenomenal and therefore uninteresting (Trigger 1989, 328; 1995).

Processualism came under increasing attack, especially from Great Britain, with critics arguing that there were significant shortcomings in both methodology and theory. The use of the term "postprocessual" came to characterize a variety of newly developed approaches that, while diverse in many ways, explicitly moved away from mainstream processual thought with its heavy emphasis on ecological and adaptationist concerns.

The Postprocessual Paradigm

In an effort to integrate individual agency, ideology, and mental states into reconstructions of culture change, scholars began to seek interpretive frameworks that would not rigidly preassign chronological or causal priority to social, economic, and political institutions. Instead, they looked for an approach that could incorporate internal social diversity, human volition, and ideology into theories of culture change. In working toward this goal, postprocessualists developed a wide range of practices.

For Ian Hodder, the most influential of the British and European advocates of postprocessualism, culture involves symbolic, material, and social behavior. As a student of Clarke, Hodder was one of the most articulate proponents of the New Archaeology, but, after a thorough reading of humanist scholars such as Collingwood and Bourdieu, he became dissatisfied with the positivist paradigm and began to investigate the utility of structural approaches for archaeology (Earle and Preucel 1987, 505). Hodder's contextual approach stands apart from most of the other processual trends and is usually recognized as the principal challenge to processual archaeology (Binford 1986, 1987). He investigates the issues of past and present symbolic systems, using ethnoarchaeology as an archaeological technique (Watson 1995, 686). One of the primary tenets of contextualism is Hodder's ethnographically well-documented claim that material culture is not only a reflection of ecological adaptation but also an active element in group interactions that can be used to disguise as well as express social relations.

The contextual approach is based on the notion that archaeologists need to examine all possible aspects of a culture if they are to understand the significance of each part. This implies an interest in culturally specific cosmologies, art styles, astronomical lore, religious beliefs, and other topics that lingered on the fringes of processual archaeology during the 1960s and 1970s (Trigger 1989, 350). Essential to this type of analysis is the idea that wherever the richness and variety of the material record is so great that it can no longer be interpreted as a response to environmental constraints or stimuli, other factors internal to the system must also be considered (Wylie 1982, 41). The intrinsic meanings with which artifacts were once imbued and the roles they may have played in complex social actions and interactions are also central to this argument (Hodder 1982).

Miller and Tilley (1984, 14) argue that ideology and power are inextricably bound up with social practices: "[T]hey are a component of human *praxis*, by which is to be understood the actions of agents on and in the world, serving as an integral element in the production, reproduction and transformation of the social." Miller and Tilley insist that we must acknowledge that people and prehistoric societies possessed the same abilities as we credit to ourselves, instead of reducing them to passive recipients of external forces (1984, 1).

In addition to criticizing the New Archaeology for its perceived inability to adequately explain variability in past human behavior, the more radical postprocessualists (e.g., Hodder 1982, 1984, 1985; Miller and Tilley 1984) also turned away from processualism's scientific positivism. The processualists, in turn, castigated their adversaries for not formulating a more constructive archaeological agenda, for deliberately obfuscating the genuine gains made during a century of systematic research, and for their failure to develop a coherent body of theory and method for interpreting the past (Yoffee and Sherratt 1993, 8). Over a period of time, this so-called debate deteriorated into a morass of charge and countercharge; the result was a major schism in the archaeological community.

In spite of the polemics, a number of scholars attempted to come to grips with these issues and move beyond the critique into the more difficult domain of archaeological practice. Although the approaches differ, most of the proffered solutions have the same basic theme—that people are actors who create, use, and manipulate their symbolic capabilities in order to make and reshape the world in which they live. In order to advance our understanding of the prehistoric past, then, the actions of individuals must be taken into account and the ideology and the working of the ancient mind integrated into contemporary reconstructions of social change.

In fact, the exploration of human cognition now stands at the forefront of archaeological inquiry. The question is not whether there is a cognitive revolution, but how empirical investigations should proceed and what methods should guide the theory structure (Bell 1994, 15). One of the fundamental challenges in archaeology is to advance the appropriate theory, methodology, and tools to understand prehistoric cognition. Researchers operating in this sphere are also concerned with cultivating an approach that will incorporate at least some of the existing methods of archaeological investigation in their effort to understand the development of cognitive processes and the early use of symbols.

The more radical of the postprocessualists, in their attempt to cast archaeology (and archaeologists) in one mold or another, miss an extremely important point; they disregard the diversity of views of those scholars studying small-scale societies. While most of the theoretical pronouncements of postprocessualists began as a kind of structural opposition to processualist views of functionalist, adaptationist, positivist, and reductionist notions of culture and material culture, these views have never been held seriously by many archaeologists (Yoffee and Sherratt 1993). Nor do most researchers accept the relativist views of the more vocal postprocessualists that Renfrew (1989, 36) labels "archaeology as wished for." And yet, there is a widespread perception among American processualists that the only alternative is this extreme form of postprocessualism. The fact is that the majority of archaeologists are not card-carrying members of one school or the other, and there are viable alternatives for those who are uncomfortable with the idea of being placed at the extremes of archaeological theory and practice.

Pragmatically, archaeology oscillates within a range of applications, and most practitioners position themselves on some middle ground. This being the case, it would seem more productive to consider this whole issue in the context of a *continuum*—a concept that allows us to explore a range of theoretical and methodological positions. In this scenario, those who prefer to follow a strict processual approach would be situated at on end of the spectrum, while those who lean toward a more extreme postprocessualist view would place themselves at the opposite end. The majority, depending on individual ideas of what form the practice of archaeology should take, would be located somewhere closer to the middle.

This continuum concept offers some advantages. By placing one's own theoretical and methodological perspectives somewhere within the middle range, a researcher can avoid the uncomfortable notion of having to hew to one extreme or the other. He or she can take advantage of the best of both worlds, recognizing the substantial contributions of processualist as well as postprocessualist advances. One's position need not be confined, of course, to a narrow band along the continuum. While a theoretical perspective may lean toward the postprocessual end of the range— if one accepts, for example, the notion that ideology is an important concept to be considered—a methodology could take a more processual direction in that it might consist of a more scientific approach to archaeology than many affirmed postprocessualists would condone. The idea of a continuum encourages a more holistic approach to archaeology, a concept advocated by many researchers. Such an arrangement also has a degree of flexibility, allowing some adjustment in one's theoretical or methodological position to accommodate newly developed concepts and advances in technology. In short, it provides some elbowroom. The ability to operate within a range along a continuum may provide a satisfactory forum for some sort of consensus that will be acceptable to the majority of practitioners. With these points in mind, I will proceed to survey some of the fundamental premises and methodological concerns of a cognitive approach and discuss a number of important concepts that fall somewhere within the mid-range of the continuum.

The Roots of Cognitive Archaeology 3

Can we use stone tools to reconstruct the evolution of language in early hominids? Does knowledge of the past require an empathic understanding of the feelings and emotions of prehistoric peoples? Are relationships between prehistoric social groups characterized by dominance and conflict, or cooperation and integration? What place did art and symbolism play in the workings of prehistoric societies? And is archaeology a science that can reconstruct some objective view of the past or, instead, merely a reflection of the present, used to satisfy our own (often unrecognized) ideological needs?

—DAVID WHITLEY

THESE ARE SOME OF THE QUESTIONS posed by postprocessual and cognitive archaeologists during the last two decades of the twentieth century. They tend to be provocative because they challenge the way archaeology was practiced in the 1970s and 1980s and contest its philosophical basis, explanatory capabilities, and methodological tools. This situation is by no means unique to archaeology; similar intellectual movements are evident in other academic fields, including the social sciences and in the humanities. In the aftermath of these challenges, some archaeologists entrenched themselves more firmly in the rationale and approach that prevailed in the 1970s, variously labeled settlement-subsistence, processual, or New Archaeology. Other scholars have committed themselves to new ways of perceiving and studying the past. Their work is also identified by such labels as contextual, radical, interpretive, and postmodern, but the main strands are most commonly referred to as postprocessual and cognitive archaeology—the terms that are used here.

Some Basic Differences

In attempting to define the cognitive approach more clearly, we must first take a careful look at the differences between processual and postprocessual archaeologies and identify those concepts that set them apart. These distinctions are, for the most part, philosophical and involve two important developments fundamental to the rise of cognitive archaeology—changes in culture theory in anthropology and the advent of a post-positivist philosophy of science.

Archaeology and the Philosophy of Science

In broad terms, the new or processual archaeology represented an attempt to transform traditional archaeology (which was primarily descriptive and concerned with defining cultural-historical sequences) into a scientific anthropology. The model of science adopted by processual archaeology was the one current and popular during the 1950s and, to a lesser extent, the 1960s. Archaeologists (and other scientists) refer to it as "positivism" (Whitley 1998a, 3). The positivist view of science first emerged during the 1920s in the form of logical positivism. In the 1930s Carnap (1936, 1937) developed a more moderate version, known as "logical empiricism," that became the accepted position for the next twenty years. According to this perspective, researchers formulated theories deductively to explain empirical generalizations, and new evidence was required to confirm or disconfirm those theories. The New Archaeology embraced this positivist approach, which held to the notion that the only true knowledge was scientific knowledge, to be arrived at through positively established proofs.

Its basic points included an interest in explaining empirical observations about human behavior by means of cross-cultural generalizations or laws and a conviction that these empirical observations (the archaeological data) are always independent of any theory. Processualists believed that the data could be used to test theories and the result would be objective knowledge about the past. They also adhered to the notion that a logical structure for scientific testing and explanation could be found in the natural sciences, such as astronomy or physics. As with other fields of study in the post-World War II era, the methodology and philosophical commitments of the positivist natural sciences were thought to be universally applicable to all disciplines, whether natural or social, including archaeology (Whitley 1998a, 3).

Binford's (1968, 17) widely proclaimed "appropriate scientific procedures" depended almost exclusively on the positivist model advocated by the philosopher of science Carl Hempel (1966; Hempel and Oppenheim 1948). This so-called nomothetic deductive positivism became the *sine qua non* for advancing the New

Archaeology as a revitalized science. If archaeologists simply followed those procedures, they could become "scientists" with the capacity for explaining the past and predicting the future. While a few archaeologists (and a number of philosophers of science) recognized that this nomothetic deductive approach to scientific explanation was flawed, Binford and his followers trivialized the views of any scholars who contested this model, labeling them "traditionalists." Philosophers of science who challenged the primacy of Hempel's model, or offered other methodologies for scientific explanation, were simply ignored in the archaeological literature (Lamberg-Karlovsky 1989, 4).

By the end of the 1960s, positivism (presumed to be the "true" and "only" science) was in a state of upheaval at around the same time that it was being adopted by archaeologists (e.g., Alexander 1982; Gardner 1985; Giddens and Turner 1987; Kelley and Hanen 1988; Shanks and Tilley 1987; Toulmin 1977). Anthropology, reflecting broader shifts taking place in the sciences, was also changing, even though a segment of it retained a concern for systems and adaptation that prevailed in archaeology (D'Andrade 1984; Ortner 1984). Shanks and Tilley (1987, 32) referred to this as the "unfortunate spectacle of archaeology embracing thoroughly discredited and outmoded ideas as the framework for its own advances." Processual archaeology, in other words, adopted a model of science and an anthropological approach just as they were in the process of being replaced in the social sciences generally and within anthropology specifically (Whitley 1998a, 3).

Many postprocessualists reacted to the New Archaeology's employment of a positivist model of science by de-emphasizing the role of scientific analysis in the investigation of the past (Yoffee & Sherratt 1993). They favored an approach, known as "critical relativism," that philosophers of science had begun to develop in the 1960s. One of its main points was that there is no single scientific method. Instead, claims to scientific knowledge are considered to be contingent on the particular beliefs, value systems, methods, and cognitive aims of its practitioners. Critical relativism, then, is skeptical of all claims to scientific knowledge because it insists that there are multiple scientific objectives and a variety of methods for achieving them (Landau 1984).

The more vocal proponents argue against any objectivity in the archaeological record. Facts can be observed only through living individuals and, therefore, facts about the past cannot be separated from the biases of present-day observers. This relativist position accommodates a variety of different concerns in archaeological reconstructions and asserts that expressions of personal opinion, political views, and other subjective elements must inevitably be a part of our interpretations (Leone 1982; Miller and Tilley 1984; Shanks and Tilley 1987). At the most extreme, relativists maintain that some archaeologists are so bound up by their own perspective and style that they cannot know the past at all—they merely present their own views of the present as if they were interpretations of the past (Miller and Tilley 1984).

Many cognitive researchers take a more moderate stance, one that holds that different individuals can, and often do, share the same perspectives, thereby allowing for some degree of objectivity (Whitley 1998c, 10). They argue that there are certain basic "facts" shared within any discipline that are independent of individual ideological biases and philosophical commitments. Those who hold this moderate position also maintain that there is a true and objective past, although we may not be able to recognize it simply by using the singular critical tests favored by processualists. Cognitive archaeologists attempt, instead, to employ a methodology that is more sophisticated than positivism while still retaining a commitment to scientific knowledge (1998, 11). This way of approaching the past also appeals to cognitive researchers because it accommodates their view of culture.

The Culture Concept

Until the mid-1950s, anthropology was dominated by the belief that most things human, including language, personality, culture, and so on, could be best understood in terms of stimulus-response relationships (D'Andrade 1984; LeVine 1984). For anthropologists, and, by derivation, archaeologists, this reflexive model of behavior was most manifest in the existing definition of culture, characterized as the patterning of behavior, with explanations of culture change framed in terms of human-environment relationships (Whitley 1992a, 60).

In his critique, Walter Taylor (1948) disagreed with this approach and advocated a more anthropological archaeology. Taylor believed that the archaeologist, as archaeologist, was nothing more than a technician digging up physical materials and their associations. The archaeologist as anthropologist, on the other hand, was uniquely qualified to produce viable cultural information concerning ancient peoples and extinct societies through time and space (Watson 1995, 685).

In 1955 Philip Phillips, a prominent Harvard archaeologist, also stressed the close ties between archaeology and the broader field of anthropology. His oft-repeated catch phrase, "American archaeology is anthropology or it is nothing," served as a rallying cry for a majority of American archaeologists for over three decades (Whitley 1992a, 59). In spite of these appeals, however, few paid any attention to the clarion call to reshape the practice of archaeology and make it more anthropological. One probable reason for this was the concept of culture that Taylor provided as the basis of his formulation.

Taylor believed (along with most cultural anthropologists of his day) that the locus of culture is mental. In this view, artifacts are not culture *per se*; they are *ob-*

jectifications of culture several times removed from the real thing. Taylor also felt that the highest goal archaeologists could strive for was to elicit culture (in an anthropological sense) from the archaeological remains, which meant the mental processes of past peoples (Watson 1995, 685–86).

Taylor's views ran counter to the basic operating assumptions held by most American archaeologists of the time. Many would not accept the notion that the original meanings (to their creators) of the material remains they excavated could be retrieved, and most were less immediately interested in this proposition than they were in basic settlement-subsistence research. Nearly two decades after Taylor completed his dissertation, another reformer made a shorter but far more successful appeal. Lewis Binford's 1962 article, "Archaeology as Anthropology," signaled the rise of a processual approach. Binford rejected the traditional anthropological culture concept because it was not appropriate to his own goals as an archaeologist. His view of culture as "mankind's extrasomatic means of adaptation" was very different from Taylor's but much more in tune with the general tenor of the New Archaeology.

Following Binford's lead, most processual archaeologists adopted a "systemic view of culture" (McGuire and Saitta 1996) that served as their link to a more scientific anthropology. The processual emphasis on predictability and generality springs from this perspective; culture is made up of subsystems that are functionally integrated into a larger whole, and stability is the normal state of social systems. Processualists viewed culture as a system of socially transmitted patterns of behavior that related human communities to their ecological settings; culture change was primarily a process of adaptation to the environment. From this perspective, technology, subsistence, and all the various aspects of social organization that can be directly tied to production are the more important cultural elements for analysis because they are the most strongly linked to adaptation. The corollary of this last point is that such cultural concepts as ritual, ideology, beliefs, and symbolism are thought to be epiphenomenal—derivative or secondary in nature—and therefore analytically irrelevant (Whitley 1998c, 3).

The connection between behaviorism and New Archaeology's "systemic view of culture" should be obvious. Culture change, one of the basic intellectual interests of processualist thought, begins with changes in the environmental (the external cause), necessitating shifts in adaptation (human behavior), which results in a new form of culture (a social phenomenon). The focus is on culture process rather than on culture history. Individuals are merely passive reflectors of forces and factors in their surrounding environments rather than intelligent human beings acting out their own ideas or intentions.

At about the same time that archaeologists were emphasizing their intellectual ties with anthropology—their "mother-discipline"—they apparently turned their

backs on major intellectual transitions that were occurring within the anthropological community. Starting in the mid-1950s, many in anthropology (and in
other human sciences) rejected the behaviorist paradigm in favor of a cognitive
formulation. Moving away from an emphasis on "normative" patterns of action,
they shifted to a definition of culture as a system of values and beliefs or, in a
word, worldview. This change in culture theory had a significant impact on the way
that most anthropologists perceived the world and in the way they interpreted it
(Whitley 1992a, 1998c).

Within archaeology, most practitioners continued to maintain a behaviorist
perspective. Processual archaeologists were seldom concerned in those early days
with human reasoning or symbolic structures; they focused instead on the more
immediately material aspects of prehistoric life. Any consideration of ideas in the
minds of the ancient actors who created the archaeological record tended to be
summarily dismissed (Renfrew 1994). Those who were committed to the idea that
subsistence behavior was the underlying foundation for cultural systems were distinctly lukewarm toward any type of a cognitive approach (Sanders 1994, 119).
For some, the realm of the mind was so nebulous and undocumented that it could
not be studied scientifically. For others, cognitive areas such as religion or belief
systems comprised dependent variables so far removed from the primary variables
of the subsistence economy as to be trivial and unworthy of study (Flannery and
Marcus 1993).

Not all archaeologists shared these views. A number of scholars felt that the
philosophy of processual archaeology added little to the understanding of culture
change. Ironically, this was a direct result of the processualist emphasis on the
study of variation within cultural systems and the subsequent identification of a
vast amount of variety in the material record. The processual approach was thus
perceived to be limiting *because* of the diversity—the inherent ambiguity and complexity in all societies—that had been revealed in the archaeological record
(McGuire and Saitta 1996). This was consistent with the notion that the materialist focus of processualism dehumanized prehistory and that ways should be
sought to include more of the values, ideas, beliefs, and cognitive processes that
make the human species unique (Flannery and Marcus 1993).

In the late 1970s and the early 1980s, the few anthropologically oriented archaeologists who were not completely swept away by Binfordian, processualist
New Archaeology received strong reinforcement from British and other European
advocates of postmodernist directions in archaeology. Just as Binford crystallized
and led the New Archaeology, Ian Hodder (1982, 1985, 1986, 1991) became the
dominant figure in postprocessual research. His contextual approach appealed to
scholars who were concerned with such diverse subjects as world-systems theory,
Marxist archaeology, and gender studies (Redman 1991). Hodder's supporters

believed it was essential to place the archaeological object in its context of ancient meaning. In doing so, they expanded the processual models of systemic context—especially those expressing a structural-functionalist viewpoint—to include broader symbolic and social domains (Redman 1991, 300).

Structural Functionalism

Postprocessual and cognitive archaeologists alike believe that structural-functionalism—the main social theory underlying processual archaeology—represents a significant problem for researchers who study traditional non-Western societies. This is because the structural-functionalism model was developed to explain the structure and operation of modern Protestant Euro-American society. From this perspective, society is thought to be organized in a fashion analogous to an organism, in that all parts work together toward the good of the whole. Since change, for the processual archaeologist, is caused by factors external to a body or system, the same view is applied to their analog—society. This approach places the emphasis on environmental factors as the cause of social change and tends to deprive individual human beings of any control over their own destiny. Change, in this view, is a condition imposed on societies by outside forces and not produced from within. Modern Western societies operate by way of institutions—politics, religion, economics, and so forth. Because we know intuitively that our own society functions within the same parameters, we assume that these concepts apply to the past. The problem for many postprocessualists is that most traditional non-Western societies may not, in fact, be structured in this way at all. Structural-functionalism, then, is a dubious model for the kinds of societies that are most commonly studied by archaeologists (Whitley 1998c, 16).

A major concern for cognitive researchers was to find a viable alternative to the structural-functionalism of processual archaeology—one that would obviate the implicit and problematic analogy with Western societies and place more emphasis on the importance of individual human intention and action (Whitley 1998c). The dominant alternative adopted by a number of cognitive researchers is historical-materialism. This concept has considerable appeal because it is a social, not a political, theory and one that models societies based on a series of functions rather than institutions, and does not presuppose an equivalence between past and present cultures. Thus, it can be applied more readily to traditional societies that may have differed in fundamental ways from Western Euro-American societies. From this perspective, social change is the result of internal conflicts between groups within society—not of external influences. This allows human actors to consciously mold their own lives and history. It can also accommodate the notion that ideology is more than epiphenomenal and that shared systems of symbols, values, and beliefs are actively created, used, and changed by individual humans (17).

A Cognitive View of Culture

At the turn of the last century, American archaeologists were profoundly influenced by the ideas of Franz Boas, who perceived culture as a phenomenon largely independent of environment, biology, and individual motives (Harris 1968). This approach, often called cultural determinism, viewed culture as a pattern of norms maintained implicitly by members of a society and obtained through historical tradition and diffusion (Earle and Preucel 1987, 503). Processual archaeology, by conceptualizing culture as a set of behavioral norms or mental templates that are transmitted from one individual to another, retained the normative view of culture, even though one of its central tenets was a rejection of the normative approach of traditional archaeology. However, instead of coming to grips with this conceptual contradiction, most processualists chose to exclude the concept of culture from any explicit archaeological consideration (Hill 1977, 103; Trigger 1984, 283–84; Whitley 1992a, 62–63).

Cognitive archaeologists believe that the prehistoric past was socially and culturally constituted and, as a result, the concept of culture must be given center stage in any form of archaeological interpretation. They insist that prehistoric cultures cannot be reduced to one-to-one analogies that uniformly equate humans with the environment. This adaptationist perspective fails to recognize that actions depend on the beliefs and values of the people who perform them. Nor do proponents of the cognitive approach believe that the explanation of the past can proceed simply with a consideration of the overt, behavioral realm.

Those who adhere to this position define culture as a shared system of symbols, values, meanings, and beliefs (Whitley 1998c, 18). But these do not constitute norms, in the sense of mental templates and prescribed patterns of behavior that are implicit in a processual archaeology. Instead, they are defined as "cognitive objects" that are actively created, used, and changed by individuals as they live out their lives; they make up the constitutive rules within which all human actions and behavior unfold. Cognitive researchers seek to identify the realm of these cognitive objects—the system of beliefs and values that comprise a culture—and, by critical evaluation, explain, interpret, and understand the prehistoric past. Since actions depend on the beliefs and values of the people who perform them, any explanation of such actions must therefore be in terms of those beliefs and values. It follows that explanations of the past, as with any social phenomena, can only be achieved by recourse to the cognitive realm (Whitley 1992a).

But how can systems of symbols and meaning at once have been created, used, and manipulated by individual humans, yet still have been sufficiently shared and patterned to allow them to be identified and studied, particularly by late-coming outsiders such as archaeologists? The answer involves the conceptual distinction between the behaviorist view of culture as a set of "regulative" rules, on the one hand, and the cognitive perspective that stresses "constitutive" rules or guidelines on the other (Whitley 1992a, 62; 1998c, 18). Regulative rules are fixed norms that work precisely as specified, with no room for deviation. Constitutive rules, by contrast, provide generalized guidelines or frameworks. Just like the rules of most games, they specify how the game must be played, but they do not determine how a particular game will turn out or who will win. This is how culture works, and it is why it can be manipulated and employed actively in the past or present and why it can be studied. Culture is a shared system of beliefs, customs, and values—mental constructs all. Culture influences behavior but, unlike behaviorist norms, does not fully govern physical actions. This is so because people think about their actions, sometimes decide to change things, and, often enough, get things wrong (Whitley 1998c, 18).

The Cognitive Approach

For cognitive scholars, the relationships that represent distinctions in social organization (e.g., commoner and elite) derive from culture-specific value and belief systems that cannot be separated from the analysis of social structure. Kinship, like economic and subsistence systems, is as much in people's minds as are beliefs and values. All of these things are, at least in part, cognitive constructs. Strictly speaking, none are observable on the ground; therefore, there is no merit to the argument that some phenomena can be identified and studied archaeologically, while others cannot (Lewis-Williams 1986; Wylie 1982). Cognitive researchers insist that to succumb to this way of thinking allows perceived inductive limits of the archaeological record to control our research (Wadley 1987). Arguments that a processual approach is somehow more concrete, less abstract, and not a part of the cognitive realm represent a serious logical fallacy (Whitley 1992a).

Cognitive archaeologists are convinced that any social inquiry must consider the cognitive and symbolic aspects of past societies. They believe that the remains of prehistoric actions are evidential and the point of inquiry is an examination of the cognitive systems behind the behavior that created the material record. They acknowledge that humans do adapt to their environment, and understand that human-land relationships might impose constraints on cultures. This does not imply that these elements are unworthy of examination or that the investigation of the cognitive realm must be methodologically different from the study of economy and subsistence. In opposition to postprocessualists like Hodder, Shanks, and Tilley, cognitive scholars do not maintain that their research is necessarily antiscientific (Whitley 1992a, 68, 72).

Some researchers insist that a variety of approaches indicates a discipline that is finally free of authoritative paradigms or the dominance of any single grand theory or method—that a healthy pluralism of methods and theories can coexist as archaeology struggles to become a more holistic discipline (Lamberg-Karlovsky 1989, 11). Others take a more cautious view, arguing that such pluralism should not include an uncritical relativism that considers all perspectives to be equally useful. Nor should it try to replace efforts at validation and a systematic approach to objectivity with some sort of ingenious storytelling, as has been said of some extreme examples of contextual archaeology (Redman 1991, 301).

Postprocessualist thinking introduced a wider range of theoretical positions, expanding the area of study beyond the usual considerations of processual archaeology. One result was a renewed interest in prehistoric cognition. Since the 1980s, those who advocate a cognitive archaeology have worked diligently to create and refine an approach that seeks explanations of human behavior at least in part by explicit reference to the human mind (Whitley 1998c, 6). Patty Jo Watson (1995, 685) summed it up nicely when she suggested, "The archaeological record can reveal ancient culture—the mental activities of long dead people—if skillfully interrogated." But how, one might ask, can things as vague and seemingly intangible as culture and cognition be reconstructed from the archaeological record? The following chapter looks at the theory and methodology of cognitive archaeologists—the tools they have developed and use to practice their craft of studying the ancient mind.

The Tools of Cognitive Archaeology

*Cognitive archaeology—the study of past ways of thought
as inferred from material remains—still presents so many challenges to the
practitioner that it seems an uncertain endeavor. That this should be so is
perhaps rather odd, for generations of archaeologists have written with
considerable freedom about the thoughts and beliefs of ancient people, about the
religions of early civilizations and about the art of prehistoric communities.*

—COLIN RENFREW

W HEN LEWIS BINFORD (1968, 22) wrote that "different kinds of phenomena are never remote; they are either accessible or they are not," he was presumably referring to cognitive elements in the archaeological record. His expressed belief that the "nonmaterial" aspects of culture were accessible "in direct measure with the testability of propositions being advanced about them," was a reflection of the high methodological ambitions of the New Archaeology. Binford and his followers believed that the use of a deductive scientific approach would allow them to move beyond descriptions of culture-history and reconstruct aspects of social and even ideological systems (Demarest 1989). Ideally, their optimism should have led to an upsurge of well-argued papers dealing with the ancient mind, but, despite the early enthusiasm, this was not the outcome.

For many archaeologists, cognitive phenomena had little relevance for the study of cultural evolution that reemerged in the 1960s and 1970s; it was viewed as trivial or secondary in nature (Harris 1964, 1968; Sanders and Price 1968). The majority of methodological and technological breakthroughs that occurred during this period were related to chronology and the recovery of subsistence evidence; it was the ecological components that captured the interest of most field archaeologists. The consensus at the time was that such things as belief systems, values, and ideology were too complex, obscure, or idiosyncratic to be perceived in the archaeological record.

This view is often attributed to Binford's own "robustly materialist position" (Renfrew 1994) and his idea that these phenomena did not comprise a truly autonomous subject of inquiry. They were, in Binford's opinion, simply a function of adaptive behavior and therefore could be explained (in scientific terms) only by appeal to adaptive principles operating at a systemic level (Wylie 1985, 90). Many of his disciples adhered to this position and argued that, while material culture may serve ideological or social purposes, it was not possible to reconstruct prehistoric beliefs and ideas. More to the point, they dismissed the anthropological preoccupation with these idiosyncrasies because they could not be subjected to proper scientific inquiry (Dunnell 1982). Any attempt to analyze prehistoric ideology and beliefs was left to those willing to apply "unsystematic and subjective interpretations" to the archaeological record (Demarest 1989, 89).

Processualism and Positivist Science

Postprocessualists contend that processualists were unable to access nonmaterial aspects of culture because they chose the wrong tools—most notably the positivist model of science. For the processualists, a positivist mode of prediction and explanation was the *only* scientific basis for interpreting archaeological data. A cultural materialist way of thinking popularized by Marvin Harris (1964, 1968, 1974, 1977, 1979) and others was explicitly reductionist, seeking to explain all culture change in terms of technological responses to environmental variations, demographic pressure, or other factors like protein deficiency (Demarest 1989). The empirical tradition of processualism also encouraged a determinist view of human behavior (Shanks and Tilley 1989, 6). The goal of determinism is to find a set of predictive laws, with the assumption that the state of variables at a given point in time can be determined so that some future state can be predicted. Explanation follows from formulation of these universal laws, arrived at through the use of the hypothetico-deductive method (Yoffee and Sherratt 1993).

The problem with hypothetico-deductive reasoning is that it presupposes a body of data that can provide a stable and unproblematic measure of the empirical truth (or accuracy) of any hypothesis. For postprocessualists, however, facts that are relevant for assessing the hypotheses important to an anthropological archaeology are not stable and immutable givens. From this perspective, the most interesting hypotheses are precisely those having to do with past events and processes that lie beyond the accessible data (Wylie 1985, 87). Therefore, post-processualists argue, a positivist methodology is totally inadequate for explaining distinctly human and cultural features that archaeologists studying prehistoric cognition find most interesting (Hodder 1982, 1983).

In a more general sense, the New Archaeology's insistence on technique and a rigorous methodology reflects a deeply ingrained belief in the omnipotence of science (Kohl 1993). The idea that anything said about the natural world from outside the sphere of science is less valuable than any result generated by science itself seems to be firmly embedded in our Western culture. The adoption of logical positivism afforded archaeology a new scientific respectability, and many proponents of processualism used this methodology as a means of legitimizing their research (Earle and Preucel 1987). The pressures of prestige and funding also encouraged this approach—"archaeological science" sounded a lot better than just plain "archaeology."

Unfortunately, according to its critics, the processualist commitment to a positivist science seemed to generate numbers rather than understanding—and it was impossible to translate those numbers into a better comprehension of prehistory (Chippindale 1993). Those researchers who insisted on uncovering universal "laws" failed to produce more than the most trivial observations (Flannery 1973; Yoffee and Sherratt 1993). The postprocessualists argue that such inconclusive and minimal results are evidence that the positivist approach stifles discovery. The more extreme positivists view the external world as a kind of primal mystery that can be perceived only through experimentation. For them, the only scientific method by which a knowable reality can be found is positivism. Postprocessualists insist, on the other hand, that positivist models unduly restrict our knowledge of the past exclusively to what we can discover empirically: they may process the data, but that is the end of the story. The results offer very little by way of imagery or intriguing clues for further investigation.

All of these anti-positivist arguments have been reviewed extensively in the processual versus postprocessual debate. The result has been a proposed dismissal of nearly all methods of scientific investigation and a movement toward a relativist position (Renfrew 1994). While both postprocessual and cognitive archaeologists are unified in their efforts to move beyond positivism, different positions have emerged. One of these involves an explicit rejection of the positivist model of science—a proposal endorsed by postprocessualists and many cognitive archaeologists. Whereas the majority of postprocessualists take this proposal as a rejection of *all* science, some cognitive researchers (whose positions are considered here) hold to a narrower view. They prefer alternative models of science that resolve the problems of positivism but still retain general scientific goals (Whitley 1998c).

The Cognitive View of Science

Cognitive archaeologists are concerned with an investigative approach that uses at least some of the existing methods of archaeological inquiry to understand prehistoric cognition. They do so with a commitment to science (Huffman 1986; Lewis-Williams 1983a; Lewis-Williams and Dowson 1988; Lewis-Williams and Loubser 1986; Whitley 1992a, 1994a, 1998c) but also with the realization that our understanding of what is meant by "appropriate methods" of scientific inquiry is itself continually evolving, as more recent developments in the philosophy of science clearly demonstrate (Wylie 1982).

These scholars argue that insofar as "science" comprises systematic knowledge, almost all academic disciplines are science. They further recognize that the practice of science may vary depending on the community one is considering (Liversidge 1995). At one end of the spectrum there is mathematics, clean and tidy and a law unto itself. Then, there is the rest of science, which is in varying degrees uncertain, hypothetical, and open to interpretation. When Sir Isaac Newton formulated and explained the mathematics of motion, he provided the philosophers of his day with a new and stunning insight: the universe obeyed certain physical laws and could be understood as a great clock. Newton's findings had a profound and far-reaching influence on all of the sciences, including the most prominent one of his time—astronomy. Some philosophers of science suggest that an undue emphasis on the experimental method is entirely inappropriate, in that astronomy, the paradigmatic science from which the scientific revolution was born, is observational and thus not truly amenable to experimentation. They argue that, if we insist the only way to study things scientifically is by compelling them to submit to experiments, the whole of astronomy would not exist, because it has never been susceptible to standard methods of experimentation. We cannot do experiments (in the sense of altering variables or controlling certain conditions) on heavenly bodies, tweaking a galaxy to see which way it goes, or giving an electric shock to a solar system to see whether it jerks in a certain way. All we can do is observe these phenomena and learn from our observations (Blacker 1998).

Truth is not always made apparent in black and white; more often than not, it is a matter of inference and the interpretation of incomplete evidence (Liversidge 1995). Outside of mathematics and formal logic, we rarely find proof of anything in science, so we should not *expect* any absolute certainty. While we can gain and lose confidence in our propositions and at times *disprove* them, we can never realize complete confirmation (Hill 1994). This is especially so for those who work with bits and pieces of the distant past where truth is often provisional, inferred, or the best guess.

Realism and Best-Fit Hypotheses

The philosophical position that many cognitive archaeologists take is a realistic one. As Trigger (1989) points out, some things *are* knowable in archaeology, and archaeological research has given us concrete information about ancient societies that has, in a number of cases, withstood the force of competing interpretive paradigms. Cognitive researchers conceive the past as existing in the physical world (much like the present), with human beings living their lives and interacting with each other and their environment very much as we do today. This perspective clearly differs from an extreme positivist position that restricts our conception of the past to that which we can learn about empirically (Renfrew 1994, 10).

This view coincides quite well with the concept of scientific *realism* and its association with a rationalist scientific method. Classical realists believe the world exists independently of our ability to perceive it—that there really is something "out there" to theorize about (Hunt 1990). Advocates of scientific realism agree that our perceptual processes can yield genuine knowledge about the external world. They contend that the job of science is to use viable methods to improve these processes and to separate illusion from reality, thereby generating the most accurate possible description and understanding of the world. The practice of developing multiple means of inquiry and testing them in multiple contexts is an integral part of this critical orientation (Cook and Campbell 1986).

From this perspective, scientific commitments are no longer based solely on empirical evidence or crucial, singular tests (Whitley 1992a). Lakatos (1969) notes that it is often unclear what constitutes a crucial test for a particular theory, except perhaps in hindsight. As Salmon (1982, 37–38) writes, "[T]here exists both confirming and disconfirming evidence for many important hypotheses." Kelley and Hanen (1988, 241) remind us that "acceptance in science is always tentative. We adopt the hypothesis that has best survived testing, always ready to abandon it if additional research shows that another is more probable." This clearly points to a scientific method that is not wedded to singular criteria (such as naïve falsification) but one that proceeds through "inference to the best hypothesis" (Whitley 1992a, 65). The conclusion that no single set of considerations applies across the board, that no solitary argument is conclusive, does not imply a relativist position in which there are no grounds for making a rational choice between alternatives (Wylie 1993, 23).

Richard Bernstein notes that arguments employed to evaluate incommensurate theories usually proceed not by "a linear movement from premises to conclusions" but by taking advantage of multiple strands and diverse types of evidence, data, hunches, and arguments to support a scientific hypothesis or theory (Bernstein 1983, 69). He believes that the "cumulative weight of evidence, data, reasons, and arguments *can* be rationally decisive." Wylie points out that explanatory and reconstructive hypotheses usually depend on a wide range of background knowledge. Questions concerning the applicability of a given interpretive hypothesis are often settled when a number of independently constituted lines of evidence converge either to support or refute the proposal. Conclusions that rely on various lines of argument derive their strength both from the diversity of their evidential support and from the fact that they comprise different dimensions of the archaeological record. Thus, the exploitation of a range of different and independent sources ensures that the elements that make up the argument are mutually reinforcing as well as mutually restraining (Wylie 1993, 23–25).

Explanation, Interpretation, and Understanding

Cognitive researchers believe that this post-positivist methodology, with its emphasis on the use of multiple criteria for scientific evaluation, provides a rational and objective verification process. This way of thinking also accommodates another important concept of the cognitive approach—the idea that archaeology is basically an interpretive endeavor. Both traditional and processual archaeologists have freely used the terms "interpretation" and "explanation"—often interchangeably. But with the New Archaeology's adoption of a positivist perspective and the subsequent rise of the postprocessual paradigm, this began to change. Positivist science dismissed the need for interpretation on the assumption that any objects studied by the physical sciences (galaxies, for example) have an existence that is independent of anything we make of them. By embracing positivism, processualists believed that archaeology could operate just like any other natural science and that recourse to interpretation was unnecessary; explanation would suffice.

Processualists who insisted on positivist hypothesis testing found it difficult to sanction interpretation, even when attempting to deal with the cognitive realm. They argued that "theories about prehistoric thinking should not simply be interpretations," because "only testable theories can deliver insight and further understanding." Thus, "since interpretations are not testable . . . they cannot deliver the type of insight that comes from passing risky tests" and there are no reliable criteria for deciding between them, or for moving beyond them (Bell 1994, 15).

Another reason that some archaeologists continue to view interpretation with suspicion is because of its close association with postprocessual thought. Ian Hodder and his colleagues endorsed the notion of "interpretive archaeologies" (Shanks and Hodder 1995) at least in part to bridge the gap between the opposing camps. The hard-core processualists would have none of it. As far as they were concerned, interpretive archaeologists professed the ability to enter the minds of ancient individuals through some kind of "active empathy." All of these efforts to somehow experience "being" another long-dead person, or having an experience to be compared with theirs, were typical of the "subjective, idealist, and interpretationist approach" used by antiprocessual, postmodern archaeologists (Renfrew 1994, 6). For most processualists, this served to reduce archaeology to a form of "self-indulgent . . . interpretive quest" (Lamberg-Karlovsky 1989, 7).

Postprocessualists contend that archaeologists have wanted to close their eyes to the interpretive side of their work in order to maintain the aura of science. In their opinion, it is postprocessual archaeology that is more scientific because it brings many hidden assumptions into the open and tries to develop an appropriate theory and method of interpretation (Hodder 1987, 517). Postprocessualists hold that all archaeology is intimately concerned with interpretation. Shanks and Hodder (1995, 8) suggest, for example, that archaeological excavations are fully interpretive. Many new students, experiencing their first "dig," find the uncertainty a bit disturbing; they have difficulty in deciding where one layer ends and another begins, or in determining whether or not a scatter of holes might once have been a house.

Weber (1975, 125) argued that, since interpretations of human actions can situate such actions within their own frames of reference, those interpretations are inherently more rational than scientific explanations of natural events, which may represent nothing more than statistical predictions. For him, the discovery of "meaning" and "interpreting" are not any different than the discovery of laws or causes in the natural world; interpretation and understanding are necessary in all domains of scientific inquiry. Cognitive scholars hold that archaeology is fundamentally an interpretive exercise, in that we all interpret the past, regardless of whether we do so through explanatory laws, symbolic explanations, or empathetic understanding, and this need not imply an extreme relativist, antiscientific approach to research. They also note that processualists have never demonstrated that their explanations are somehow more scientific or more objective than interpretations put forth by cognitive archaeologists (Whitley 1992a, 73).

Some researchers, including those who admit that prehistoric cultures and the human minds that created them are legitimate areas of study, will not concede that there is any method of examining the thought processes of prehistoric people. Those who insist that such endeavors are indeed possible point to the fact that all archaeologists, of whatever persuasion, routinely discuss concepts in prehistoric minds when they say, for example, that a particular object gave prestige or social status to ranked individuals. Even statements concerning ancient economies and the use of settlement areas make assumptions about past attitudes toward dirt, space, and so forth (Hodder 1986). This is not an entirely foreign concept. Gordon Childe (1949) long ago extended his own materialist analysis of society to include cognitive elements of human behavior. He believed that archaeologists must treat artifacts as concrete expressions of human thought and ideas and that religion, beliefs, magic, and ritual all leave their marks on the archaeological record no less conspicuously than does technical knowledge.

Most cognitive archaeologists hold that prehistoric culture, which is to say beliefs, values, or worldview, is inseparable from other cognitive abstractions such as social organization and subsistence. They insist that cognitive systems are effectively expressed, at some level, in all aspects of material culture (Whitley 1992a, 75). The problem, of course, is that values and belief systems are most often represented by symbols, and the creators of these images are no longer around to explain their purpose or meaning.

The Use of Analogy

Cognitive researchers argue that the notion that beliefs and values can only be uncovered by speaking with informants represents a misconception concerning the nature of anthropological research (Whitley 1992a, 76). From their perspective, oral accounts are simply the raw data that anthropologists use in developing their own interpretations of a particular culture; but they are only part of the process followed by ethnographers. Such commentaries can be more productive when used in conjunction with behavioral evidence, and behavior and actions are revealed in the archaeological record.

While many archaeologists recognize the value of combining the study of archaeological data with that of ethnographic oral traditions and historical records, there are differing opinions concerning the appropriate method for accomplishing this task. Most cognitive archaeologists advocate the use of analogical inference, but this methodology has been the object of uneasy mistrust in the archaeological community for a long time. The idea that sound interpretations can be based on ethnographically informed analogical models is simply not acceptable to many hard-core processualists. With the advent of a self-consciously "scientific" archaeology in the 1960s (and its reaction against more traditional forms of research) analogy became anathema. Binford (1967, 10) insisted it was a mistake to assume that by "placing analogy on a firmer foundation," we could increase our knowledge of archaeologically documented societies; no improvement in our understanding of present contexts could possibly enhance the empirical credibility of the claims an interpretive hypothesis makes about the past.

Wylie (1985, 87) makes the point that hypothetico-deductive testing, even in the most ideal applications, does not completely eliminate our dependence on inductive forms of inference. This argument has been made in an archaeological context by Salmon (1975, 1976), Hill (1972) and, in direct rebuttal of Binford's view, by Sabloff, Beale, and Kurland (1973). Wylie further believes that, contrary to claims made by its perennial critics, analogical inference is not radically faulty or categorically misleading. There are criteria and several associated methodological strategies for strengthening and testing analogical inferences that clearly provide a basis for weeding out and decisively rejecting those cases of false analogy that originally inspired a reaction against analogy (Wylie 1985, 107). Just as explanatory and reconstructive hypotheses inevitably depend on a wide range of background knowledge (Wylie 1993, 23), sound analogical inference should be based on multiple sources. There is simply no support for the idea that there has to be a one-to-one analog between source and subject (Wylie 1985, 106). Furthermore, analogical inference does not lead to "ethnographic despair" when no single, complete analog for a particular subject is available (Wylie 1988, 231). As a result, many prehistoric cases that have no exact equivalent in the ethnographic record may be approachable and interpretable in light of well-founded analogical inference (Whitley 1992a, 77).

Concepts of Time

This way of thinking raises another consideration in the minds of many archaeologists—one that serves as a presuppositional stumbling block whenever the topic of cognitive systems of the past is considered. It has to do with change over time: the idea that the specific meaning of any particular object for living individuals or groups is lost forever. Put another way, the real significance of any object, in an ethnological sense, has disappeared by the time it becomes part of the archaeological record. There is an assumption that, because time has elapsed, change has necessarily occurred. According to cognitive archaeologists, this way of thinking mistakenly confuses the fact that, since change occurs over time, time is somehow causally implicated. These scholars remind us that change is a condition to be demonstrated empirically, rather than assumed *a priori* (Huffman 1986, 85). They point out that cognitive systems of belief, values, and ritual tend to be very conservative and resistant to alteration, even in the face of acculturation and social disruption (Whitley 1992a, 78).

Richard Bradley holds that dates are only one way of measuring time and, without a clearer conception of time itself, it may be more difficult to make the transition from chronological studies to interpretations (Bradley 1991, 209). He stresses the fact that archaeologists have always faced problems of chronological resolution. Even with the latest advances in dating techniques, it is still unlikely that prehistorians will be able to work with blocks of time of less than fifty years or so, and often these units are longer. Social change may occur through a series of short-term events, but they can only be recognized by researchers working with a longer time scale. Archaeologists may be able to perceive environmental changes at one scale and the behavior of individuals at another, but they lack the chronological precision that allows an investigation of human intentions. Ingold (1984, 12) argues that without this information prehistorians can only investigate events such as cultural adaptation and are prevented from studying social evolution.

Countering this argument, Bradley (1991, 210) points out that many features found in the archaeological record are very long-lived indeed. Examples include art styles, the construction of megalithic monuments, and the deposition of votive offerings in water. All three phenomena have one feature in common; they show evidence of ritual rather than subsistence. This is significant not only because ritual plays such a central role in prehistoric archaeology, but also because it may involve a conception of time that is quite different from everyday affairs. Bloch (1977) notes that more than one sense of time often exists in the same society. Routine, everyday activities may be conducted according to a more practical understanding of time, whereas ritual may involve a very different perspective of the world. Bloch makes a distinction between mundane conceptions of time that determine the conduct of everyday affairs, such as the sowing and harvesting of crops, and ritual time, which involves the merging of the past with the present.

Bloch suggests there is a direct relationship between the different ways of experiencing time and the presence of social distinctions that can be protected by means of ritual. The reason for this is that ritual tends to maintain social divisions by making them part of a timeless natural order. Nevertheless, the fact that rituals retain so much stability does not imply that societies stay the same; if ritual assists in maintaining the social order, it can also be manipulated, and this is of particular importance to the archaeologist (Bradley 1991, 211). Since ritual can operate over the long term, archaeologists do not have to be restricted solely to the study of adaptive behavior. By playing off ritual time against the archaeological evidence of sequence, we may, in fact, be better equipped to explore the nature of social evolution. By observing the interplay of ritual time and mundane time, we can more carefully examine some of the fundamental changes that took place in prehistoric societies. Our long time-scale is no longer such a disadvantage; in this context, it could be a strength (212).

As persuasive as they may be, discussions about interpretation, time, and analogy still leave some archaeologists with a degree of skepticism. These theoretical and methodological devices and constructs have, after all, been quite thoroughly debated, defended, and berated for a number of years. There is, however, a recent addition to the cognitive archaeologist's tool kit that has not been subjected to the same type of scrutiny: cognitive neuroscience.

Neuroscience Research

Not long ago, Steven Mithen wrote,

> The character of past cognition must be largely inferred from the archaeological record. And to draw such inferences archaeologists need to engage with, or rather become participants in, the cognitive sciences. This is essential since we cannot pretend to understand the ancient mind without entering debates concerning the character of the modern mind. (1994, 29)

Until quite recently, there was very little in the way of cognitive research that could be usefully deployed, even by archaeologists interested in investigating the prehistoric mind. During the last few years, however, significant advances have been made in cognitive neuroscience. Using high-speed imaging devices, radioactive tracers and new theories concerning mental activity, medical researchers are trying to uncover the fundamental architecture of the human mind; and their efforts are not limited to neurons, synapses, and chemical processes. They are now exploring the mind's ability to develop complex belief systems and probing into the neurobiology of religious experience in search of a scientific perspective on the sacred. Scientists are seeking, in the actions of genes, the origins of virtue, altruism, moral behavior, and human consciousness. For better or for worse, this research is encroaching upon what some might consider humanity's last hold on uniqueness (Hotz 1998).

Cognitive archaeologists are using these studies to augment and advance their own research. They are convinced that the integration of neuroscience data, as well as information from other related disciplines, enhances an approach that affords access to a realm of the past heretofore thought archaeologically unapproachable. They believe they have developed a viable and appropriate method and theory for the investigation of prehistoric cognitive processes and the early use of symbols, an approach that can be particularly rewarding when applied to a study area that has, until recently, been marginal to mainstream American archaeology—rock art.

Neuroscience and Rock Art

For cognitive scholars, the special merit and unique characteristic of rock art as the subject of archaeological inquiry is its directness. These images reflect ancient worlds as ancient minds envisioned them; they are neither stray fragments of garbage from middens nor chance remains of prehistoric architecture. They are specific material expressions of human concepts, of human thought. Through this medium that we collectively refer to as "rock art," we see how different cultures, at various times in the past, represented and interpreted change *for themselves* (Chippindale and Taçon 1998, 1).

This approach obviously shifts the focus of inquiry away from human-land relationships toward the cognitive realm and, while not denying the significance of technological innovation, adaptive processes, or environmental issues, emphasizes an anthropological archaeology with culture as a central consideration. Cognitive scholars reject the notion that art and symbolism in general, and rock art in particular, are epiphenomenal and therefore analytically irrelevant. They insist that this type of research has reemerged as an intellectually viable subject, that the investigation of the symbolism reflected in the rock art is currently in the methodological forefront of archaeology in general and at the substantive lead of hunter-gatherer studies specifically. In this respect they also argue that all of the traditional complaints about the cognitive approach being methodologically weak, inherently unscientific, or theoretically depauperate no longer hold up under close scrutiny (Whitley and Loendorf 1994, xv).

Cognitive archaeologists are convinced that explanation of the prehistoric past can only be achieved through recourse to the cognitive sphere and that rock art studies provide a unique and viable access into the realm of the prehistoric mind (Whitley 1992a, 70). In the next two chapters I will trace the development of rock art research in both the Old and New Worlds. I will begin with European Upper Paleolithic cave art and look at some of the approaches and theoretical underpinnings that researchers have used in their efforts to uncover the meaning of these ancient and enigmatic drawings and engravings.

The Evolution of Rock Art Research   **5**

THE URGE TO DECORATE seems to be one of the defining characteristics of all modern humans. We know of various pieces of "art" from earlier contexts (like the exquisitely ground and polished mammoth tooth from Tata in Hungary) that date from between 78,000 and 116,000 years ago, but art does not appear as part of a coherent system until sometime after 35,000 B.P. (before present). This phenomenon is associated with human evolutionary and technological changes in Europe, Africa, and Asia, and the colonization of America and Australia during the latter part of the Pleistocene period. From that time on, humans have consistently decorated themselves, their tools and, where available, rock surfaces. Scholars still debate the implications of this artistic watershed and the way it might be related to the need for—or creation of—new types of social communication. Whatever the final outcome, a reasonable portion of the art created over many millennia has survived in the archaeological record and provides material evidence of the artistic endeavors or, more generally, the symbolic activities of all human societies (Morwood and Smith 1996).

Evidence for the postglacial cultural transformation of the world is scant in most places. For some aspects, like the prehistory of song and dance, we find hardly a trace. An enormous amount of ancient art involving perishable materials like wood, bark, fibers, feathers, or hides, as well as body painting or tattooing, has been lost forever. There is one record that is far more enduring. The incredible corpus of ancient rock paintings and engravings still extant around the world is a testament to visual art as a medium for better understanding the profound human events that shaped our histories (Chippindale and Taçon 1998, 1). Although the archaeological record normally provides an incomplete sample of the material remains of the past (Trigger 1989, 357), rock art is a rare exception.

The Art

Vast quantities of art have undoubtedly disappeared or deteriorated as a result of flaking and weathering, action by animals, insects, algae and other organisms, human activity, damage from fire or deposits of soot, geomorphological processes, and tectonic events. And yet, millions of engraved and painted rock surfaces survive at thousands of sites around the globe. Rock art is present in all but a few countries. (Holland has almost no rocks, and although Poland does have rocks, no art has yet been detected [Bahn 1998, xxvii].) Even in previously well-documented areas new images and entirely new sites are still being discovered; the carvings of axes and a dagger at Stonehenge, for example, were not noticed until 1953 (1998, xxi). Some of these finds, most notably the more recent discoveries at Grotte Cosquer and Chauvet Cave in France, are remarkable. Others, especially those located in the remote rock shelters in Africa and Australia and at many sites in the New World, may not be quite as spectacular but are no less significant.

A large portion of the parietal art (i.e., engravings and paintings found on rock surfaces or walls) that does survive still exists in its original form. Unlike other artifactual material, it has not been subjected to extensive and often complex postdepositional influences: natural and human processes that frequently affect the preservation of archaeological data (Trigger 1989, 358). Rock art, then, is not a "distorted reflection of a past behavioral system" (Schiffer 1976, 12) in the same sense as other artifacts that were deposited in the archaeological record, survived over a long period of time, and then actually recovered. Thus, the elimination of any distortions caused by formative or cultural processes is of less concern, especially when compared with other materials like stone tools and other objects that are likely to be curated, reused, and transported over long distances (Binford 1983, 269–86).

Parietal art has another advantage over other kinds of artifacts because it is found in the place where it was created; it is still precisely where the prehistoric artists put it and meant it to be (Leroi-Gourhan 1986, 10). This attribute allows us to study rock art in terms of unchanged physical parameters (Clottes and Lewis-Williams 1998, 62). Nevertheless, the art cannot speak for itself, and the messages have, for a variety of reasons, become distorted or difficult to grasp. Even if, after carefully excavating the surrounding area, conducting delicate pigment analyses and precisely recording the images, we come to understand the chronological and technical elements of prehistoric art, intriguing and perplexing questions still exist: who created it, under what circumstances, and for what purpose.

Early Research

Although many archaeologists, particularly in North America, have been reluctant to accept rock art studies as a respectable endeavor, a scholarly interest in rock art is certainly not new. The earliest known written reports are found in *Han Fei Zi*, written about 2,300 years ago by a Chinese philosopher named Han Fei. One of the first references to the rock art of Europe appears in 1548 when one of the Borgia popes, Calixtus III, strictly forbade cult ceremonies in a cave containing pictures of horses (Bahn 1998, 4). Presumably, the good prelate was referring to a painted Ice Age cave—an appropriate place to begin a discussion of the development of rock art research in the Old World.

Long before parietal art was recognized, various decorated objects were recovered from habitation layers in French caves. These were portable or "mobiliary" art—bone, antler or ivory images that people carried with them—as opposed to the drawings on rock walls. The first pieces of Upper Paleolithic portable art, an engraved pseudoharpoon and a perforated antler baton, were discovered in 1833 in the cave of Veyrier, close to France's border with Switzerland. Other engraved objects were uncovered in the 1840s and 1850s, but there was no real conception of how old this prehistoric art might be; the early finds were simply considered to be "pre-Roman." No one recognized the great age of these pieces until the discovery of engraved bones and stones in a number of rockshelters and caves in southwestern France during the 1860s. These objects were found with Paleolithic stone and bone tools and remains of Ice Age animals (a well-known engraving from La Madeleine, for example, depicts a mammoth carved on a piece of ivory tusk) and this association proved their antiquity (Bahn 1998, 57).

The identification of Paleolithic *art mobilier* did not, however, lead to an awareness of the age and significance of the art found on the walls of caves. It is often said that Europeans began their fascination with parietal art in 1879, after a young girl and her father investigated a cave at Altamira, near the north coast of Cantabria (Grant 1967, 3). In November of that year a Spanish landowner, Don Marcelino Sanz de Sautuola, was looking for Old Stone Age tools, bones, and hearths on the floor of the cave. His daughter, Maria, noticed drawings of large animals on the chamber ceiling and exclaimed to her father, "Mira, Papa, bueyes!" (Look, Papa, oxen!). Noting that the paintings were very similar in style to images seen in Upper Paleolithic portable art, Sanz de Sautuola published a small pamphlet that suggested the art of Altamira was of a comparable age (Bahn 1998, 58–59).

Even though images of animals had been observed in the cave of Niaux in France some thirteen years earlier, this was the first serious attempt to evaluate the age of parietal art (Krupp 1997, 116). But because Altamira's elegant 12,000-year-old paintings were not thought to be "primitive" enough to satisfy prevailing misconceptions about prehistoric art, the experts decided they must be a hoax. Most of the archaeological community refused to take Sanz de Sautuola's views about the antiquity of Altamira seriously; they dismissed him as naïve or a fraud.

His peers ridiculed him until his death in 1888 (Bahn 1998, 60; Clottes and Lewis-Williams 1998, 38).

Altamira's refined polychrome paintings of bison, horses, and other beasts were finally accepted as genuine in 1902 (Krupp 1997) when Emile Cartailhac, an expert who had previously challenged the cave's authenticity, finally admitted his mistake (Clottes and Lewis-Williams 1998, 38). Although Cartailhac received all the accolades, it was Edouard Piette, one of France's greatest prehistorians at the turn of the twentieth century, who had earlier (and against all odds) accepted the authenticity of Altamira. Due to his previous experience with mobiliary art, Piette was in a much better position than his contemporaries to recognize that Altamira belonged to the Upper Paleolithic—the Magdalenian in particular. He developed his considerable expertise while excavating at Gourdan, Lortet, and Arudy in the Pyrenees in the 1870s (Clottes and Lewis-Williams 1998, 38). It was Piette who found, in the late 1880s, the famous painted pebbles in the cave of Le Mas d'Azil. One of the doubts raised about Altamira was that the cave was too humid and the rock too friable to have preserved painting for so long. The stratigraphic position of the Azilian pebbles, however, offered proof that ochre could adhere to rock for thousands of years. The final breakthrough occurred in 1895 with engravings found in the cave of La Mouthe, in the Dordogne region of France. Paleolithic deposits blocked the entrance to the gallery where the images were located, thus providing evidence that the engravings must be of the same age (Bahn 1998, 60).

The Search for Meaning

From the first discovery of prehistoric painting at Altamira to the stunning finds at Grotte Cosquer and Chauvet Cave in the 1990s, researchers have tried to uncover the meaning of this Ice Age art and the function of the painted caves. Numerous attempts have been made to understand it; each one has brought something new, been elaborated upon, and had an influence, even if it has been rejected as a global explanation. It is therefore critical to look at the earlier interpretations; in spite of their inadequacies and errors, they comprise the bases of current thought (Clottes and Lewis-Williams 1998, 61). The major themes found in the explanations of cave art include: art for art's sake, totemism, hunting and fertility magic, and modern structuralist theories. Researchers confronting the enigmas of parietal art anchor their interpretations on the same basic foundations: the content of the art, the archaeological context in which it occurs, and ethnological comparisons made to more recent traditional societies that create or created rock art and about which we have fairly precise information (Clottes and Lewis-Williams 1998, 61).

Art for Art's Sake

When French paleontologist Edouard Lartet found a sculptured antler in the form of a bird engraved with the head of a bear in the cave of Massat (Ariège), he was perplexed. This refined portable art did not fit the image of primitive and prehistoric humans shared by most people in the mid-nineteenth century. Because of this, the first explanations were simple: these engravings and sculptures had no purpose other than to decorate arms and tools—for pleasure alone. This is the so-called theory of art for art's sake. Several things influenced this way of thinking, including Rousseau's notions concerning the "noble savage" (Clottes and Lewis-Williams 1998, 65). The people of prehistory, according to the ethnographers of the time, lived effortlessly in a world of plenty; artistic creativity was associated with free time and abundance.

Our Western tradition of museums and art galleries that proudly possess and display collections of work by acclaimed artists still prompts some to endorse the notion that the cave paintings represent art for art's sake. The principle of public exhibition is, however, a modern one; the painted caves of France and Spain were too poorly lit to function as museums and too redundant to be interpreted as some expressive artist's personal statement (Krupp 1997, 119). Moreover, these interpretations could not account for paintings and engravings in deep cave chambers, far from any dwellings (Clottes and Lewis-Williams 1998, 66).

Totemism and Hunting Magic

In an attempt to identify motivations other than simple ornamentation or purely aesthetic endeavors, researchers turned briefly to totemism, a concept that implies some kind of strict and privileged correlation between a human group and an animal species or specific plant. Assuming that the proprietors of Ice Age art recognized some sort of ancestral bond with certain animals (and thus avoided eating them), the paintings were seen as clan emblems that identified territorial rights within the cave (Krupp 1997, 118). Critics of this explanation note that some of the animals appear to be wounded by spears, which would not be compatible with the respect due a totem. Furthermore, if these images were really clan emblems, one would expect to find homogeneous art centered around a particular animal in each cave, rather than the mixture of animals seen at each site (Clottes and Lewis-Williams 1998, 66).

The prevailing explanation for the Upper Paleolithic images for at least the first half of the twentieth century was one that appealed to the premises of sympathetic magic. This new way of interpreting the art was partly due to the fact that, by the early 1900s, ethnographers were offering a different image of so-called primitive humans. The creators were no longer seen as carefree noble savages living in a world of plenty but, instead, as weak creatures struggling to get along in a hostile environment. In this scenario, magic arts had a very practical objective—that of aiding in survival. The art of this era was therefore utilitarian (Clottes and Lewis-Williams 1998, 68). The theory of sympathetic magic is based upon a proposed relationship or identity between an image and its subject. In acting upon the image, one also acted on the person or the animal represented. The three primary goals of magical practices were the hunt, fertility, and destruction.

Hunting magic, by taking possession of the image of the desired animal—and thus of the beast itself—was aimed at making plentiful hunts possible. It was thought that the predominantly animal images were painted or engraved as part of sympathetic magic to ensure success in the hunt or to effectively challenge those animals that were dangerous (Conkey 1989, 136). From this perspective, the images of incomplete beasts were intended to diminish their powers and thereby facilitate their capture. This magic was applied to the great hunted herbivores such as mammoths, horses, bison, aurochs, ibex, and deer. Destructive magic was directed toward animals that were considered dangerous to humans: felines, rhinoceri, and bears. Through fertility magic, people were thought to assist the procreation of useful species by depicting pregnant females or animals of the opposite sex in precoupling scenes (Clottes and Lewis-Williams 1998, 69).

This concept met with lasting success because it represented progress over the previous theories and also because of the influence of Henri Breuil, one of the towering figures of Old World prehistory in the first half of the twentieth century. The Abbé Breuil, often referred to as the "pope of prehistory," was renowned for his tracings of both cave and portable art, mostly in Europe, but also in southern Africa. His interpretation of Paleolithic art as a reflection of fertility and hunting magic was based on a somewhat simplistic use of selected ethnographic analogies (Bahn 1998, 66–67). Nevertheless, the notion of hunting magic was subsequently adopted and enlarged upon. Breuil popularized this idea to such an extent that it became crystallized into a sort of dogma until the end of the 1950s (Clottes and Lewis-Williams 1998, 68).

Critics note that, if sympathetic magic was, in fact, the principal motivation in Paleolithic art, we would expect to find a large number of the spellbound animals marked with "arrows" or wounds, along with pregnant females and explicit sexual couplings (Clottes and Lewis-Williams 1998, 70). We also know that the animals depicted in the caves had but a small part in prehistoric diets (Krupp 1997, 118). Furthermore, there are many elements—often fundamental ones— that cannot be made to fit the concepts of hunting, destruction, or fertility magic. In this context it is impossible to explain the stenciled hands, the isolated and caricatured human figures, and the depictions of composite creatures—the type of monsters that did not exist in nature and which one could not, therefore, wish would either multiply or die (Clottes and Lewis-Williams 1998, 71). Despite its having fallen out of favor, sympathetic magic theory has not disappeared completely. It is still alive and well in popular consciousness; some guides in those decorated caves that are open to the public continue to propose it to visitors as an irrefutable explanation (Clottes and Lewis-Williams 1998, 72). Most scholars, however, consider this interpretation to be inconsistent and unsatisfactory, and it was eventually replaced by structuralism.

Structuralism

The structuralist approach rejects the idea of using ethnological theory as a basis for interpretation and instead advocates a return to the caves and the works found there. Attempts at explaining Paleolithic art from a structural viewpoint began in the 1940s with the work of Max Raphaël, a long-unrecognized precursor of this method of analysis (Clottes and Lewis-Williams 1998, 73). Raphaël (1945) was struck by what he saw as the ordered and composed whole of parietal art. Instead of a disparate accumulation that a variety of distinct magical practices would have produced over centuries, he noticed combinations and compositions. Raphaël's successors, most notably Annette Laming-Emperaire and André Leroi-Gourhan, went much further. They believed that the caves themselves played an important role in the perception people had of them and in the way they were used.

Beginning in the 1960s, Leroi-Gourhan revolutionized interpretation of the Paleolithic images by rejecting ethnography and making a structuralist analysis of cave art's contents. To his way of thinking the caves were not simply collections of individual images, as Breuil had thought, but carefully planned homogeneous compositions laid out according to a preconceived blueprint (Bahn 1998, 66). In other words, he assumed there had to be some underlying structure or a set of structural principles that generated the resultant imagery (Conkey 1989, 140). To establish these patterns more firmly, all of the different parameters had to be related to each other, and, to accomplish this, Leroi-Gourhan used statistics, based on counting images. He studied sixty caves, established an inventory, and compared their elements (Clottes and Lewis-Williams 1998, 74).

Believing that the figures were an assemblage of graphic symbols and that the collection was neither writing nor pictogram, Leroi-Gourhan (1982) suggested that the mode governing the assemblage was that of a *mythogram* in which figures are arranged around a central point, just as if it were a picture. He concluded that bison, aurochs, mammoths, and horses formed the basis of the bestiary, and that they were frequently combined and tended to occupy the central panels. Complementary animals like ibex and deer followed in their wake and were most often placed in secondary positions. The more dangerous animals, like rhinoceri, lions and bears, were relegated to the cave depths (Clottes and Lewis-Williams 1998, 74).

This system was considered to be binary in that certain animals were seen as always being associated with others; the basic couple was the bison (or auroch) and the horse. Leroi-Gourhan suggested that this involved some kind of sexual symbolism; signs and animals had male or female values that were both complementary and opposed. In his opinion, the bison and aurochs were female symbols and, inversely, horses were considered to be masculine (Leroi-Gourhan 1986, 15-16). In his system, the number, gender, posture, shape, and rendering of the animals was of little or no consequence; it was only the subject matter that counted (Clottes and Lewis-Williams 1998, 75; Krupp 1997, 120).

The critics of structuralist concepts are vocal and many. They reproach structuralists for using an elementary level of interpretation, arguing that suggestions that the drawings reproduce a system of thought or myths explain nothing about why they were created in the depths of the caves. There is no referential context of social action, and there are no actors, intentions, reasons, or questions as to why these structural mythograms might have been meaningful to their particular makers, users, and viewers (Clottes and Lewis-Williams 1998, 75; Conkey 1989, 145; Eagleton 1983, 112).

We should keep in mind that the intellectual atmosphere that prevailed during the period that structuralism developed was one of emerging tension between ethnology and archaeology, with most of the early interpretations being derived from direct parallels with ethnographic groups observed during the nineteenth and twentieth centuries. In the earlier theories (hunting magic, totemism, and so forth), the people producing the art were thought to be hunter-gatherers who were decidedly *not* like modern humans of the civilized world. They were, instead, prescientific, prereligious, and not to be understood in the same terms and concepts (Conkey 1989, 136). Leroi-Gourhan's structural reading of Paleolithic art changed this way of thinking by confirming and extending the universal foundation of fully human thought back into the Upper Paleolithic Era (153).

The intellectual climate spawned in part by Leroi-Gourhan's structuralist approach has insisted that Upper Paleolithic studies be premised on an acceptance of the cognitive complexity of the people who produced the art. This atmosphere also encouraged the idea that all forms of rock art can be an object and a construct of archaeological investigation, no matter what one's paradigm might be (Conkey 1989, 147). In this context it is also interesting to note that liberation from sympathetic magic hypotheses was gained through statistical and quantitative analysis. The application of these quantitative methods (which were fully accepted by the New Archaeology of the 1960s) to a new set of data represented "a move away from the empiricist paradigm to an exploration of anthropological theory"

(Lewis-Williams 1983a, 5). It was, then, a theoretical shift in the way archaeological data—human material culture—are conceptualized (Conkey 1989, 150).

It is important to note that Leroi-Gourhan did not produce his structural account and then simply let it stand. As he himself insisted, this was nothing more than a "clearing of the terrain" that revealed a more complex Paleolithic thought process than traditional interpretations had led us to believe. He also asserted that "the cave's decor does really form a decor, that is to say, a framework within which something magically or mythically unfolds" (Leroi-Gourhan 1986, 10). In 1966 Leroi-Gourhan wrote a particularly informative essay on how he viewed this enterprise. Here it becomes quite clear that his goal all along was "accessing traces of metaphysical thought" (Michelson 1986). In the early 1960s, however, ideas like this were deemed incompatible with the emergence of an Anglo-American New Archaeology and its denial of "mind." The irony here is that processualist thought was grounded in anthropology, but it missed the link with the most anthropological of Europe's prehistorians—Leroi-Gourhan (Conkey 1989).

Despite their general failure to interpret Paleolithic art as a whole, the preceding theories have greatly influenced current studies. Scholars now realize that it is no longer possible to draw superficial ethnological parallels, even though studies of the hunter-gatherer societies that created rock art are a rich vein to tap. We can no longer ignore the importance of the caves in the choice of sites and also in the significance of the paintings. The placement of the drawings in terms of the relief and topography are fundamental to modern studies. The types of animals depicted respond to a logic quite different from a culinary one (Clottes and Lewis-Williams 1998, 78–79).

Shamanism

For a closer look at the development of the most recent theories having to do with the interpretation of Paleolithic art, we must move a continent away, to southern Africa. It was here that David Lewis-Williams, a cultural anthropologist at the University of Witwatersrand, began his research. In an attempt to decipher the meaning of historic and protohistoric San rock art, Lewis-Williams combined an analysis of available ethnographic data on ritual, myth, and linguistics with the archaeological record of painted images. He determined that the painted motifs referred to the supernatural visions and experiences that medicine men received while in altered states of consciousness (Lewis-Williams 1982, 1983a, 1985). Intrigued with the implications suggested by the fact that the painted forms originated in hallucinatory trance states, he began an investigation of the neurophysiological effects of altered states of consciousness on visual and graphic imagery (Lewis-Williams 1986).

His research was based on the premises that the human neurological system is a biological universal and that neuropsychological effects of altered states can be presumed to be equivalent cross-culturally and through the antiquity of Homo sapiens' occupation of the earth. Experiments dealing with the effects of altered states of consciousness in Western laboratory subjects support this position (Reichel-Dolmatoff 1978; Siegel and Jarvik 1975, 81–104). Building on these data, Lewis-Williams and his student, Thomas Dowson, abstracted a series of recurring, fundamental visual forms (which they referred to as "entoptic phenomena") that are experienced cross-culturally during altered states. They also described a set of principles of perception by which these forms are seen, as well as the stages through which trance subjects' visual hallucinations proceed (Lewis-Williams and Dowson 1988).

They tested their model against two separate corpora of rock art, both of which were known to have been created by shamans and to be related to altered states experiences. The shamanistic art was from two continents: the San rock art (Lewis-Williams 1980, 1981, 1982) and the engravings of the Coso Range in the western Great Basin of North America (Whitley 1988). A close correspondence between the expectations of their neuropsychological model and the San and Coso rock art gave them increased confidence in the inferential value of their model for interpreting prehistoric art.

With these data at hand, Lewis-Williams and Dowson compared the expectations of their model with the rock art of the Upper Paleolithic. They found a close correspondence between the recurring entoptic forms and the so-called geometric signs of the cave art. They also found a correlation between their model and the Paleolithic art in terms of the principles of perception and the compositional style and graphic logic by which many of the geometric forms were combined with iconic images, and in the way the iconic images themselves were rendered. This inference opened the door to the cognitive belief systems of Upper Paleolithic people (Lewis-Williams and Dowson 1988).

Since its introduction, the neuropsychological model has gained a number of proponents. It has been refined, tested, and expanded, particularly with regard to European Upper Paleolithic art. In 1998 Lewis-Williams, in collaboration with the world-renowned rock art authority Jean Clottes, published a book titled *The Shamans of Prehistory: Trance and Magic in the Painted Caves*. Advocating a combined neuropsychological and ethnographic approach, Clottes and Lewis-Williams summarize their current interpretation of the Ice Age cave art:

> The way in which each individual cave was structured and decorated was a unique result of the interaction of four elements: the topography of the cave, its passages, and chambers; the universal functioning of the

human nervous system and, in particular, how it behaves in altered states; the social conditions, cosmologies, and religious beliefs of the different times at which a cave was used; and, lastly, the catalyst—the ways in which individual people and groups of people exploited and manipulated all of these elements for their own purposes and advantage (1998, 101).

Clottes and Lewis-Williams acknowledge they were not the first to consider Upper Paleolithic art in the context of shamanistic practices. Mircea Eliade (1964), Joan Halifax (1982), Weston La Barre (1972), Andreas Lommell (1967), and other researchers had earlier suggested that paintings at Lascaux, Les Trois-Frères, and other sites represented shamans and their supernatural helpers (Clottes and Lewis-Williams 1998, 79). They were, however, the first to place shamanism at the center of a broader framework that, for them, brought the diverse and puzzling evidence of this art into a coherent, flexible pattern.

This explanation, like the ones that preceded it, has its critics. All of the components used in its development—analogy, ethnography, neuropsychological modeling—have come under fire in the past and continue to be debated. The idea that the art was created by shamans and reflects the hallucinatory visions experienced during trance has probably been the subject of more controversy and scrutiny than any of the preceding theories. Following a review of the development of rock art research in the Americas, subsequent chapters will consider all of these elements more closely.

Rock Art Research in the Americas 6

E VER SINCE THEIR GREAT ANTIQUITY WAS ACCEPTED, the Upper Paleolithic art and artifacts of Europe have enjoyed a privileged position in our evolutionary scenarios. At least in part, this is because these materials and images have been associated with the activities of early humans for more than a hundred years. Some researchers would have us believe that the prestige of the Franco-Cantabrian materials led to the widespread dissemination of every theory having to do with their creation and meaning, and that these ideas were exported and applied to rock art in every part of the globe (Clottes and Lewis-Williams 1998, 69; Conkey 1989, 136). The implication is that Paleolithic research provided the intellectual foundation for rock art studies throughout the world, but this is not the case. American rock art research has a long tradition of its own—and one with a very different intellectual context.

The Early Years
When explorers and missionaries from Western Europe began to colonize and investigate various parts of the globe, they reported on anything of interest that they encountered, including primitive markings on rock surfaces. During the sixteenth century, Spanish priests traveling in the New World commented on rock art in many parts of Latin America, including Brazil, Colombia, Venezuela, Paraguay, and Peru, as well as several sites in Mesoamerica (Bahn 1998). In the mid-seventeenth century, the renowned Jesuit missionary and explorer Jacques Marquette made one of the first references to North American rock art when he noticed painted winged monsters on a cliff near Alton, in present day Illinois. Other discoveries followed. In 1711 Padre Eusebio Kino described the Painted Rocks at Gila Bend, Arizona. Cotton Mather, the renowned New England intellectual, published an archaeological

report in 1714 that included a description of the abstract designs and highly stylized human figures on Dighton Rock on the east bank of the Taunton River in
Massachusetts (Molyneaux 1977). Father Silvestre de Escalante, while attempting
to find a land route from Mexico to Monterey in 1776, observed carved rock images in western Colorado (Bahn 1998).

During the nineteenth century, North America pioneers pushing westward observed and recorded a number of rock art sites. As early as 1804, Bishop James
Madison wrote an account of a rock outcrop near Burning Springs in western Virginia that bore images of humans and animals. The first sketch of California petroglyphs was made at a site in Lassen County, near the northeast boundary of the
state. There, on October 1, 1850, J. Goldsborough Bruff recorded strange and abstract motifs that he found carved in basalt rock (Read and Gaines 1949). The
earliest written record of rock art in Utah dates from 1852; it was published in
Lieutenant J. W. Gunnison's book *Mormons or Latter-Day Saints*. In 1853 Henry
Schoolcraft published a rendering of images from two rock art sites, one on the
south shore and another on the north shore of the Agawa Bay region of Lake Superior. The Reverend Stephen Bowers, one of the early investigators of the Chumash paintings in southern California, sketched images of two sites near San
Marcos Pass in 1877 (Bahn 1998, 52).

The major American researcher during this time was Lieutenant Colonel Garrick Mallery, an Army officer in command of Fort Rice on the Upper Missouri
River. Relying on contributions from hundreds of observers, Mallery compiled a
remarkable record of the "picture writing" made by aboriginal inhabitants of the
United States and published the first comprehensive work on rock art in North
America (Mallery 1893). In spite of this work, there was relatively little interest
in New World rock art in the early decades of the twentieth century. Scholars of
the time generally considered rock art as a minor facet of the archaeological record
that did not lend itself to those methods of analysis being applied to more conventional cultural material such as architecture, ceramics, or lithics (Hedges 1992,
67). Even the extensive body of petroglyphs and pictographs in the far western
United States was almost completely overlooked. Alfred Kroeber (1925), in his
book *Handbook of the Indians of California*, gives little attention to the subject except
for a brief reference to some pictographs in southern California. *Primitive Art*, the
seminal work of Franz Boas (1927), neglects rock art in the major considerations
of form, symbolism, and style; except for some minor asides, this book gives the
topic no treatment at all.

In 1929 Julian Steward's *Petroglyphs of California and Adjoining States* was published
by the University of California at Berkeley. This monograph was the first work
from a prominent American anthropologist to deal specifically with petroglyphs
and pictographs. This regional synthesis followed Mallery's methodology in that

it used randomly acquired descriptive texts as baseline data. These source materials, which had been piling up for years in the Department of Anthropology at Berkeley, were "largely the contributions of private individuals" (Steward 1929, 52). Steward was the first to classify design elements and their geographic distribution. He focused on establishing a series of rock art "areas" that were presumably meant to identify some type of cultural affiliations (Whitley and Loendorf 1994, xii) but offered only general inferences concerning their interpretation. Steward (1929, 53) admitted that he was "able to make personal visits to only a few sites" located in Santa Barbara and Inyo counties in California. Referring to these areas he wrote, "more intensive study of the petrography . . . is necessary to establish more detailed relationships" (Steward 1929, 55).

More than thirty years later, Campbell Grant, a dedicated avocational, made an effort to answer Steward's plea. Grant conducted extensive field research in both areas and wrote a remarkably popular book on each (Grant 1965; Grant, Baird, and Pringle 1968). Even though these books were favorably received by the general public (*Rock Drawings of the Coso Range* had six printings between 1968 and 1987), most field archaeologists working in far western North America still viewed rock art research as a marginal endeavor. Overviews of the Desert West (Jennings 1964) and the Great Basin region (d'Azevedo et al. 1966; Jennings and Norbeck 1955) make no mention of the rock art. In an article by Fowler (1980) that traced the history of Great Basin anthropological research from 1776 to 1979, there is no commentary on rock art studies.

This marginalization of rock art research in America went hand in hand with changes that were taking place within archaeology during the 1960s and 1970s. The New Archaeology was primarily concerned with cultural ecology and evolution; research focused on subsistence aspects of human societies and viewed culture as an adaptation to the environment. This approach was also associated with an emphasis on quantification and a scientific methodology. The humanist interest in prehistoric aesthetics suffered as a result, and rock art studies were usually left to amateurs (Earle 1994). It is not surprising, then, that Grant and his colleagues (all amateurs) were among the first to offer a specific explanation for the rock art of the Coso Range in east-central California, nor is it entirely unexpected that their interpretation was of hunting magic.

The Search for Meaning

Most researchers in North America reduced art and symbolism to adaptive adjuncts and viewed rock art as a secondary activity that must be associated with some "significant endeavor such as hunting" (Hedges 1992, 68). Julian Steward was the first American archaeologist to offer a "hunting magic" hypothesis for the petroglyphs of the Great Basin. In his 1929 monograph he observed that the images of mountain sheep may have been associated with the hunt or with the magical increase of the herd (Whitley 1998b, 132). Although Steward was cautious about this theory and recognized that it failed to explain a large portion of the art, others pursued it with considerable enthusiasm.

In a report in *Science*, Heizer and Baumhoff (1959) contended that they had "proved" the hunting magic hypothesis when they found correlations between Nevada petroglyph sites and game trails. These scholars expanded this concept in a 1962 book titled *Prehistoric Rock Art of Nevada and Eastern California*. Their work, which was focused on sites in northern Nevada (particularly a concentration of petroglyphs known as the Largomarsino site), traced its lineage to Mallery and built on Steward's previous work in neighboring California. However, this study was radically different from its predecessors on two counts. First, it was based on field investigations that were specifically undertaken to produce the book. Although ample avocational contributions were incorporated, most of the data were newly acquired in the course of an independent three-year project (Heizer and Baumhoff 1962, 5–15). Second, its goal was purportedly interpretation, namely an attempt to explain the social function of Great Basin petroglyphs. The main thrust was to link rock art sites by content and location to the critical role of increasing-the-herd rituals as a critical function in prehistoric Great Basin life.

Heizer and Baumhoff's work encouraged others to conduct a number of area and site-specific studies. Foremost among these was Grant's research that resulted in the publication in 1968 of *Rock Drawings of the Coso Range*. In this examination of Coso rock art, Grant and his colleagues suggested that "most of the immense number of sheep drawings were connected with hunting magic—the drawing of the sought-after animal would help bring the hunter success" (Grant, Baird, and Pringle 1968, 113). They also thought it was possible that the images might have been created as "art for art's sake," arguing that "the steady improvement in technique . . . demonstrates that the creators took satisfaction in a job ingeniously conceived and well executed. Where one man would abrade a barely recognizable sheep . . . some of the later artists made highly stylized life-sized sheep, laboriously pecked all over." Therefore, they concluded, "the drawings satisfy the innate desire of the creator to make a pleasant image on a rock where nothing had existed before" (115). When Julian Steward wrote the forward to this book, he stated that the authors "have made a very convincing case . . . for the association of the rock pictures with hunting magic" (Steward 1968, ix).

Amateurs and professionals alike accepted the hunting magic hypothesis. For many processualist archaeologists, it appeared to validate the notion that subsistence was the primary concern of primitive hunter-gatherer societies. Cultural traditions, beliefs, art, and symbolism were merely adaptive mechanisms that reflected this concern for food procurement. The logic behind this interpretation seemed to be unassailable. Bighorn sheep were food; they were in the art; and therefore the art had to do with food, as everyone knew it must (Whitley 1998b, 133). In those rare instances where rock art was given any consideration, hunting magic thus became the explanation of choice.

People had, of course, been speculating about other possible meanings for the images carved in stone long before the advent of processual archaeology and, for that matter, well before archaeology was recognized as an academic discipline. Missionaries in Latin America knew that certain rock art sites were religious in nature and in some way sacred to the indigenous people. Believing that the images were the objects of superstitious worship, they either destroyed the sites or engraved crosses in high and prominent places to show the superiority of Christianity (Bahn 1998, 10).

In North America, travelers and researchers have commented on the heads or faces carved at the foot of the Great Falls on the Connecticut River in Vermont since their discovery in 1789. These engravings have been described variously as Indian chiefs, family groups, symbols of male authority, memorials of noteworthy past events, idle artwork, and, most significantly, the work of shamans recording their vision experiences (Bahn 1998, 20). Garrick Mallery, the author of the first comprehensive study of North American rock art was, in several respects, ahead of his time. He took the position that the art should be viewed as only one part of a much larger continuum of activities whereby humans left a graphic legacy in stone as well as in other media. Mallery's (1893) discussion of shamanism and its association with rock art was among the first of its kind and, even today, remains a remarkably literate and readable example of the genre.

Little known (or perhaps conveniently overlooked) is the fact that Heizer and Baumhoff's (1962) work linking the Largomarsino petroglyphs with hunting magic was an elaboration of a 1958 paper by Baumhoff, Heizer, and Elsasser that related this rock art to shamanistic practices. Baumhoff and his colleagues knew that Great Basin Shoshoneans purportedly sought supernatural power through visions and dreams at specific power spots, especially springs or water holes that might be inhabited by "water babies." The authors' knowledge of the association of petroglyph sites with permanent springs led them to propose that "native curing doctors (shamans) may have been responsible for the rock markings" and that their motivation may have been acquisition of supernatural power (Baumhoff, Heizer, and Elsasser 1958, 4). This proposition was, however, omitted from the 1962 book.

In the late 1960s, a detailed analysis of the rock paintings situated on the Lower Pecos River in Texas placed the rock art in the context of a hypothesized shamanic society (Kirkland and Newcomb 1967). A comprehensive study of the

Petersborough petroglyph site in Ontario, Canada, published in 1973, also put forward a shamanic origin for the engraved images found at this location. Incorporating archaeology, ethnography, and art history, this work gave a detailed iconographic interpretation grounded in Algonkian shamanism with reference to shamanism on a worldwide scale (Vastokas and Vastokas 1973). Although this interpretation was considered highly speculative (Hedges 1992), the authors argued that "even speculation may provide . . . an insight into the problems of rock art research and suggest to the archaeologist new avenues of approach in his efforts to reconstruct the prehistory of North America" (Vastokas and Vastokas 1973, 5).

The Emergence of a Cognitive Approach

Unfortunately, the New Archaeology was ascendant, and few took this proposal very seriously. There were no commitments that encouraged a broad interpretive framework for the study of North American rock art and certainly none that took into account ritual or religion. It was not until the 1980s, when researchers began to question the processualist paradigm and to acknowledge the importance of symbolism, individual human agency, beliefs, and ritual, that rock art resurfaced as a subject worthy of legitimate archaeological inquiry. Since that time, David Whitley has been a driving force in promoting the expansion of rock art studies in far western North America and the principle advocate of a cognitive approach that incorporates a shamanistic interpretation. Much of Whitley's research has focused on the western Great Basin. Before considering his work more closely, we will look briefly at the physical environment, the prehistoric inhabitants, and the rock art of the Coso Range.

Physiographic Setting

The Mojave Desert and the easternmost edge of California are part of western North America's basin and range territory, a region with internally draining rivers and valleys, none of which exit to the ocean. Toward the end of the Pleistocene, roughly 12,000 years ago, wetter conditions created great river and lake systems that filled the lower-lying areas. In the southern part of Inyo County, Owens Lake overflowed toward the south and formed a series of lakes that included China Lake, Searles Lake, and Panamint Lake, evidenced by ancient shorelines and partially dissected lake beds (Clements in Harrington 1957).

The Coso Range lies in east-central California, at the westernmost edge of the Great Basin. The Cosos are bounded on the west by the Sierra Nevada, on the north by Owens Lake, on the east by the Argus Range, and on the south by Indian Wells Valley. Coso Peak, rising 2,475 meters above sea level, is the highest point in the range. Southwest of Coso Peak, there is evidence of volcanic activity, both ancient and more recent. For tens of thousands of years the Pleistocene history of this region reflects a struggle between the fairly steady force of stream erosion as well as the less frequent, but more powerful, eruptions of intracanyon volcanic flows (Duffield and Smith 1978). A number of cinder cones have ruptured the granitic rock structure, and immense basaltic flows have been extruded and then faulted, forming the cliffs of smooth volcanic rock used for rock engravings.

The Inhabitants

This was the land of the Numa. At the time of Euro-American contact—about mid-nineteenth century in this part of North America—Numic-speaking peoples occupied the Coso Range and most of the Great Basin. Numic comprises a group of related languages that is part of a larger Uto-Aztecan stock, a family that includes such disparate and well-known cultures as the Gabrielino in the Los Angeles Basin of southern California, the Hopi in northern Arizona, and the Aztec in central Mexico. Numic includes six different languages divided into three generalized groupings: northern Paiute, ranging from the Owens Valley in eastern California northwards through the western portion of Nevada and into southeastern Oregon; Shoshone, extending from the Coso Range across Death Valley, through central Nevada, southern Idaho and northern Utah into western Wyoming; and southern Paiute, found primarily in the Mojave Desert south of the Coso Range, southern Nevada, southern and central Utah, and the western part of Colorado (Bettinger and Baumhoff 1982; Goss 1977; Lamb 1958). People living in the immediate vicinity of the Coso Range were known as "Coso" or alternatively "Panamint" Shoshone (Steward 1938).

The inhabitants confronted one of the harshest environments found in North America. Population density, considering the relative paucity of natural resources, was necessarily low and quite widely dispersed. These people were hunter-gatherers who employed a classic pattern of seasonal aggregation in the winter months followed by dispersal into single or extended family units during spring and summer. These small groups would usually congregate to harvest pine nuts in the fall. The result was much more movement and a wider ranging territory than was normally the case for other Native California groups. These circumstances also contributed to greater linguistic and cultural homogeneity, in sharp contrast to the more typical California pattern where languages, or at least dialects, seemed to change with every new valley (Whitley 2000).

Numic society consisted of loosely organized bands representing allied family groups that were led by a headman. Although the headman governed by consensus and was often the oldest and, therefore, the wisest member of the band, this leadership position usually ran with a particular family line (Bettinger 1982; Whitley 2000). The headman was also the religious leader—the Man of Power, or shaman. Generic Numic terms for "headman" and "shaman" were exactly the same, as were terms for "headman's assistant" and "shaman's assistant" (Whitley 1998b, 34). The role of political, social, and religious leader was, then, entrusted to one individual.

As part of a linguistic continuum that ranged from southeastern California to the eastern edge of the Great Basin, Numic-speaking inhabitants shared a remarkably homogeneous culture in terms of worldview, beliefs, concepts of kin relationships, and other matters. This was a widespread phenomenon that extended well beyond language groups, different environments, and various subsistence activities. While the immediate Coso Range was the principle habitat of the Coso Shoshone, their lifeways were quite similar to surrounding related groups, and it is likely that intermarriages with their neighbors and regular travel outside their home territory tended to mitigate any cultural or geographic boundaries. We can, therefore, infer that the rock art was probably not the product of any single group of inhabitants living in the Coso Range, but was instead part of a more general pattern of Numic use of the landscape. Northern and Southern Paiute, Kawaiisu, and other peoples may thus have been responsible for some of the petroglyphs (Whitley 1998b).

The Rock Art

Steward (1968, vii) observed that "[t]he Coso Range seems an improbable place to find such elaborate, distinctive, and abundant art." Improbable as it may seem, the Coso Range, by most accounts, contains the most profuse and important array of rock art resources to be found in California, the Great Basin, and perhaps all of North America (Clewlow 1998, 14). Although many scholars consider Nevada's Largomarsino site, with roughly 600 elements, to be unusually endowed in a Great Basin context, it pales in significance when compared with the main Coso canyons. In a study of six sites in close proximity to each other, Grant and his colleagues counted over 1,000 elements apiece; the inventory of the entire area numbered nearly 15,000 elements (Grant, Baird, and Pringle 1968, 119). Wilke and Rector (1984) believe that the actual number might be three times the original Grant figure. No wonder then, that this region has served as an academic testing ground for all manner of speculations, hypotheses, and inferences put forward in many past and current scholarly studies.

The rock art in the Coso Range was not officially "discovered" until the 1920s (Grant, Baird, and Pringle 1968, 14). Steward included images from Little Lake, on the western edge of the Cosos, in his 1929 work. The first published account of Renegade Canyon (now known as Upper Renegade and Little Peglyph) appeared about ten years after the initial discovery (Johnston 1933). The earliest description of the area currently known as Big Petroglyph Canyon was written more than a decade later (Smith 1944). During this interval, a large part of the Coso Range came under the jurisdiction of the United States Navy and, beginning in 1943, visits by the general public were no longer allowed. Thus, many of the earlier scholars were not familiar with the main concentrations of rock art. This restriction was not eased until 1964, and even now access to the sites is limited.

From the earliest scholarly investigations, researchers have tried to define the petroglyphs in terms of style. Heizer and Baumhoff (1962) classified them as Great Basin Curvilinear and Rectilinear Abstract or Great Basin Representational, designations that could be used throughout the Great Basin. Grant and his colleagues (1968) placed the rock drawings into four recognizable styles: naturalistic, stylized, abstract, and pit-and-groove. Whitley (2000) moves away from this concept of style and, in its place, considers all Native California rock art in terms of a series of "artistic traditions" that emphasize the distribution, the techniques used to create the art, and the function and meaning as demonstrated ethnographically.

Under Whitley's scheme, the Coso petroglyphs are categorized as Great Basin Engraved, a variant of his Great Basin Tradition. This form is found in the Mojave and Colorado deserts and the adjacent western edge of the Great Basin in California. Great Basin Engraved art comprises pecked motifs in the form of geometric designs and representational images. At the majority of sites outside of the Coso Range, geometric images predominate; they include concentric circles, grids, dot patterns, zigzags, curvilinear meanders, spirals, and circular designs that contain fairly complex interior patterns. Representational forms are most often found in smaller proportions and are usually comprised of bighorn sheep, human figures, weapons, bags, prints and tracks, vulvas, lizards, rattlesnakes, and an occasional canine or mountain lion.

The bighorn sheep (*Ovis canadensis*) is one of the hallmarks of the Great Basin Engraved variant. These animals are depicted in a variety of ways: with horns facing forward or in profile; with fairly realistic, somewhat rectangular, bodies; or as highly stylized boat-shaped (or navicular) forms. Based on the fact that only males of this species achieve large, incurving horns (and not until sexual maturity at about seven or eight years of age), experts suggest that a large majority of the bighorn engravings are intended to represent sexually active males (Whitley 2000). Although the sheep are occasionally shown impaled by spears or arrows, they are more commonly depicted as imaginary forms that have long meandering horns, two heads or two sets of horns, or elaborate internal body markings.

al species other than bighorn sheep are relatively rare, with
s occurring most frequently after sheep. Rattlesnakes, fol-
monly found throughout far western North America, are
tically as zigzag lines or diamond chains. Other species of
or birds, appear occasionally, but this is the exception rather
than the rule. Dogs (or coyotes) are quite rare but, when they are portrayed, they
exhibit a characteristic tail-erect posture. Mountain lions are usually depicted with
the tail paralleling the back.

Humans are rendered as simple stick figures, larger solid-bodied forms, or
large and elaborate "patterned body" images. Stick figures may be horned or wear
feathered headdresses; they are sometimes depicted with exaggerated digits. The
solid-bodied images are often phallic and may have oddly shaped heads. The patterned body figures typically have rectangular torsos filled with complex geometric designs. The heads of the patterned body humans are frequently highly
schematicized—either reduced to small circles or shown as spirals or concentric
rings. In either case, they may have headdresses that are often feathered. Most of
the human figures are male. Females are represented about 1 percent of the time
(Whitley 2000, 1998b) and are most often depicted with a round or pear-shaped
body in combination with pendant labia. Vulva forms are present at some sites;
they are approximately life size and usually shown as an oval or inverted "U," partly
bisected by a short vertical line.

Items reflecting material culture are usually restricted to weapons and what
appear to be skin bags, sometimes referred to as "medicine bags." The weaponry
includes bows and arrows (invariably shown in the hands of a human), atlatls (a
throwing board or kind of weapon used to propel a spear) that may be shown in
use or as isolated motifs, and occasional projectile points, blades, and knives. The
atlatls are rarely depicted realistically. Most often they are in the form of geometric designs: straight vertical lines (thought to represent the shaft of the atlatl) bi-
secting a small circle at the lower end, sometimes having a hook at the upper end.
These images are very common in the Coso Range and emphasize the importance
of men's objects.

There are occasional, but quite remarkable, examples of the combination of
animal and human forms. Patterned body figures, for example, are sometimes depicted with bird-claw feet. Stick-figure humans may have torsos or legs that seem
to be transforming into the zigzags of a rattlesnake. Mountain sheep may have
flat, plantigrade human feet, rather than hooves. Some of the solid-body "hunting" humans appear not so much to be wearing bighorn sheep headdresses, but
rather to have bighorn sheep heads.

In a general sense, the Great Basin exhibits a widely shared assemblage of
components, in that examples of all the motif types are often present at every

site. There are, however, major quantitative differences from one site to the next. Generally speaking, the representational forms found in the Great Basin Engraved variant are usually much less common than the geometric elements. The images in the Coso Range are an exception. In this comparatively small area, 26 percent of the engravings are geometric forms and 74 percent are representational (Grant, Baird, and Pringle 1968, 119; Whitley 1998b, 114). In the Cosos, there is considerable variation in the distribution of motifs. At one site (Little Lake) on the western edge of this region, the tabulations are 76 percent geometric and 24 percent representational—almost a complete reversal of the Coso pattern as a whole (Whitley 1998b, 115). Regardless of the site-to-site variability, bighorn sheep account for 51 percent of the representational engravings in the Coso Range, and it is the preponderance of these images that has influenced most interpretations of the rock art.

Beginnings of a Shamanic Interpretation

Noting that the Coso Range contained more bighorn sheep drawings than all of the other sheep sites in North America combined, Grant and his colleagues (1968, 34) suggested that "[i]t is hard to account for such a concentration unless we postulate the gradual development in the Coso region of a sheep cult." This way of thinking was based on the perception that the economically important game animals were often treated ceremonially by many North American tribes, the idea being that the spirit of the slain animal had to be placated so that it would return to the hunter in a new body, ready to be killed again (Grant, Baird, and Pringle 1968, 41).

Whitley (1982b) was one of the first to dispute this hypothesis. In 1981, while finishing his doctoral dissertation on the study of rock art in North America, he had an opportunity to examine bighorn sheep symbolism among the Numic speakers of the western Great Basin. In his first published article, Whitley suggested that hunting magic was too narrow an interpretation for the bighorn sheep motifs found in the canyons of the Coso Range. Based on his examination of the mythology of the Numic-speaking Western Shoshone, he offered a slightly different viewpoint, proposing that "the evidence points to the bighorn sheep as symbolic of male success in hunting and in sexual activities in a general sense, and not to the prehistoric existence of a cult with attendant ceremonial regalia and esoteric rituals" (Whitley 1982a, 269).

Years later, Whitley acknowledged that this conclusion was somewhat superficial and, in fact, barely scratched the surface of the meaning of the art (Whitley 1998b, 139). Nevertheless, his first publication contained the basic elements of a cognitive approach—one that emphasized the importance of a developed chronology for the production of the rock art, the appropriate use of the ethnographic record, and, most importantly, the idea that the rock art reflected the ideology and belief systems of a particular culture.

Working within these guidelines, Whitley concluded that shamans created much of the rock art in the Coso Range. The engraved images were related to the acquisition of supernatural power and portrayed the hallucinations that shamans perceived during trance or altered states of consciousness generated specifically to access the spiritual world (Whitley 1992a, 1994a, 1996, 1998a, 1998b, 2000). Obviously, this hypothesis did not spring full-blown overnight. Rather, Whitley arrived at it after years of intensive field work and deliberation, a period when concepts about the creation and meaning of the images were evaluated and refined. Whitley was breaking new ground, and it was during this time that he developed and refined his innovative theory and methodology for a cognitive archaeology.

The most critical underlying element of this entire approach is that, even though American and European rock art studies came from very different research directions, they both led to the same phenomenon: shamanism. This construct has become one of the major focal points for cognitive archaeologists and therefore warrants more detailed examination.

Shamanism

Do you believe that the sciences would ever have arisen and become great if there had not been magicians, alchemists, astrologers and wizards, who thirsted and hungered after abscondite and forbidden powers?

—FRIEDRICH NIETZSCHE

THE ORIGINS OF SHAMANISM are hidden deep in the mists of our primordial past. Joan Halifax, an anthropologist who has worked with healers and shamans around the world, suggests that the lifeway of the shaman must be nearly as old as human consciousness itself, predating the earliest known civilizations by many millennia (Halifax 1982). While we may never know exactly when or how the phenomenon of shamanism began, we can assume that the presence of individuals with particular healing skills was a significant element in the development of human culture. Disease, emotional problems, and traumatic injury, as well as social and philosophical dilemmas, had to be dealt with just as surely as infant helplessness. Those with the abilities to confront and cope with these problems must have been esteemed, and it seems likely that persons with special powers were often shamans. We can only speculate about the techniques of early healers, but the full range of skills must have developed over a long period of time (Bean and Vane 1992, 8).

A number of experts believe that the roots of shamanism reach back at least as far as the Paleolithic period (Eliade 1964; Furst 1977; Kirchner 1952; Lommell 1967; Wilbert 1972) and archaeological data seem to support this contention. The 1960 discovery of skeletons in Shanidar Cave in Iraq, for example, provides intriguing evidence for the presence of a curer in Paleolithic times. Soil samples taken from Shanidar IV, a male burial estimated to be over fifty thousand years old, contained numerous clusters of anthers representing eight species of flowers; seven of them have known medicinal properties (Leroi-Gourhan 1975). Most scholars are convinced that the flowers were included purposefully (Leroi-Gourhan 1989; Solecki 1989), and, if they were placed with the remains because of their healing properties, as many surmise, is it such a giant leap to infer the beginnings of some type of shamanistic activity?

Others believe that the origins of shamanic beliefs and practices were probably concurrent with the emergence of the earliest fully modern humans (Bean and Vane 1992; Clottes and Lewis-Williams 1998; Halifax 1982; Ripinsky-Naxon 1993). Whatever the time depth, we can infer the antiquity of shamanism from the fact that it is a near-universal phenomenon, one that was present among hunter-gatherer groups throughout the world (Bean and Vane 1992, 8; Clottes and Lewis-Williams 1998, 19; Ouzman 1998, 33; Whitley 1998a, 15).

Cognitive researchers have also established a link between shamanism and another near-universal phenomenon—rock art. If we accept the idea that at least a part of the rock art found around the world was created by shamans and that the images reflect the belief systems of their creators, then it is essential that we try to comprehend the essence of shamanism and the ideology that was a fundamental part of nearly all ancient cultures. This is admittedly a very difficult task. While it may be appropriate, as Renfrew (1994) suggests, to think of the past as really existing in the physical world, with human beings living their lives and interacting with one another and their environment much as we do today, we must also realize that the world of the shaman was very different from our own.

Early Contact and Studies

Beginning in the sixteenth century, explorers from Western Europe began journeying to distant parts of the world, where they encountered strange, bizarre, and sometimes terrifying religious beliefs and practices. The majority of these people came from a social and intellectual background that was determined, for the most part, by strict religious dogma. Their confidence in the unassailable truth of their own religious convictions led them to consider the beliefs of others as degenerate, evil, and, quite literally, satanic (Clottes and Lewis-Williams 1998, 11). They were often met by shaman-priests: people who were responsible for dealing with foreigners, outsiders, and any other strange or potentially dangerous elements in their universe (Bean 1992a, 2).

The Roman Catholic priests who accompanied the Spanish conquistadors during the subjugation of Central and South America encountered people who spoke of intense spiritual experiences that could be attained only through the consumption of intoxicating beverages. They often fell into a trance and, in this state, believed that they left their bodies and went on journeys to supernatural realms where they braved fearsome spirits and monsters (Clottes and Lewis-Williams 1998, 11). In the 1600s, French Jesuits, who were active as missionaries among the natives of New France, faced serious competition for the Indians' souls from their doctors, or "medicine men," as the priests called them. They were referring to certain individuals who, by virtue of their supposedly supernatural abilities, cured the sick and also performed a variety of mysterious deceptions. As a result, they were frequently called "conjurors" in the Jesuit records. Gradually, the missionaries acquired a more balanced understanding of these activities and recognized that, from the Native American perspective, medical skill was only one of the expressions of the supernatural abilities of medicine men. Accordingly, the notion of "medicine" was expanded to include all manifestations of supernatural power (Hultkrantz 1979, 84).

On the African continent, French missionaries François Daumas and Thomas Arbousset journeyed to what are now South Africa and Lesotho. There, in the 1830s, they found people who danced until they fell to the ground, totally exhausted, and covered with blood that poured from their nostrils. The horrified priests were convinced that these dancers were "worshiping" some supernatural being (Arbousset and Daumas 1846, 246–47).

The earliest recognition of "classic" shamanism (the form in which it was first described) occurred in central and northern Asia. Russians, exploring the vast territory of the Tungus people in the eastern part of Siberia during the seventeenth century, linked the term šaman, with a person who moved between different worlds on supernatural errands (Krupp 1997, 36). E. Ysbrant Ides, a Dutch diplomat who accompanied the Russian embassy sent by Peter the Great to China from 1692 to 1695, was the first to identify and describe a Tungus shaman (Laufer 1917).

Based on the work of early Russian ethnographers, researchers began to recognize the similarities between Siberian shamans and Native American medicine men. This led, in turn, to comparative ethnographic studies that placed the shaman in a specific cultural framework. Franz Boas was one of the first ethnographers to be mentioned in this context. Trained in an academic environment that was concerned with the archaic nature of shamanism, Boas chose to examine cultural particularity. For him, the influence of culture on an individual's actions and the role of culture in shaping a person's thoughts were of singular concern (Boas 1938, 673).

Following his earlier ethnographic work dealing with the native peoples of Canada and the American Northwest Coast, Boas began a project known as the Jessup North Pacific Expedition. Beginning in 1901, members of this expedition sailed slowly up the Pacific Coast to Alaska and then across the Bering Strait to Siberia. They established contact with various Northwest Coast tribes, with the Alaskan Eskimos, and with Neo- and Paleo-Siberian groups (Grim 1983, 17). The major fieldworkers, Waldemar Borogas and Waldemar Jochelson, wrote extensively about the shamanic practices they witnessed. One of their most significant contributions was the notion that shamanism was archaic, that is, a primitive or early religious experience maintained in a culture in spite of later developments. They concluded that shamanism originated in northern Asia and similarities to shamanic activities in North America were the result of migrations of an earlier period (Bogoras 1902, 1904; Jochelson 1905, 1924). Their work is still a major source for the ethnography of the region and has had a lasting influence.

American studies of shamanism, including works by Robert Lowie (1948) and Paul Radin (1914) were heavily influenced by the *Reports of the Jessup North Pacific Expedition*. Both of these scholars thought of shamanism as a primordial religious expression that offered important insights into the contemporary world. When Alfred Kroeber wrote his classic work, *Handbook of the Indians of California* (1925), knowledge about the status and role of shamans was somewhat limited and not yet understood as part of a holistic system. Nonetheless, a number of scholars (e.g., Gayton 1930; Kelly 1936, 1939; Park 1938; Whiting 1950) made substantial contributions to our understanding of shamanism during the second quarter of the twentieth century.

Most of the academic community, however, continued to take a conservative approach to shamanism and failed to appreciate many of its facets (Bean 1992a, 2). It was not until the works of Mircea Eliade were published in the early 1960s that the study of shamanism began to attract the attention of students of religion as well as anthropologists. Perhaps an equal stimulus was the publication, beginning in the late 1960s, of the works of Carlos Castenada, who was himself a reader of Eliade. The counterculture of the 1970s and its fascination with Native American religions and other non-Western philosophies was another significant factor. Since that time, our understanding of the shaman's role in society has increased considerably, and many scholars have worked diligently to enhance and improve that knowledge.

Some writers, however, oppose the application of the concept of shamanism on a global scale. Alice Beck Kehoe, for example, argues that "the terms 'shaman' and 'shamanism' should be limited primarily to Siberian practitioners so called in their homelands" (Kehoe 2000, 102). She insists that "[i]t is confusing and misleading to use a simple blanket word, lifted from an unfamiliar Asian language, for a variety of culturally recognized distinct practices and practitioners" (52–53). But practices that we refer to as "shamanistic" and practitioners we call "shamans" are not nearly as disparate, on a worldwide scale, as Kehoe and others would have us believe.

The Shamanic Universe

Although the topographical details of the shaman's universe may differ from culture to culture and from place to place, the fundamental structure is the same. Throughout the world the shamanic cosmos is usually vertically tiered. In its simplest form there are three levels: the plane of everyday life, a realm above, and a realm below (Whitley 2000). The upper world is occupied by powerful anthropomorphic beings—frequently seen as the primary creators—with whom humans can interact for their own well-being. The upper world might also include astronomical personages like the Sun, Moon, constellations, significant stars, theriomorphic creatures who were the forerunners of all the animal species, and other beings who have no counterpart in the mundane world (Bean 1975, 26).

The underworld is situated below ground and is often entered through caves or cracks in rocks. It is inhabited by superordinary creatures—spirits, ghosts, and monsters—that are usually considered to be more malevolent toward humans than those of the other two realms. These beings take many forms and are associated with water, springs or underground rivers and lakes. They frequently have reptilian or amphibian shapes, such as serpents or frogs, or the distorted humanoid appearance of hunchbacks, dwarfs, giants, cyclopes, or water babies (Bean 1975, 26).

People reside in the middle world—usually conceived as circular, floating in space, and surrounded by a void or by water (Krupp 1997, 35). Most cultures perceive the middle world as lying at the geographical center of the universe, and both human beings and a variety of nonmortal entities with considerable power dwell in this middle realm (Bean 1975, 26). Spirits frequently inhabit distinctive features of the middle world: mountains, caves, rivers, springs, rocks, trees, and other special places (Krupp 1997, 35).

The universe is also organized directionally; the world has a center and an edge. That boundary might be an echo of a circular horizon or have corners that correspond to the world's cardinal directions. The most common scheme used by people to organize the space they inhabit has to do with quarters, a notion encouraged, perhaps, by the symmetry of the human body. Not everyone uses the same four directions, but most people partitioned the land with some form of directional system (Krupp 1997, 17).

The center of the world, sometimes referred to as the *axis mundi* or world axis, represents the threshold between the different realms. Even though this cosmic center was considered to be everywhere, peoples of all times and places have created finite representations, frequently in the form of a World Tree or a Cosmic

Mountain. These symbols are the point of contact between the upper and lower worlds and intersect the separate realms of existence: the underworld is penetrated by the roots of the Tree and is in the belly of the Mountain; the middle world is transected by both, and the crown of the World Tree and summit of the Cosmic Mountain are each received by the heavenly realm (Halifax 1982, 84). A sacred pole, a cosmic pillar, or the World Tree is the device used by shamans to ascend into the company of spirits, to reach the higher cosmic plane, a bridge, or star. World Tree ideology is thus an important element in maintaining shamanic contact with the supernatural world. For some cultures, the World Tree is connected to the World River that acts as a link between all three realms and must be traversed by the shaman to reach any one of them (Ripinsky-Naxon 1993, 120).

This, then, is the traditional shamanic cosmos, with roots that reach deep into antiquity—a universe structured by a center, directions, boundaries, and time—and animated by the power of spirits and other creatures. This universe hosts a variety of spirits that help, hinder, or ignore the affairs of people (Krupp 1997, 35). Although these beings may occupy the heights of heaven and the catacombs of the underworld, this does not mean that the three realms are entirely discrete, nor that shamanistic societies make any distinctions between the real and the supernatural as Westerners do (Clottes and Lewis-Williams 1998, 29).

When we contemporary humans talk about the ideas of the ancients, or even about our own religious concepts, we make a distinction between natural and supernatural power. For us, all natural phenomena seem to exhibit a physical and scientific relationship between cause and effect. Things that break the rules are said to be supernatural, and scientific analysis banishes the supernatural from all rational thought. Spirits and gods, then, must exist outside of the natural world. For the ancients, however, this universe, with all its spirits and other mystical creatures, was entirely natural. The mysterious or magical was just another element that was part of the environment, an example of one channel of power. In this landscape the shamans were pivotal, and for them the connection between power and the cosmos was entirely obvious—all power was rooted in the natural order.

The Concept of Power

The cosmologies of most small, self-sufficient social systems—groups that need to deal directly with the natural world—are remarkably similar. Power is the most important precept. Power most often originates in a void where two potent entities, usually male and female, come together in some cataclysmic event that produces a dynamic creative force. In some cases, power and creators appear simultaneously in the cosmos—without explanation—and a creative force then proceeds to form or alter the world. In each instance the creator (or primary creators) uses power to accomplish a variety of acts that lead to a number of other creations, including human beings. The final outcome is a hierarchically structured social universe, a cosmological model where the nature of power is defined and rules governing the interaction with power sources are established (Bean 1975, 26).

In this cosmos, power is omnipresent. It is the principal causative agent for all phenomena throughout the universe. Power is sentient, possesses will, and potentially exists in all things. It is distributed differently through all realms of the world; some things may possess more power than others, but anything that reveals some form of "life" or demonstrates the will "to act" has a certain degree of power. A rock that suddenly moves downhill may thereby exhibit an ability "to act," and thus reveal itself as a source of power (Bean 1975, 27).

The topography of space and time concentrates power in the middle world. It is the point of contact—the nexus—between the upper realm of celestial objects and sky spirits and the lower realm of subterranean waters and caves of predatory monsters and spirits of death. Since humans inhabit the geographical center of the universe, they are ideally situated to bring power from the other realms into play in the middle world. Because all power is sentient and personalized, people are able to interact with power, or the conduits of power, much as they would with other humans (Bean 1975, 27). Those who possess knowledge of the guidelines or rules that govern power can acquire, manipulate, and wield this power throughout the universe. In small-scale hunter-gatherer societies, access to supernatural power is most often reserved for those who stand at the apex of the power hierarchy: the shamans (Bean and Vane 1992).

The special role of the shaman is interaction with the sources of power. Their goal is to preserve the cosmic equilibrium by acquiring and applying knowledge and power. Shamans use supernatural power to solve problems. Specialists in magical defense and spiritual cures, they work on contract, spirit by spirit, soul by soul. They escort the dead and carry messages to and from the Otherworlds. Using clairvoyance and divination, shamans can see and find what other humans cannot and foretell events that have not yet occurred. They act as venture capitalists in supernatural power, but they do not option power for its own sake. The focus of their activities is an interaction with sources of power for the benefit of the people. Supernatural power, enhanced by magic and gained during altered states of consciousness, is one of their tools. Ordinary power, acquired through observation of the natural world, is another. By maintaining direct contact with all the cosmic forces of the universe the shaman can explain and make sense of both the measured order of ordinary times and the catastrophes of drought, thunder and lightning, earthquake, and flood, as well as a variety of more intangible threats to the well-being of the community.

Form, space, and time are all rendered mutable and malleable under the influence of power. A shaman has the ability to draw a land form toward him or travel through space, transformed into some other creature, such as a bird, bear, or mountain lion. He might use power to bring sacred time into the present so that he can interact with supernatural beings from that otherworldly time. He may also transcend space, shortening or lengthening distances through the use of power (Bean 1975, 28).

Before he can accomplish any of these tasks, the potential candidate must first answer a "call" to the shamanic way of life. A primary requisite of this call to power is a separation from the mundane world; the neophyte has to turn away from the secular life, whether voluntarily, ritually, or spontaneously through a sickness, and look inward toward the unknown. The initial call to power places the candidate in the realm of chaos, where power exists in an untransformed state (Halifax 1982, 6).

Becoming a Shaman

Although the details vary among cultures, the path toward shamanism appears to have a common underlying pattern. Individuals who have the need or the desire to respond to such a call have done so in similar ways, undergoing analogous ordeals and rites of initiation that indicate to us the transcultural nature of the shamanic experience (Ripinsky-Naxon 1993, 71). Whether this unique role was hereditary or not, sought out by or forced upon the candidate, its assumption usually begins with some event that calls attention to the fact that the prospective shaman must be set apart or consecrated (Bean and Vane 1992, 9).

A potential initiate might discover his calling through some inner personal crisis. He might find his selection underscored by a physical or mental anomaly, such as an extra digit on a hand or foot or an extra tooth; he might be susceptible to spells of possession or fainting (Ripinsky-Naxon 1993, 71). Superior skills or unusual talent, either mental or physical, were thought to be signs of a shamanic calling. Thus, the best hunter, the fastest runner, or the brightest or most creative child might be considered a likely candidate. A young person who was alert, curious, and ambitious was sometimes seen as a potential shaman and therefore guided in that direction. An escape from danger, like an escape from illness, might also be a sign of supernatural power.

The essential elements of shamanic initiation show remarkable similarities in a variety of cultures. The ordeal most often begins with isolation, usually in some remote place, where the aspiring neophyte is subjected to psychological and physical stress in order to gain the appropriate spiritual disposition. The idea is to induce a "shamanic state of consciousness" (Ripinsky-Naxon 1993, 49) that will dispatch the initiate on the profound soul-journey to the Otherworld.

During this time the candidate inevitably experiences a ritual death and rebirth. Spears and arrows sometimes pierce his navel; quartz crystals signifying supernatural power may be shot into his body. He might be "killed" by ghosts or spirits, have internal organs removed, and his skeleton dismembered. This trance state is the gateway to a singular introspective experience, aiding the novice in attaining a profound awareness of his own existence. Recognizing the mortality of the physical body is essential for the soul's transcendence to a more spiritual level of consciousness: one must "die" in order to advance to another plane. The entire process represents "an ecstatic metamorphosis" (Reichel-Dolmatoff 1979a, 54) and, according to Eliade (1964, 76), "*It is only this initiatory death and resurrection that consecrates a shaman*" (emphasis in the original). Thus, if the neophyte emerges successfully from all these ordeals, he will have been reborn and acquired "shamanic enlightenment." At some point in the transcendental voyage, the new shaman will ideally encounter "power animals" or supernatural spirit helpers—entities that are likely to remain his lifelong assistants (Ripinsky-Naxon 1993, 86).

Although the initiation rite may take only a short time, the full acquisition of shamanistic knowledge and power usually requires many years and is achieved only after a number of tests or trials, along with instruction from master shamans. Although the former neophyte is now a *bona fide* shaman, training and enlightenment do not end here. His mentor continues to instruct him in shamanic techniques and lore as well as in the oral traditions and myths of his people. He introduces the new shaman to the mysteries of curing and the use of magical plants, teaching him, at the same time, the methods used in their preparation (Ripinsky-Naxon 1993, 87).

Aspects of the initiatory episode are repeated, at least in part, whenever the shaman enters the shamanic state of consciousness. Having learned to cope with the dangers, the full-fledged shaman is now more firmly in control of the situations encountered and more likely to increase the intensity of each experience as his career goes forward (Bean and Vane 1992, 12). The overriding goal of this lifelong training and refinement of skills is, as noted previously, the acquisition and use of supernatural power. Knowing that power is distributed throughout the cosmos, the shaman must be familiar with the terrain of this world and of the ones beyond so that he can transport himself supernaturally to wherever power resides. The common route is trance.

Altered States of Consciousness

The word "trance" derives from the Latin *transitus*: a passage. The verb root is *transive*, meaning "to pass over." Trance is literally defined, then, as an entrance to another world. The term *shaman*, in turn, is a transliteration of the Tungus-Mongol word šaman (Eliade 1964, 4) and functions as both a noun and a verb. The noun-word šaman comes from the Indo-European verb-root ša-, which means, "to know" (Ripinsky-Naxon 1993, 69). As a noun it refers to "one who is excited, moved, raised"; used as a verb it means, "to know in an ecstatic manner" (Czaplicka 1914, 144). Thus the shaman is, by definition, one who attains an ecstatic state. Most specialists, therefore, consider trance to be a prerequisite for any kind of true shamanism (Grim 1983, 50; Ripinsky-Naxon 1993, 96).

Anthropologists who have apprenticed themselves to shamans and entered altered states under their direction tell us that the experiences of a person in trance are so compellingly "real" that they should be viewed as a "nonordinary reality." This is not to imply that shamans in altered states lose consciousness or become temporarily comatose. While there is a general impression that a state of trance is a state of unconsciousness or nonconsciousness "what we are really trying to establish," as Johan Reinhard (1975) points out, "is that the shaman is in a nonordinary psychic state which in some cases means not a loss of consciousness but rather an altered state of consciousness." Eliade (1964, 223) argues that shamanic ecstasy is less of a trance than a "state of inspiration"; the shaman sees and hears spirits and may be "carried out of himself" because he is journeying through distant regions, but he is not unconscious. The experienced shaman can enter into a deep ecstatic trance—one that may exhibit the superficial appearance of induced death—yet continue to maintain control over his personality. He retains his cognitive perception of purpose and becomes actively involved in encounters with the supernatural creatures of the Otherworld (Ripinsky-Naxon 1993, 86).

Altered states of consciousness may be induced spontaneously, by sensory or physical deprivation such as sleeplessness and fasting (the classic vision quest), through various techniques of meditation, or by intensive and prolonged dancing. Repetitive movement can promote altered states of mind, especially when coupled with rhythmic sound or music, light flicker, and fatigue. More often than not, ingestion of hallucinogenic substances plays an important part in shamanic ritual. Indeed, it seems that in many cultures the use of psychoactive drugs is the preferred method for reaching trancelike states conducive to the sensation of seeing and contacting the supernatural. Although other methods may be employed, the use of hallucinogens appears to be the easiest and fastest technique for achieving perceived visions and supernatural experiences.

Magical Flight

According to Mircea Eliade (1964, 5) the core of shamanic practice is the acquisition of supernatural power through ecstatic trance, "during which [the shaman's] soul is believed to leave his body and ascend to the sky or descend to the underworld." This fundamental principle expresses the idea that, whether engaged in finding a remedy for some patient captured by disease, servicing the needs of some wandering soul, negotiating with the spirits for the seasonal return of game, or setting out on a quest for knowledge of future events, the shaman makes a dangerous voyage to the Otherworlds (Ripinsky-Naxon 1993).

Thus, the special skill of the shaman is his ability to journey between the mundane world, where the rest of the community is confined, and the spirit realm. Responsible for conducting business across transcendental borders, he must travel to distant and threatening places in all of the realms. When the shaman enters an altered state of consciousness, he is truly transformed, attaining the capacity for supernatural flight. During these magical journeys the shaman sheds his ordinary identity and makes contact with powerful spirits—supernatural allies willing to endorse his cause. When he travels to the spirit world, he becomes the powerful animal or creature whom he calls on for supernatural aid (Grim 1983, 52). In his mind and in the belief of his people, the transformation is literal. The visual and sensory imagery of these trance states, especially with the use of hallucinogens, is taken as proof that the supernatural world has been attained (Hedges 1992, 71).

The true shaman, then, attains his knowledge, position, and power through trance, vision and soul-journey to the Otherworld. We must also understand that these states of enlightenment are reached through inner personal crisis, during an altered state of consciousness, and not by purposeful study or the application of a corpus of systematic knowledge. In other words, while those of us in "literate" societies get both our religion and our religious proofs from books, people in non-literate communities usually rely on direct confrontation with the supernatural for evidence of all religious reality. An altered state serves as a device whereby the shaman is able to transcend intellectual and cultural boundaries—creating new ideas and seeing things in different ways and in new combinations. Trance and magical flight allow the shaman to interact with spirit beings and discover the true nature of life and pathways to the land of the dead, so that the living may be reassured about the future. The shaman's journey, then, like the World Tree, acts to maintain the relationship between the cosmic worlds.

While worldview provides the landmarks for the visionary journey of the shaman's soul, the shaman also has the ability to influence that worldview. As the healer, mystic, and intellectual leader of the community, he alone possesses a store of knowledge concerning all things necessary for human existence. The shaman acts as a seer or clairvoyant, foretelling natural as well as man-made events and is expected to intervene with the spirits to abort the recurrence of disaster in the future. Custodian of sacred tradition and myth, the shaman functions as the memory of his people—a mythologue and genealogist. As an epic singer, he is the chanter of tribal lore. In addition to being the ritual practitioner, his complementary function is keeping a calendar for all the important phases that define the lifeways of his people (Ripinsky-Naxon 1993, 64). The shaman is entrusted with overseeing the community's complete well-being, caring for individuals as well as the group, and maintaining a balance within his society and nature. When physical and spiritual conditions are not in equilibrium, as evidenced by illness, natural calamities, or any other form of disaster, the community expects the shaman to restore harmony, balance, and beauty.

Shamanism and Culture

If we accept the concept of human agency—the notion that individuals played some part in shaping their histories—then we must surely recognize the vital role of the shaman in ancient society. Equipped with an impressive store of empirical knowledge as well as a profound insight concerning human behavior, the shaman holds a central place in his society, not merely as a healer of disease, but also as a harmonizer of natural and social dysfunctions or imbalance. Using ritual, the shaman structures the perennial quest for purpose and metaphor. He formulates meanings, relevant on both the individual and social levels, that afford ideological worth and ecological possibility to human existence (Ripinsky-Naxon 1993, 65).

Processualists who maintain a behaviorist perspective tend to emphasize the relationship of the shaman to the biological environment. They underplay his role as an agent in formulating and manipulating existential realities and therefore deprive shamanism of its socially transcendent character. Clearly, the shaman's knowledge and abilities are of real consequence when applied to culture-environmental issues, but to ignore all symbolic elements is to deny the full integrative potential of shamanism as a dynamic factor in the cultural process. Culture change, abstract or material, is not independent of other factors. Shamanism is part of a much broader dimension, where the relationship of a society to its milieu is reflected not so much in techno-environmental considerations but through a system of metaphors and social organization. It is an idiomatic expression of culture, rather than merely a behavioral response, and involves a social community that accepts a certain mode of behavior suited for a beneficial relationship with the prevailing conditions. Once it is socially approved, this mode becomes the preferred—perhaps even the ideal—response to a prescribed situation (Ripinsky-Naxon 1968, 225).

The goal of archaeology is to resuscitate deceased cultures. If we are successful, we not only bring to life the dead culture's subsistence strategies and technology but also recapture its soul—the worldview that provided meaning and vitality. It should be clear by now that cognitive scholars take the position that culture is better defined by its beliefs and art than by its potsherds and stone tools (Whitley 2000). Fundamental to this approach is the notion that the experience acquired by shamans in visions is a major component of culture change. With this in mind, it is time to take a closer look at the way that cognitive archaeologists deploy the tools of their trade to interpret rock art.

Using the Tools of Cognitive Archaeology 8

THE THEORY AND METHODOLOGY of a cognitive approach to archaeology were developed in a variety of ways. In a few cases, resourceful individuals, willing to explore new avenues of inquiry, created them out of whole cloth. More often than not, however, researchers, exploring various ways of looking at the material record, relied on previous archaeological studies, as well as work from related disciplines such as anthropology, ethnology and linguistics. They also adopted ideas pioneered by practitioners in other branches of the natural and social sciences: microbiologists, philosophers, psychologists, neurologists, physicians, and students of the history of religion, among others. In the following pages, I will take a closer look at some of these concepts and discuss how they are employed in rock art research. Before doing this, however, I must first consider a subject dear to the hearts of archaeologists of any persuasion—chronology.

Chronology and Rock Art

One of the primary reasons for our fascination with rock art is the fact that so much of it was produced in truly prehistoric times, well before the advent of written records. Ever since the paintings at Altamira Cave were authenticated and dated to the Upper Paleolithic, scholars and amateurs alike have shown a paramount interest in the age of parietal art. As a result, techniques for dating the rock art have been an important part of any new analyses. The spectacular finds in the last decade of the twentieth century offer prime examples. New dating techniques applied to Grotte Cosquer and Chauvet Cave in France, as well as the Côa valley petroglyphs in Portugal, have given us a different perspective of the art's distribution over time and helped to enhance our understanding of European Paleolithic images (Clottes 1998, 112). The age of these drawings clearly influences our interpretation and chronological issues are, therefore, just as important for cognitive archaeologists as they are for other prehistorians.

Rock Art Chronometrics in Europe

Until the 1980s, it was not possible to date parietal art directly. For nearly a hundred years, researchers in Europe used the time-honored methods developed by Abbé Breuil and his successors to identify chronological sequences. They studied superimpositions, defined a set of stylistic criteria that always appeared in the same sequence, and compared the undated art with that which was thought to be securely dated (Clottes 1994, 1998). The use of superimposition relies on the idea that each time period had a distinct set of themes, techniques, or conventions, just as each culture is defined by a distinct set of tools. The regular recurrence of these stylistic conventions on top of or beneath other images could then be used to establish a succession of styles or periods. The problem is that there are a limited number of examples of superimposition, and the duration of stylistic conventions is usually not known (Clottes 1998, 112). Traditionally, researchers used caves that had been securely dated as solid points of reference when comparing one case to another. Caves with openings blocked by deposits that obviously precluded later entrance, paintings or engravings inside caves or rockshelters covered over by an archaeological layer, or fallen wall fragments or collapsed roof panels found in or under the Upper Paleolithic strata were considered to be well dated (Clottes 1994, 1). The difficulty here is the implicit assumption that a negligible amount of time elapsed between the moment the art was made and the moment when it was sealed up or covered over.

Thus, until recently, most chronological attributions for Upper Paleolithic art rested on slim evidence. Leroi-Gourhan, the creator of a widely used interpretive system for the analysis of cave art, observed that "the thorniest terrain was that of the dating of the figures" (Leroi-Gourhan 1965, 31). This changed in the 1980s with the introduction of new and improved methods for direct radiocarbon dating and pigment analysis. Even though it has been available for more than fifty years, conventional radiocarbon dating has rarely been used for determining the age of rock art. Because a relatively large amount of organic material was needed for a single sample, too much of a painting would have to be sacrificed. By the early 1990s, technological innovations, most notably the development of radiocarbon dating by means of accelerator mass spectrometry (AMS) had reached a point where analysis could be done with a very small sample. The amount of material required for the chemical analysis of pigment is even less than that needed for the new radiocarbon dating procedures. In recent years, both of these methods have been applied to Upper Paleolithic cave art, with impressive results. Direct dating played a major role in settling a debate about the authenticity of the art at Grotte Cosquer (Clottes 1998). At Chauvet Cave, a series of radiocarbon dates from the images and torch marks revealed several human incursions, each one separated by a few millennia; the earliest, around 31,000 years ago, was considerably older than anticipated (Clottes 1996).

Rock Art Chronology in North America

Upper Paleolithic art differs substantially from North American rock art and, as a result, difficulties that are encountered in dating the European art are compounded in the United States. Most of the Upper Paleolithic art is found deep in caves, as opposed to the small rockshelters or exposed rock surfaces in the New World. Since it is unlikely that a painted or engraved panel covered with an archaeological level or any painted caves blocked by archaeological deposits will ever be found here, the traditional European methods are usually not applicable in North America.

The sophisticated direct dating techniques used today had not been developed when the first American archaeologists began venturing into the area of rock art. While these researchers were certainly concerned with chronological sequences, most attempts to fit the art into some sort of temporal framework were still grounded in the nineteenth-century Darwinian concept of the "evolution of art styles" (Whitley 1998b, 129). This held that if animal species evolved from simple to complex, the same must be true for human societies, including the social institutions and other characteristics of human culture. In this scenario, the art began as crude scratchings that became more regularized over time; simplistic representational styles developed and eventually became more sophisticated and complex. This notion went hand in hand with nineteenth-century attitudes toward people from traditional, small-scale, and non-Western cultures. They were, after all, *primitives*.

Although Julian Steward (1929) was the first to introduce an embryonic form of this evolutionary perspective to American rock art, it was Heizer and Baumhoff (1962) who brought it to fruition. Although their theory was largely implicit, they believed that the earliest rock art in the Great Basin consisted of motifs that were the most "primitive"—pit-and-groove petroglyphs thought to be at least 5,000 years old. These simple motifs were no more than shallow ground pits (or cupules) and short, gouged-out lines in rock surfaces. Heizer and Baumhoff's next phase involved abstract forms—curvilinear designs that gradually became rectilinear geometric motifs. Finally, about 2,000 years ago, prehistoric artists developed the ability to create representational art, such as bighorn sheep.

The problem with their theory is that it ignored empirical evidence as well as certain aspects of North American and world prehistory. Scholars had known since the 1930s that the technical and artistic skills of North America's prehistoric inhabitants did not necessarily evolve from rudimentary to complex. The earliest known culture at the time was identified as "Folsom" and dated to around 10,000 B.P. The fluted spear point, so characteristic of this culture, was a finely made tool that represented a sophisticated stoneworking technology, particularly when compared with other point types found in much of the Great Basin. The so-called Pinto or Little Lake forms, for example, are usually characterized as large, crude, often asymmetrical projectile points. If style and sophistication were the sole criteria, these Pinto forms would, according to Heizer and Baumhoff's evolutionary scheme, predate Folsom points. We know this is not the case. The widely distributed Pinto points appeared in the Great Basin sometime after 7000 B.P. and persisted until about 3500-3200 B.P. (Basgall, Hildebrandt, and Hall 1987; Gilreath, Basgall, and Hall 1987; Jenkins and Warren 1984).

Furthermore, the initial dating of the Paleolithic caves of France and Spain had proved conclusively that humans were capable of making very sophisticated figurative images—and from a much earlier time than Heizer and Baumhoff dated the purportedly earliest Great Basin rock art. If carried to its logical conclusion, their evolutionary scheme would have the ancestors of modern western Europeans producing representational figures thousands of years before ancestors of modern Native Americans developed the same aesthetic capabilities.

Campbell Grant used a different approach to establish approximate dates for the creation of some of the engravings in the Coso Range. Like many researchers who encountered these petroglyphs, he noticed the depiction of both the atlatl and bows and arrows. Based on the work of Farmer (1955), Grosscup (1960), Kelley (1950), and Morris (1936), Grant estimated that bows and arrows were introduced into this part of the country sometime between 2,500 and 2,000 years ago and had replaced the atlatl over a period of 500 years (Grant, Baird, and Pringle 1968, 51). He proposed that the introduction of the atlatl, with its increased hunting efficiency, led to the decimation of the bighorn sheep herds and a subsequent demise of the hunting cult. Grant (1968, 58) also guessed that the rock art was produced until about 1,000 B.P., a date he admitted was an arbitrary choice made to coincide with a hypothesized Shoshonean migration out of the area due to overkilling of the sheep. Heizer and Baumhoff (1962, 234) had suggested a slightly longer span of rock art production, to about 500 B.P.

David Whitley had empirical evidence to the contrary. He was aware that Euro-American themes and motifs, such as horses, carts, and western hats, had been documented at a few sites in the Great Basin (Bard 1979; Benton 1978; Garfinkel 1978; Ritter, Brook, and Farrell 1982). In his doctoral dissertation, he made note of a rendering from the Birchim Springs site in the Coso Range that depicted a quadruped with a rider wearing what appeared to be a Euro-American type of hat (Whitley 1982b, 170–76, fig. 67). Whitley had also identified possible horse and rider motifs in Lower Renegade Canyon and Sheep Canyon. Clearly then, some representational petroglyph production did occur in the Cosos historically, possibly as late as the middle of the nineteenth century. Whitley reasoned that, if at least some Great Basin rock art was historical or recent in age, then the existing dating schemes were incorrect. He spent a good portion of the next few years investigating various techniques for dating rock art, particularly the engraved petroglyphs of the Coso Range.

Dating Techniques

Researchers can draw inferences about the age of rock art in three ways. The first is the one just discussed: finding time-specific themes or subject matter in the images. Thus, the rock art depicting quadrupeds and riders or human figures wearing Euro-American-style hats confirms the idea that some of the art was made after the "discovery" of the New World. Images like this obviously postdate the initial appearance of Europeans in western North America in the sixteenth century and may postdate widespread cultural contact in the late eighteenth or early nineteenth centuries (Whitley 1996, 35). Recognizable representational images also provide an aid to relative chronological placement, as shown in the case of the atlatl and bow and arrow motifs (Whitley 1987, 164).

Another clue is the condition of the painted images in relation to other art found at a particular site. In very broad terms, a more deteriorated or fainter pictograph should be older than one that shows less deterioration and is brighter. Researchers should, however, use caution when considering microenvironmental and other factors that can affect the condition of the images at a given site. Rock art that is directly exposed to weather, for example, cannot be compared fairly to art that has been protected from such conditions, even when in close proximity (Whitley 1996, 35).

While the relative condition of rock art depends on a number of factors, archaeologists can draw helpful inferences by using variations of this technique. Through a comparison of older and newer photographs, for example, a number of researchers have detected a visible deterioration of some paintings in southwestern and south-central California in the last fifty to one hundred years (Whitley 1996, 36). Grant, working in the coastal regions of California, recognized significant changes in the condition of pictograph panels when the images were compared with photographs taken near the end of the nineteenth century (Grant 1967). Whitley noted that, of eleven painted historic period motifs in the Kern River Valley area of east-central California recorded in the 1960s, only two were found to be extant when the site was revisited twenty or thirty years later (Whitley 1987,

164). Realizing that most of the painted art found on small, poorly protected overhangs would not last beyond a few centuries due to the effects of erosion, he concluded that much of the pictographic art in California was created in the last five hundred years.

For petroglyphs, a heavily revarnished engraving should be older than one that is lighter and less revarnished (Whitley 1994a, 361). Researchers have cross-checked this relative condition with time-sensitive subject matter to achieve slightly stronger inferences about the age of the art. As an example, atlatl motifs in the Coso Range that should date to 1,500 B.P. or more typically exhibit moderate to heavy revarnishing, whereas bow and arrow engravings that are less than 1,500 years old generally have little or no obvious revarnishing (Whitley 1996, 36).

Finally, specific dates for particular petroglyphs and pictographs can be determined through the use of direct chronometric techniques. In 1981 Whitley and geomorphologist Ron Dorn began a research project in the Mojave Desert area of the western Great Basin. Much of their effort was directed toward dating rock varnish that accumulates over time on petroglyphs (Dorn and Whitley 1983, 1984; Whitley 1992c; Whitley and Dorn 1987, 1993). The age of the rock varnish can be established in two different ways (Dorn 1994, 13). One method measures the proportions of major inorganic trace elements in the varnish, some of which leach out at a known rate over time while others remain more stable. A technique called electron microprobe analysis measures the bulk chemistry of varnish samples and yields what are called "cation-ratio dates" (Whitley 1996, 37).

The second method (UML dating) allows researchers to analyze the micro-stratigraphic layering of the rock varnish by examining the micromorphology of the varnish under a scanning electron microscope (Dorn 1998, 77). During the Pleistocene or Ice Age, before about eleven thousand years ago, environmental conditions were wetter and less dusty in the Far West. Varnish that accumulated under those conditions exhibits a rounded, lumpy shape (like a cluster of grapes), called "botryoidal" when viewed in microscopic cross section. Varnish that formed in the drier, dustier conditions of the last eleven thousand years, by contrast, exhibits a flat, layered structure called "lamellate" when examined microscopically (Dorn 1998, 76; Whitley 1996, 37). In the Coso Range, the arid Holocene (the last eleven thousand years) supported the vast accumulation of lamellate varnishes. The analysis of varnishes on engravings of Pleistocene age shows a microstratigraphy of lamellate on top of botryoidal (Dorn 1986). Thus, a petroglyph engraved more than eleven thousand years ago typically shows botryoidal layers of varnish overlaid with layers of lamellate; an engraving made more recently would have only lamellate varnish (Whitley 1996, 37). Researchers can use these changes in microscopic structure as another independent check on radiocarbon and cation-ratio dates (Liu and Dorn 1996). While technicians continue to refine and improve these direct dating methods, problems still exist. Dorn (1998, 81) and Whitley (1996, 38) stress that all these techniques are still considered experimental. The potential for contamination, uncertainty about the contemporaneity of the organic matter, and the complexities of calibration all contribute to the enduring difficulty of dating the rock art.

Nevertheless, by the mid-1980s, Whitley had accumulated and analyzed a large enough body of chronometric data to allow him to argue with some confidence that the petroglyphs of the Coso Range were first made approximately ten thousand years ago and that their production continued minimally into the last three hundred years (Whitley 1987, 165). The cation-ratio dates that he and Dorn had collected (Whitley and Dorn 1987) confirmed Whitley's long-standing belief (based on historic motifs found in a few of the images) that at least some of the petroglyphs were created during the historic period. Whitley was also certain that the ethnographic inhabitants of the region were the creators of the historic period rock art (Whitley 1987, 165). This conclusion was based partly on the work of Alan Garfinkel (1982), who had argued for an *in situ* continuity in the rock art of the region. From this, Whitley inferred that the Coso Range petroglyphs continued to have symbolic importance and that the petroglyph canyons were used as ritual locations into the historic period (Whitley 1982b, 267). Taking this reasoning one step further, he argued that, since at least some of the Coso petroglyphs were produced in historic times, the use of symbolism that had been identified in the historic oral traditions could reasonably be applied to the Coso rock art.

The Ethnographic Record

Whitley was not suggesting (at that time) that the known ethnographic record offered any direct insights concerning the creators or the meaning of the paintings and engravings. Scholars had argued for decades that there were no available ethnographic data about the rock art. Heizer and Baumhoff (1962), Grant (1968), Steward (1968), Heizer and Clewlow (1973), and Wellman (1979) all insisted that there was no ethnography relating to the petroglyphs. Implicit in Grant's (1968) hypothesized terminal dates for the creation of the rock art in the Cosos was the notion that the images had been produced by cultures other than the ones that inhabited the region in protohistoric or historic times: "The practice of making . . . pictures had disappeared long before the first anthropologist began questioning the Indians of the area" (Grant, Baird, and Pringle 1968, 32). This idea, shared by a number of researchers, was based on the work of earlier Great Basin ethnographers, particularly Julian Steward. Commenting on Grant's work, Steward declared that his own extensive study of the Shoshonean Indians of the region revealed that they knew nothing of the authorship or meaning of the petroglyphs, and that their culture was "unlikely to manifest itself in this medium" (Steward 1968, viii). His statement that "Grant and his coauthors quite convincingly suggest that the climax of the Coso Range rock art must have been achieved at a fairly remote time" obviously reflected his own views about the creation of the art. Although Whitley had effectively overcome the well-entrenched belief that the engravings were entirely prehistoric, he still accepted, on the strength of the earlier contentions, the absence of any direct ethnography concerning far western rock art (Whitley 1994b, 84).

Armed with evidence that at least some art was made during the ethnographically known period, and reasoning that this reflected a continuity of production from prehistoric times, Whitley decided that the ethnography that was available (the "historic oral traditions") could somehow be integrated into the study of rock art. This approach represented the thinking of the time. By the early 1980s, the trend in California research had been to associate specific rock art sites with particular myths found in the ethnographic record. Whitley recognized that such correlations were difficult to establish and suggested that it might be possible to gain a better insight into the ideology and beliefs of the creators of the rock art through an analysis of the myths themselves: "A symbolic approach to the analysis of rock art in light of mythology is more likely to provide useful interpretive results than particularistic correlations between myths and specific rock art sites" (Whitley 1982a, 268).

At around the same time that Whitley was exploring this new approach, a South African researcher, David Lewis-Williams, published a landmark work on rock art (1981), *Believing and Seeing: Symbolic Meaning in Southern San Rock Paintings*, that had to do with the pictographs of southern African bushmen. Although trained as a cultural anthropologist and not an archaeologist, Lewis-Williams' research confronted a number of the same problems that Whitley faced in North America. The San bushmen were hunter-gatherers and were similar to the Numic-speaking people of the western Great Basin in social structure and in the kinds of environments they inhabited. Although their polychrome rock paintings had been recognized for years as particularly sophisticated examples of hunter-gatherer art, the interpretation of the images remained elusive. Further paralleling the North American case, African archaeologists had argued for decades that there were no ethnographic data that could be used to understand this bushman art. Lewis-Williams proved that this was wrong. Using a symbolic anthropological approach to interrogate the ethnographic record, he developed a convincing interpretation for the creation of the paintings. For Whitley, this way of thinking was "the single greatest intellectual breakthrough, worldwide, in the history of rock art studies" (Whitley 1998b, 140–41).

Whitley realized that Lewis-Williams' work facilitated employment of an ethnographically informed analytical approach to rock art research. It was also quite clear that the use of concepts derived from symbolic anthropology required a complete mastery of the pertinent ethnographic record. In 1987, after a few years of excavation in the Coso Range, Whitley began a two-year postdoctoral fellowship at the Rock Art Research Unit of the University of Witwatersrand in Johannesburg, South Africa, under the direction of David Lewis-Williams. He spent those two years researching the ethnographic data of far western North America (Whitley 1998b, 140).

The outcome was remarkable. Shortly before beginning his ethnographic quest, Whitley had written that the "absence of ethnographic information in east-central California is . . . symptomatic of rock art ethnography in much of California and the Great Basin. Except for a few rare instances, no ethnographic information exists on the making and use of this type of cultural remain" (Whitley 1987, 162). Contrast this statement with the opening lines of an article published just a few years later:

> The ethnographic record of the rock art of far western North America is arguably the most complete and detailed of any in the world. It identifies not only those who made the art in this region but also the context in which the art was produced and what it was intended to symbolically and ideologically portray. (Whitley 1994b, 81)

Whitley had obviously found a very different way of looking at the ethnographic data, and this new perspective can be traced directly to David Lewis-Williams. In a 1983 work, Lewis-Williams suggested that the key to using ethnographic records in the interpretation of rock art was the use of a "metaphoric model." Whitley recognized fully the implications of this approach:

> Once it is acknowledged that many ethnographic concepts are expressed metaphorically, and an effort is made to decipher relevant metaphors in texts that pertain to rock art, a coherent interpretation of otherwise enigmatic ethnographic statements can be obtained. (1994b, 82)

Whitley illustrated this principle in action by applying the "metaphoric model" methodology to one of the fundamental issues concerning the interpretation of the petroglyphs and pictographs of the Far West—the identity of the creators of the art. He knew that ethnographers throughout the Great Basin and its peripheral regions had recorded comments that some of the rock art was made by a particular being referred to as a "rock baby," "water baby," or "mountain dwarf" (Driver 1937, 86; Hultkrantz 1987, 49; Lowie 1924, 296; Steward 1943, 282–83; Voegelin 1938, 61; Zigmond 1977, 71). Some ethnographers dismissed their informants' knowledge of the rock art because they likened these "rock babies" to our own brownies, fairies, or wood sprites (Voegelin 1938, 61). Others took it as an indication that their informants knew absolutely nothing about the rock art and concluded that it must be very ancient (Steward 1968, viii). Whitley, using the metaphorical approach to examine the ethnographic record, found that these beings were, in fact, powerful supernatural helpers of the shaman. Furthermore, these and other creatures—and the power attributed to them—were acquired by shamans during vision quests undertaken while in altered states of consciousness (Whitley 1992a, 86; 1994b, 82; 1998b, 142). Ethnographic evidence also revealed that the informants made no distinction between the shaman's actions, his dream helper, or visionary altered states (Applegate 1978, 27; Gayton 1948, 32; Siskin 1983, 22). To claim, then, that a water baby created the rock art was simply to assert metaphorically that it was the product of a shaman.

Alice Kehoe believes that any claims that paintings and engravings were made by shamans to depict what they saw in trance represent an extreme case of the universal application of the term "shaman." She contends that "No one has documented a shaman . . . actually making rock art of such visions" (Kehoe 2000, 4). Whitley provides evidence to refute this argument, pointing out that not all of the ethnographic information concerning rock art was metaphorically "disguised." While conducting his research, he found a small but important portion of the record that contained direct references to the rock art (Whitley 1994b, 82). One informant, for example, stated that a rock art site "depicted a man's dream" (Gifford 1932, 52). Another informant confirmed this by declaring that shamans created the art: "They painted their 'spirits' on rocks to 'show themselves, to let people see what they have done.' The spirit must come first in a dream" (Driver 1937, 126). Whitley (1994b, 82) argued that these explicit references were particularly valuable because they afforded another independent check on the translations of the metaphors.

These findings comprised a significant breakthrough for rock art research in the western United States, but they were only the beginning. Once the identity of the creators of the images was established, the next question to be considered was the content—what exactly the shamans were depicting in the rock art. In this regard, excepting rare but direct important references to "dreams" or "spirits," the ethnographic record was silent. Searching for answers, Whitley turned his attention to developing studies that involved the effects of altered states of consciousness on mental imagery.

The Neuropsychological Model

More than fifty years ago, neurologists and pharmacologists discovered that the visionary images people experienced during altered states of consciousness were similar at certain basic levels. Anthropologist Thomas Blackburn (1977) was the first to realize the importance of this observation for North American rock art research. Blackburn reviewed neuropsychological data developed in the laboratory along with studies of the hallucinatory images that shamans in lowland South American societies described and drew for anthropologists. He recognized a rather broad correspondence between many of the geometric patterns found in both studies. Blackburn argued that the similarities between the South American images and certain Chumash pictographs from the Santa Barbara area of southern California provided additional support for the (then unproven) hypothesis that the art was made by shamans and that it depicted visions experienced in altered states of consciousness. Subsequent research (e.g., Hedges 1976, 1982, 1983; Wellman 1978) further strengthened the connection between California rock art and visionary experiences.

Lewis-Williams merged his analysis of existing ethnographic data with the archaeological record of San rock art and reached the same conclusion: the painted motifs in southern Africa referred to visions that medicine men received during trance (Lewis-Williams 1982, 1983a, 1985). Recognizing the implications of these findings, he turned his attention to the neurophysiological effects of altered states on visual and graphic imagery (Lewis-Williams 1986). This portion of his research was based on the fact that the nervous system is a human universal. As a result, all humans react to altered states of consciousness in certain limited ways, and mental images that originate in trance-state experiences can be predicted to be broadly similar. Experiments with Western laboratory subjects support this conclusion (Reichel-Dolmatoff 1978; Siegel and Jarvik 1975, 81–104), and these findings allowed Lewis-Williams to focus his investigation of mental imagery on features of altered states that were not subject to cultural influences, but instead completely controlled by the human nervous system.

Previous research (Asaad and Shapiro 1986; Horowitz 1964; Klüver 1926, 1942; Knoll et al. 1963; Oster 1970; Richards 1971; Siegel 1977, 1978; Siegel and Jarvik 1975) had shown that, under certain circumstances, the visual and neurological systems generate a series of luminous percepts independent of light from external sources. These phenomena take geometric forms such as grids, zigzags, catenary curves, dots, and spirals. Since they are derived from the human nervous system, all people who enter altered states of consciousness, no matter what their cultural background, are liable to perceive them (Reichel-Dolmatoff 1972).

Based on these findings, Lewis-Williams and his student Thomas Dowson developed a neuropsychological model—a set of predictions of the kinds of mental imagery that occur most commonly during altered states. For the first component of their model, Lewis-Williams and Dowson selected seven of the most common visual percepts experienced during altered states of consciousness: a basic grid or lattice, sets of parallel lines, dots and short flecks, zigzags, nested catenary curves, filigrees, and spirals (Lewis-Williams and Dowson 1988, 203). They used the term "entoptic phenomenon" (or "entoptics") for these geometric percepts to emphasize the fact that these visual sensations derive primarily from the structure of the optic system. They emphasized that entoptic phenomena are distinct from hallucinations, which are not generated within the optic system. Unlike entoptics, hallucinations include iconic visions of culturally influenced images such as animals, as well as somatic and aural experiences (202).

The second step was the formulation of the seven general principles that govern the way subjects perceive mental imagery generated during altered states: simple replication of the image; the fragmentation of an image into component parts; the integration of two or more images into one (particularly the integration of entoptic and representational forms); the superpositioning of one image over another; the juxtapositioning of two images alongside each other; reduplication or multiple replications of images; and finally the rotation of images off a horizontal plane. These principles apply to both entoptics and iconic hallucinations and in some cases link the two; a grid, for example, may be integrated with an animal, or one species may be blended with characteristics of another (Lewis-Williams and Dowson 1988, 203).

Finally, Lewis-Williams and Dowson outlined three separate stages in the progression of mental imagery during altered states of consciousness. In the first stage, subjects experience only entoptics. During the second stage, the brain tries to recognize or decode these various forms by matching them against a store of experience, just as it does in a normal state of consciousness. It is during this stage that the entoptic forms are interpreted as culturally meaningful images, perceived as recognizable shapes of people, animals, and monsters. As subjects move into the third stage, marked changes in imagery begin to occur. At about this time, the representational forms become more fully integrated with the entoptics, often with the iconic imagery projected against a background of geometric forms. During this third stage, individuals may begin to have bodily hallucinations in addition to the visual effects (Lewis-Williams and Dowson 1988, 203–4; Whitley 1998b, 150–53).

To test the efficacy of their neuropsychological model, Lewis-Williams and Dowson applied it to two bodies of shamanistic art from two different continents: the paintings of the San bushmen in southern Africa, and the engravings of the Coso Range in western North America. Their focus on shamanistic art was essential to the argument because it emphasized what they believed to be "the most important and overriding feature of shamanism . . . altered states of consciousness" (Lewis-Williams and Dowson 1988, 204). They found that all of the entoptic forms were present in both the San and Coso art and took this as an initial confirmation of the utility of their model for explaining one component of the images. Using several examples, they demonstrated that the other segments of their model—the principles of perception and the stages in the development of the mental imagery—were also present in the art. The fact that the model clarified and ordered depictions in both the San and Coso cases increased their confidence in its explanatory value when applied to Upper Paleolithic art (211).

The reasons for selecting the San case for their model are obvious. Lewis-Williams had been investigating this art for several years (Lewis-Williams 1980, 1981, 1982, 1985, 1987) and recognized that the ethnographic record for San shamanistic practices was quite detailed. Their choice of the Coso art for a second assessment of the model was not coincidental. Whitley was associated with Lewis-Williams' Rock Art Research Unit at the time that the model was being developed and his input is quite apparent. In addition to citing Whitley directly, Lewis-Williams and Dowson used a number of the same references that we find in Whitley's later work. Commenting specifically on the use of the Coso material, the authors mention "the paucity of direct ethnographic references to rock art in this area," but concluded, "it is sufficient to justify using it in a second, though subsidiary, evaluation of our model" (Lewis-Williams and Dowson 1988, 205). Because their work was published in *Current Anthropology*, it was subjected to the scrutiny of scholars from around the world. Responding to comments that questioned the shamanistic origin of the Coso images, the authors asked Whitley (1988, 238) to review the ethnographic data that verified this premise.

Lewis-Williams and Dowson realized that "cultural expectations" affect the imagery to a considerable extent. For this reason they stressed the fact that their model was derived entirely from neuropsychological research and concentrated on entoptic phenomena as a feature of altered states that was completely controlled by the human nervous system. Since these visual images are produced within the human nervous system (a biological universal), they are liable to be perceived by all people who enter an altered state, regardless of their cultural background (Lewis-Williams and Dowson 1988, 202). They also realized that their inference that the rock art was created by shamans to portray images seen in trance states was not a final conclusion but merely a platform for addressing outstanding issues (238). Referring to the Coso case specifically, they suggested that several points might be clarified when the North American ethnography was more intensely used in interpreting the rock art (211). Whitley, deeply involved in research concerning Far West ethnography and working in a milieu that fostered new ways of looking at interpretive issues, accepted the challenge.

Interpretation of the Coso Rock Art

During the next few years, Whitley published several articles concerning the Coso images, their shamanistic origins and the interpretative aspects of the art. In 1992 he wrote a significant chapter for Schiffer's *Archaeological Method and Theory* series that outlined the theoretical and methodological tenets of a postprocessual approach to the study of archaeological data. Quite understandably, Whitley relied heavily on Lewis-Williams' work in formulating his own cognitive paradigm.

Whitley realized that, if culture-specific elements influenced the depictions (as Lewis-Williams and Dowson had suggested), then the only way to get at their meaning was through a thorough comprehension of the beliefs and worldview of the people who produced the images. This was the key to understanding the art of prehistoric people, and it led Whitley to argue for an anthropological archaeology with culture as a central concern, just as Walter Taylor had done nearly fifty years earlier. Culture, from this perspective, was not defined in the behaviorist terms of processual archaeology but instead as a system of values and beliefs—a society's worldview. This concept of culture shifted the emphasis of social inquiry away from a purely behavioral realm to one that would allow specific reference to the human mind and the actions of individuals (Whitley 1992a, 60; 1998c, 6).

Lewis-Williams and Dowson also addressed an important methodological issue—the traditional empiricist position that the proper strategy for all rock art studies was to collect and classify the data and then induce explanations from them. They rejected this approach because they believed it was based on a false notion of science—one that demanded "proof" of any assertions. They insisted that proof is a concept appropriate only to mathematics or irrefutable deductive arguments and concluded, "A call for proof is therefore inappropriate in rock art research, and researchers must use forms of argument appropriate to the human sciences." Realizing that many scientific disciplines were operating outside the rigidly demarcated areas of proof and disconfirmation, they argued that "best-fit" hypotheses were more appropriate for cognitive analysis (Lewis-Williams and Dowson 1988, 234).

Lewis-Williams and Dowson knew that some philosophers of science (e.g., Copi 1968; Hempel 1966) had proposed other legitimate criteria for judging hypotheses, such as predictive potential, the quantity and diversity of data explained, testability, and compatibility with well-established research. Whitley recognized that such an approach was ideally suited to his own work and saw it as a viable alternative to the scientific positivism that was so firmly entrenched in processualism. He also knew that a post-positivist philosophy of science had emerged at around the same time the New Archaeology came into vogue—one that rejected the positivist emphasis on falsification or verification as the preferred means of testing theories. Whitley adopted the post-positive axiom that the goal of science is not necessarily to discover truth, but to move increasingly closer to it. He was convinced that the best way to accomplish this was to use empirical evidence to select the best from a series of competing hypotheses, an idea that was very close to Lewis-Williams and Dowson's notion of "best fit" (Whitley 1998c, 11).

The desire to be more "scientific" had also turned processual archaeology away from another traditional interpretive device: ethnographic analogy. Lewis-Williams and Dowson, aware of this prejudice, argued that their proposition (that the nervous systems of all prehistoric people responded, in certain altered states, in ways closely similar to modern humans) provided a "relation of relevance" that strengthened their use of analogy. They believed that the presence in Paleolithic art of geometric forms that were similar to entoptic phenomena, the combinations of entoptic and iconic forms, and the range of predictable transformations clearly implied altered states of consciousness comparable to shamanistic San and Coso trance states that generated geometric forms in the rock art (Lewis-Williams and Dowson 1988, 236). Alison Wylie, a respected proponent of analogical inference, defended this approach, arguing that their model was further strengthened by the use of two different but mutually reinforcing sources (Wylie 1988, 231).

Whitley, as the provider of one of those reinforcing sources, realized that ethnographic analogy offered a sound foundation for archaeological interpretation. He believed that building an ethnographically informed analogical base was essential for the development of his cognitive approach. Ethnographic interpretations could then be used to identify relevant relationships and, once the methodologically sound analogy had been constructed, the prehistoric past could be truly accessed (Whitley 1992a, 77).

During the early 1990s, Whitley brought all of these concepts to bear as he formulated a broad interpretation for the rock art of the western Great Basin. His fundamental premise was that Numic shamans and shaman-initiates created the art. The motifs were graphic expressions of visions experienced while in altered states of consciousness (Whitley 1994a, 361). While in these trance states, shamans entered the supernatural world to acquire power, usually manifest in the form of supernatural helpers, songs, and ritual paraphernalia. Because certain spirit beings conferred special kinds of power, it was possible to relate particular images to specialized shamanistic activities. Whitley found, in the ethnographic record, a strong association between the rain shaman and the mountain sheep— the dominant image in the Coso Range (Whitley 1994a, 362).

The ethnographic literature revealed that mountain sheep, along with natural phenomena like rain, thunder, and lightning, were said to be the specialized spirit helpers of the rain shaman. Moreover, much of the ritual paraphernalia obtained during vision quests derived from mountain sheep products such as horns and hide. Whitley stressed the idea that the mountain sheep vision of the rain shaman was not simply a dream of a sheep as a beneficial spirit helper. Because visions experienced in altered states of consciousness could not be described in "normal" terms, shamans in the Great Basin, like all humans who confront the problem of an inexpressible event, reverted to metaphors to explain their visions. Whitley (1998b, 154) found that one of the most important metaphors for an altered state is death or killing. In support of this notion, he cited ethnographic material (e.g., Kelly 1936, 139; Steward 1941, 259) that associated the killing of mountain sheep with rainfall and supernatural power. He argued that killing a mountain sheep was a metaphor for the acquisition and application of a particular kind of shamanistic power—weather control (Whitley 1994a, 363).

Recognizing that this interpretation of the Coso petroglyphs provided one reading of the art, Whitley suggested that existing ethnohistoric and ethnographic records could be used to gain additional information concerning the social context of the images. He believed that, even though Numic-speaking people were usually viewed as the archetypal egalitarian society, asymmetrical social relations did in fact exist. One of these was a degree of gender inequality resulting from the sexual division of labor and the institution of marriage. In Numic society, the men hunted big game while women gathered plant foods and foraged for small animals. Meat obtained by men was communally shared, whereas a woman's contributions were reserved for her immediate family (Whitley 1992a, 83; 1994a, 364).

For Whitley, the implications of this sexual division of labor and pattern of circulation were extreme. Because of the differences in the way that plant foods gathered by women and large game hunted by men were distributed, women were economically independent. Women did not need husbands because the division of big game throughout the camp guaranteed them some portion of this meat. Men, whether they hunted or not, would always receive a share of hunted game, but they could get the essentials of their diet—plant foods—only if the wife was diligent in gathering (Whitley 1992a, 85; 1994a, 365). For the male, then, a wife was necessary to maintain a steady supply of dietary staples. The less desirable alternative was to incur debts to other married males.

Thus, while marriage tied women to a fairly strict plant-gathering regimen and burdened them with primary child care responsibilities, it freed the men from their reliance on other males. Marriage also structured asymmetrical relationships between groups of men—bachelors and husbands (Whitley 1994a, 365). Prestige was measured partly by the number of wives maintained and the economic status that accrued as a result. While there were no true chiefs among Numic speakers, older married males did have a degree of influence and authority.

Ethnographic studies showed that another asymmetrical relationship was created by access to supernatural power. Although Numic culture was viewed as egalitarian (and thus at the lowest stage of sociopolitical evolution), authority and leadership were vested in certain individuals. The most common leader was the village or band headman, a person who ruled by consensus rather than by exercising dictatorial prerogatives (Whitley 1994a, 366). Whitley's research also revealed that, almost invariably, headmen were shamans. This did not necessarily mean that all shamans were headmen, but it was only through the acquisition of shamanistic power that men could truly become political actors and gain prestige and status in Numic society.

With this ethnographically informed perspective of Numic culture at hand, Whitley focused on the relationship of the Coso engravings to Numic subsistence patterns and social systems. Archaeological research in the western Great Basin, including Whitley's own work in the Coso Range, showed evidence of a subtle transition, beginning about eight hundred years ago, from a generalized, mobile hunting and gathering strategy to a less-mobile, seed-oriented gathering and foraging economy. Whitley inferred from this that the existing social relationships must have been threatened, in that the increasing emphasis on plant foods provided by women, combined with the diminished importance of game hunted by men, had the potential for altering gender relations (Whitley 1994a, 367). Over time, this change made women more economically independent. Conversely, since a man's independence (from other men) would now be predicated on marriage and the resulting control of women's gathering activities, it increased male dependence on women and marriage.

Whitley suggested that the response to this changing subsistence pattern involved a dramatic increase in the production of rock art. Chronometric studies revealed that a majority of certain classes of engravings were produced roughly within the last thousand years. These images included anthropomorphs, mountain sheep, weapons, and "hunter" motifs—depictions that were previously thought to be evidence of a sympathetic hunting magic cult. Whitley's ethnographic studies had, however, shown that no such cult existed among the Numa (Whitley 1994a, 367). Instead, the ethnography revealed that these motifs were metaphors for the shaman and his relationship with the supernatural world, and the bighorn sheep was specifically associated with the rain shaman. Thus, Whitley argued, the changing subsistence system appeared to have precipitated a dramatic increase in weather-control shamanism (368).

This response emphasized male—particularly the male shaman's—control over women's subsistence activities. By metaphorically killing a mountain sheep and recording this supernatural act in rock art, the shaman stressed his importance to women's plant gathering. This also served to emphasize, through the selective use of masculine symbols, the continued significance of male hunting, even when this component of their subsistence strategy was substantially diminished (Whitley 1992a, 86). Therefore, Whitley contends, the Numic shaman not only controlled nature (causing seed plants to grow through rain rituals) but also encouraged the stability of social relations. Shamans, by reaffirming male dominance, were able to perpetuate the established gender asymmetry despite the increased importance of women's contributions to the diet.

Furthermore, changing subsistence practices precipitated an alteration in relationships among males (Whitley 1994a, 368). The acceleration of shamanistic activities, reflected in the rock art motifs, allowed the emergence of shamans as part-time ritual specialists, charged with maintaining the dominant position of men in relation to women. This, in effect, set the stage for asymmetrical relationships between men in that those favored with power—shamans—held an advantage over those who were without. Access to the supernatural, and the accumulation of esoteric knowledge and power that went with it, gave the shamans an edge in terms of prestige and respect. Whitley, stressing the idea that political authority was identified with shamanic power, concluded that the combined circumstances triggered the emergence of incipient sociopolitical organization among the Numa (369).

Using an ethnographically derived interpretation of Coso society and its rock art, Whitley developed an understanding of the last few thousand years of prehistory in this region. While his primary concern was to show how cognitive theory and method could be effectively deployed, an underlying objective was to overcome the adaptationist contention that Numic culture was mostly "gastric" in nature (Steward 1938, 46). He emphasized the idea that subsistence change is not simply a mechanical or even evolutionary alteration in diet. From a cognitive point of view, a subsistence system should be perceived as a conceptual entity, only indirectly expressed in the archaeological record. Whitley (1994a, 370) believes that, in order to study subsistence change, one must commit to the study of prehistoric cognition. Without denying the impact of man-land relationships or the significance of technological innovation, this approach clearly emphasizes an anthropological archaeology and the need to consider the cognitive realm.

Cognitive research, however, is not just about rock art. Interpreting rock art from a cognitive perspective, whether the art of the Ice Age caves, paintings of the San bushman of southern Africa, or the engravings of the western Great Basin, leads to the phenomenon of shamanism. The study of rock art, and the resulting evidence that the creation of much of the art found around the world can be attributed to shamanistic practices, has opened a new research direction that can be extremely valuable for the study of ancient cultures.

The Nonarchaeological Case for Shamanism   9

IN EARLIER CHAPTERS we saw how cognitive researchers developed a shamanic interpretation of the archaeological record, particularly the rock art, through the use of a neuropsychological model that was based on the fact that the human nervous system is a biological universal. When Lewis-Williams and Dowson first presented their model, they stated explicitly that it was derived entirely from neuropsychological research and not from the rock art. The validity of the model, they argued, could then be determined only by neurological studies. Fortunately, this type of research, as well as studies in the fields of microbiology, biochemistry, genetics, and other related disciplines, has increased significantly in recent years and thus affords us not only an opportunity to more carefully evaluate the validity of the neuropsychological model but also broader insights into altered states of consciousness, prehistoric cognition, and shamanism.

Altered States, Shamanism, and Science

We know that the central focus of shamanistic activity is the vital human contact with a transphenomenal power—a condition gained by specialized techniques and mechanisms. These methods include meditation and the induction of altered states of consciousness, either through the use of external agents such as hallucinogenic drugs, or by internal means like fasting, sensory deprivation, and rhythmic movement. We also know that the basic elements of altered states experienced by shamans are remarkably consistent over time and space and in a variety of cultures (Ripinsky-Naxon 1993, 82). Mircea Eliade, discussing the universality of shamanistic trance, wrote, "We have termed the ecstatic experience a 'primary phenomenon' because we see no reason whatever for regarding it as the result of a particular historic movement. Rather, we would consider it fundamental in the human condition, known to the whole of archaic humanity" (Eliade 1964, 504). Erika Bourguignon (1968) offered further empirical support for this proposition when she found that fully 90 percent of a sample of 488 societies from around the world, with varying degrees of complexity, had some form of institutionalized altered states.

Peter Furst (1982, 4) believes that the shamanistic altered state shares so many basic features over time and space as to suggest common neurological, biological, and psychological origins. Is there any evidence that altered states of consciousness may in fact be "fundamental in the human condition?" Research on human brain function is beginning to shed new light on the biological and neurological aspects of trance and offers at least some tentative explanations of how and why people enter into altered states of consciousness.

A growing body of evidence suggests that the human brain may be naturally calibrated to transcendence. Andrew Newberg and his colleagues at the University of Pennsylvania are using a technique that involves single positron emission computed tomography (SPECT) to peer deep into meditating minds. Interestingly (and contrary to the processualist position that ideology, belief systems, and the like were epiphenomena that could not be subjected to scientific inquiry), Newberg chose to investigate the neurobiology of meditation precisely because it is a spiritual state that is easily duplicated in the laboratory. As part of this study, researchers scanned the brains of several Buddhist monks who were in a state of prolonged meditation. To facilitate photography of the neural activity during this meditative period they injected each monk with a slightly radioactive tracer chemical that quickly infuses into the brain cells, where it illuminates neural activity for the SPECT camera. The images revealed distinctive changes in brain activity as the monks settled into a meditative state. In particular, activity diminished in those parts of the brain involved in generating a sense of three-dimensional orientation in space (Newberg, d'Aquili, and Rause 2001). The loss of this sense of place could conceivably account for a spiritual feeling of release into another realm beyond time and space. The implication is that a vital element of the religious experience of transcendence may be hard-wired in the human brain.

At the University of California, San Diego, Center for Brain and Cognition, researchers are trying to uncover the fundamental architecture of the human mind. Testing patients who suffer seizures that result from temporal lobe epilepsy, they have found provocative hints of "dedicated neural machinery" that affects how intensely humans respond to spiritual or mystical experiences. During seizures, test subjects report overwhelming feelings of union with the universe. Researchers determined that these people also have heightened (and completely involuntary) neural responses to certain religious symbols and language. Their conclusion is that something strange has happened in the temporal lobes of these subjects—

something that intensified their reaction to religious terms and icons (Ramachandran and Blakeslee 1999).

Anthropologist and neuroscientist Marc Hauser of Harvard University believes that the ability to form complex belief systems may be linked to the brain's prefrontal cortex, an area that seems to be responsible for the most sophisticated aspects of the human mind and its relationship with the universe around it. In his opinion, the most crucial part of the brain is the region that has grown the largest in our evolutionary history—the prefrontal cortex—and ours is about 200 percent larger than one would expect for a primate our size (Hotz 1998). The prefrontal cortex is also critical for linking up with concepts like religion. Current neurophysiological research, then, appears to be telling us that the human brain has a certain affinity for altered states.

While altered states can be deliberately induced in many ways, the use of hallucinogens appears to be the preferred method for many cultures. This may be so simply because ancients discovered long ago that the use of drugs is a particularly reliable and rapid way to achieve altered states of consciousness (Dobkin de Rios 1996, 6). Whatever the reason, most researchers agree that the use of psychoactive (i.e., acting on the psychological processes) substances to enter nonordinary states of consciousness for the purpose of interacting with the supernatural world is a very ancient and widespread human practice (Dobkin de Rios 1996, x; Harner 1973a, xiv; 1981, xi, xiv; Ripinsky-Naxon 1989, 220). Once again, there is a growing body of scientific evidence that provides some clues as to why this may be so.

The Use of Hallucinogens

Andrew Weil, a Harvard-trained physician, believes that our appetite for "high states" has its origin in the human nervous system and is independent of any external substances. Weil is thoroughly convinced that the "desire to alter consciousness periodically is an innate normal drive analogous to hunger or the sex drive" and that the desire for intoxication is a universal and natural phenomenon, an intrinsic part of the human condition, rooted in mammalian, and therefore human, biology (Weil 1972, 17). Research psychopharmacologist Ronald Siegel tells us that the quest for intoxication through drugs is a primary motivational force. He believes that the human nervous system is arranged to respond to chemical intoxicants in much the same way it responds to other types of stimuli: "Throughout our entire history as a species, intoxication has functioned like the basic drives of hunger, thirst or sex, sometimes overshadowing all other activities in life" (Siegel 1989, 10). Thus, we should not be surprised to learn that hallucinogens have played a vital role in the cultural and spiritual practices of ancient societies for many millennia.

The Ethnography of Drug Use

Early Sanskrit and Chinese writings tell about the hallucinogenic properties of *Datura*, a psychoactive plant that occurs in both hemispheres (Schultes and Hofmann 1972). The use of hallucinogenic plants such as henbane, mandrake, and belladonna was once a common practice in the Old World. This fact is little known in current times because the use of these substances was often associated with medieval witchcraft, which the Church deemed heretical. The agents of the Inquisition zealously suppressed these practices, observing that many of the things that witches confessed to, like flying through the air and engaging in orgies with demons at Sabbats, were patently impossible. These cases were, however, well documented and much of our data about the role of hallucinogenic plants in late medieval Europe come from records of the Inquisition (Harner 1973d, 125).

In Siberia, the earliest known eyewitness account of the intoxicating fly-agaric mushroom dates to 1658 and is found in the journal of a Polish prisoner, Adam Kamienski Dluzyk, who wrote, "They eat certain fungi in the shape of fly-agarics and thus get drunk worse than on vodka" (Ripinsky-Naxon 1993, 163). In the eighteenth and nineteenth centuries, travelers and natural scientists wrote about the shamanistic use of this mushroom in tribal Siberia. One of the members of the Jessup North Pacific Expedition, Waldemar Jochelson, revealed that this plant was used by shamans to facilitate communication with the supernatural, to divine the future, and to determine the cause of illness. He wrote that "fly-agaric produces intoxication, hallucinations, and delirium. Many shamans, previous to their seances, eat fly-agaric to get into ecstatic states" (Jochelson 1905, 583).

In the New World, Europeans first witnessed the use of a hallucinogenic snuff among the Taino Indians of Hispaniola. Friar Ramón Pané, who had been commissioned by Columbus "to collect all ceremonies and antiquities," wrote in detail concerning this drug and its place in Indian society (Schultes 1972, 24). The Spanish conquerors of Mexico found the Indians engaged in religious cults in which deities were worshiped with the aid of hallucinogenic plants. There is no doubt that these were drugs nor about how they were employed, since Spanish chroniclers of the period railed vehemently and often against these pagan rituals (Schultes 1972, 7).

Among the sources containing taxonomic and ethnobotanical information, as well as those that describe the medicinal properties of many hallucinogens are the manuscripts of Fray Bernardino de Sahagún, known collectively as the *Florentine Codex*; the writings of Fray Diego Durán, whose original manuscript in the National Library in Madrid is referred to as the *Codex Durán*; the writings of the physician Francisco Hernández; and the illustrated herbal compendium dating to the middle of the sixteenth century, known as the *Codex Badianus*. Archaeological and ethnohistorical fieldwork conducted in later years not only corroborated these accounts, but also widened our perspectives by adding cultural and temporal depth to the ethnopharmacological practices. Scholars believe, for example, that the Chicimecas, the original Aztec group, as well as the Toltecs, were acquainted with hallucinogenic substances as far back as 2400 B.P. (Dobkin de Rios 1996, 141).

In South America, the Ecuadorian geographer Villavicencio was the first to report on the existence and effects of a hallucinatory drink made from tropical forest lianas. He observed that "this beverage is narcotic . . . in a few moments it begins to produce the most rare phenomenon. It . . . appears to excite the nervous system; they feel vertigo and spinning in the head, then a sensation of being lifted into the air and beginning an aerial journey" (Villavicencio 1858, 372–73). Students of Andean prehistory also acknowledge a rich natural laboratory of drug plants from Peru (Cooper 1949). The Nazca, for example, used hallucinogenic cactus, species of *Datura*, and *wilka* snuff. These and other psychoactive plants are employed in Peruvian healing throughout the coast and tropical rain forests today and appear to have been in continuous use throughout prehistoric periods (Dobkin de Rios 1996, 59).

The study of the effects of mind-altering drugs began to attract serious scholarly attention at the end of the nineteenth century as a result of scientific investigation into the phenomena of hallucinations and mystical experiences by leading figures of the day, such as Francis Galton, J. M. Charcot, Sigmund Freud, and William James (Ripinsky-Naxon 1993, 142). More recent research concerning the neurological and biological aspects of consciousness and brain-mind functions has increased our understanding of the effects of hallucinogens on the brain and nervous system. Because psychoactive agents are very similar to certain natural substances already present in the brain, the study of their effects on brain function and experiences affords an excellent opportunity for exploring and understanding the relationship of brain to mind in a contemporary setting. More importantly, this type of research can provide some remarkable insights into prehistoric cognition in a shamanistic context.

The Psychoactive Flora

Hallucinogenic compounds are present in plant roots, stems, leaves, seeds, and flowers. Schultes tells us that the most common of these belong to either the nitrogen-containing alkaloids derived from the amino acid tryptophane or the nonnitrogenous compounds dibenzopyran and phenylpropene (Schultes 1972, 6). The best known and most widely researched nonflowering psychoactive plants belong to the agaric family (*Agaricaceae*) and include the various species of mushrooms. Families of flowering plants known to contain hallucinogenic substances include several members of the morning glory family (*Convolvulaceae*), mints (*Labiatae*), the cacti (*Cactaceae*), the pea family (*Leguminosae*), *Malpighiaceae*, *Myristcaceae*, and *Solanaceae*.

The ethnographic literature reveals not only that hallucinogens were widely employed in prehistory, but also the types of plants that were used to achieve altered states of consciousness. Botanists and pharmacologists have now isolated the psychoactive substances in most of these plants. Following is a brief summary of some of the species within the families listed above, including plants that were used most frequently to induce altered states of consciousness in the prehistoric past:

Agaricaceae. The Spanish conquerors of Mesoamerica observed several ritual cults in which the Indians worshipped deities with the aid of hallucinogenic substances. One of the most important—and for the Spaniards the most loathsome—was the cult of *teonanacatl*, the Nahuatl name for mushrooms meaning "flesh of the gods" (Schultes 1972, 7). Later studies by qualified botanists identified these plants as species of *Psilocybe, Conocybe,* and *Stropharia.* Researchers isolated psilocybin, a hallucinogenic substance, from several species (Farnsworth 1968).

Cactaceae. In terms of hallucinogenic properties, the most significant species in this group is *Lophophora williamsii*—peyote cactus. de Sahagún (1950) was one of the first known Europeans to discuss peyote seriously, noting that the Chichimecas and Toltecs had used it for many hundreds of years to "see visions." Among the tribes of northern Mexico, its medicinal powers were so great that it was considered a vegetal incarnation of a deity. Schultes (1972, 15) refers to the peyote cactus as "a veritable factory of alkaloids." The best-known psychoactive substance in the peyote cactus is mescaline, a vision-inducing alkaloid that works primarily on the visual areas of the brain's cortex. Certain species of columnar cacti of the high Andes are also know to contain mescaline. Schultes (17) tells us that certain Peruvian Indians prepare a vision-inducing hallucinogenic drink from *Trichocereus pachanoi*, known locally as the San Pedro cactus.

Convolvulaceae. One of the most important sacred hallucinogens among the Mexican Indians at the time of the Conquest was *ololiuqui*, the small, round seed from a vine known in the Nahuatl language as *coxihuitl*, or "snake plant" (Schultes 1972, 17). This plant was subsequently identified as *Rivea corymbosa* (morning glory) and the seeds contain derivatives of lysergic acid (Hofmann 1963).

Leguminosae. Among the most famous of the New World drugs is the snuff made from a South America tree named *Anadenanthera peregrina*. This potent hallucinogen was so widely recognized in anthropological circles that, until recently, almost all the narcotic snuffs of South America were attributed to this plant, even in areas where it does not occur. The hallucinogenic ingredients include several tryptamine derivatives (Schultes 1972, 24).

Mescal beans are the seeds of a shrub found in the American Southwest and Mexico, known botanically as *Sophora secundiflora*. In the sixteenth century, the Spanish explorer Cabeza de Vaca wrote that these beans were used as articles of trade among the Indians of Texas (cited in La Barre 1964). The Stephen Long Expedition of 1820 reported that the Arapaho and Iowa tribes used the red beans as a medicine and a narcotic. A well-developed mescal bean cult existed among the Apache, Comanche, Delaware, Iowa, Kansa, Omaha, Oto, Osage, Pawnee, Ponca, Tonkawa, and Wichita (Dobkin de Rios 1996, 53). The hallucinogenic ingredient is cytisine or related alkaloids (Schultes 1972, 31).

Malpighiaceae. The South American Indians in the western Amazon, the Orinoco, and on the Pacific coast of Colombia and Ecuador use an extraordinary hallucinogen prepared from the bark of vines, *Banisteriopsis caapi*. This narcotic drink is variously known as *caapi, ayahuasca, yagé, natema,* or *pinde,* depending on the region and the cultural group, and it enters deeply into almost every aspect of the lives of the people who ingest it (Reichel-Dolmatoff 1972; Schultes 1972, 35). The principal psychoactive constituent is harmine, an alkaloid structurally related to indole derivatives like mescaline and psilocybin (Harner 1973b, 5).

Myristcaceae. One of the most recently discovered hallucinogens is a toxic snuff that is prepared from the bark and resin of several species of *Virola* found in the northwestern Amazon. The resin contains a high concentration of tryptamines that causes very rapid intoxication. Within minutes after a large dose is blown into the nostrils—often through bamboo or bird-bone tubes—the subject experiences visual hallucinations, a deep stupor, and the sensation of floating in air or flying (Schultes 1972, 44).

Solanaceae. Possibly the most important group of plants used by humans to contact the supernatural belongs to the order *Solanaceae*. This family includes economically significant plants such as the tomato, potato, and pepper, as well as other species that are highly regarded (and also feared) for their hallucinogenic properties. The genus *Datura,* known by a variety of names such as jimson weed, devil's apple, angel trumpet, thorn apple, and Gabriel's trumpet, is a member of this group. Other hallucinogens from this family that bear a close resemblance to *Datura* in their effects include mandrake (*Mandragora*), henbane (*Hyoscyamus*) and belladonna, or deadly nightshade (*Atropa belladonna*) (Harner 1973d, 128; Munz and Keck 1959; Schultes and Hofmann 1972). All of these plants contain quantities of atropine and the closely related tropane alkaloids hyoscyamine and scopolamine (Claus and Tyler 1965; Henry 1949; Hoffer and Osmund 1967; Lewin 1964).

The literature from 1492 to the present leaves little doubt concerning the use of tobacco by American Indians in religion, curing practices, and ceremonies. Although the New World plant *Nicotiana* is not one of the true hallucinogens from the botanist's or pharmacologist's point of view (Wilbert 1972, 55), its active ingredients, especially the alkaloid nicotine, can induce dramatic psychodynamic effects. There is ample evidence that tobacco has been used in many parts of the New World to trigger shamanic trance states that are very similar, perhaps even identical, to those induced by the true hallucinogens (Furst 1990, viii; Schultes 1972, 54).

Although there were thirteen different species of native tobacco growing wild in Australia at the time of European contact (Goodspeed 1954), the tobacco-like substance known as *pituri* was probably more important to the early aborigines (Dobkin de Rios 1996, 23). This narcotic is prepared from cured leaves of the *Duboisia hopwoodii* shrub and mixed with an alkali ash from *Acacia* wood (Mulvaney and Kamminga 1999, 97). Small doses of this mixture, which contain scopolamine and hyoscyamine, give rise to hallucinations and illusions of detachment from time and space (Lewin 1964).

As a result of more recent research, we are beginning to understand why substances as different as mescaline or psilocybin produce similar mental states and how certain compounds can unlock forgotten doorways into worlds of experience that have, until recently, confounded science.

Hallucinogens and Brain Function

Most of the psychoactive compounds such as tryptamine, bufotenine, and psilocybin are structurally related to serotonin—a neurotransmitter that helps brain cells, called neurons, send and receive information. Serotonin is involved in a variety of functions in all areas of the brain and central nervous system, such as appetite control, sleep, memory and learning, cardiovascular activity, mood, behavior (including sexual and hallucinogenic behavior), and depression (Borne 1994). Serotonin acts as a chemical messenger; released from the axon of one neuron and transmitted across a synaptic gap to tiny points known as "receptors" on other neurons, it allows the brain cells to "talk" to each other (Burton 1998). Studies show that psychoactive compounds act directly on the specific receptor sites that receive serotonin, thus interfering with serotonin's normal activity. By mimicking the actions of serotonin, the hallucinogens thus act as serotonin inhibitors, effectively reducing interference with their own chemical activities and thereby altering the normal chain of chemical events in the neural system of the brain (Jacobs 1987; Ripinsky-Naxon 1993, 144).

Serotonin is sometimes characterized as the gyroscope of the mind-brain; one of its main functions is to regulate the flow of information through the neural system. Its role is neither to inhibit nor promote neural communication but rather to maintain a balance, ensuring that the entire neurological system stays within normal limits (Porush 1993). But when hallucinogens stimulate these serotonin receptors, they disrupt the delicate balancing act that cycles messages coming in from the exterior world, destabilizing serotonin's homeostatic control and loosening the brain's grip on what it normally perceives as reality. The stream of hallucinogen molecules, bombarding key serotonin receptor sites and sending signals unprovoked by external stimuli, also disrupts the messages going out to the motor cortex of the brain. Suddenly, the mind seems to float free, enjoying (or being overwhelmed by) images that no longer come from the physical world alone but from some new origin outside normal reality.

These findings demonstrate that the chemical effects of hallucinogens cause the brain to undergo a massive and global change—a major ecological shift for which the brain appears to be inexplicably ready. These substances seem to have a unique ability to fundamentally transform the functions that we consider to be uniquely human—the way we think, feel, and act. They alter and shift cognitive and symbolic capacities, aesthetic sensibilities, and our linguistic and imaginative abilities—the very kinds of brain functions that constitute the fabric of what we experience as "mind." Knowing this, we can now more readily comprehend why a shaman in a hallucinogen-induced trance state might feel that he is in contact with the supernatural, since the messages his brain receives are not connected to "normal" reality and cannot be correlated to the environment his senses tell him is there. Understanding the effects of drugs on the human brain and nervous system allows us to evaluate the stages of trance and other aspects of shamanistic altered states from a neurological and biochemical perspective.

Hallucinogens and the Stages of Trance

In developing their neuropsychological model, Lewis-Williams and Dowson (1988, 203) examined three stages in the progression of altered states of consciousness.

During the first stage, subjects experience "entoptic phenomenon" (or "entoptics") (Siegel 1977, 132; Siegel and Jarvik 1975, 111). This term refers to visual sensations derived from the structure of the optic system—perceptions that are independent of any influence from external sources.

Beginning in the 1920s, Heinrich Klüver began a systematic analysis of these percepts. Working under laboratory conditions, Klüver (1942, 177) concluded that they had form, and abstracted a number of recurring form elements from his subjects' reports of altered states of consciousness. He determined that the major categories of these form constants are grating, lattice, fretwork, filigree, cobweb, tunnel, honeycomb, funnel, cone, and spiral (Klüver 1966, 66). Other researchers (e.g., Horowitz 1964; Richards 1971; Siegel 1977) verified Klüver's findings and identified additional recurring form elements. They discovered that these visual phenomena take geometric shapes in the form of grids, zigzags, dots, circles, and catenary curves. Entoptics, even those produced by simple pressure on the eyes, can consist of relatively simple designs or quite elaborate patterns. While we know that sensory deprivation, fatigue, hyperventilation, rhythmic movement and the like are generating factors (Klüver 1942; Horowitz 1964, 512–18; Sacks 1970; Siegel and Jarvik 1975), hallucinogens invariably produce these abstract patterns (Oster 1970). Barber (1970, 32) suggests that psychoactive agents may lower the threshold for the perception of these entoptic phenomena.

During the second stage of trance, subjects attempt to make some sense of the entoptics by elaborating them into iconic forms (Horowitz 1964, 514; 1975, 177, 178, 181). In normal states of consciousness, the brain receives a stream of sensory impressions and decodes the visual images by matching them against a store of experience. But with drug-induced altered states, the process is chemically disrupted. The human nervous system itself becomes a "sixth sense" (Heinze 1986) that produces a variety of images, including entoptic phenomena. The brain tries to recognize and decode these forms just as it does the impressions supplied by the nervous system in a normal state of consciousness. The brain's cortex is now not only being pressed to deal with this alien input but also finds itself stimulated by a flood of hallucinogens that disrupt its ability to carry out normal functions. The result is a flow of images scripted and edited into an entirely new show.

As subjects progress to the third stage, marked changes in imagery begin to occur (Siegel 1977, 132). Subjects experience an increase in lattice, kaleidoscopic, and tunnel forms. Entoptic phenomena give way to iconic images, a shift that is accompanied by a sharp increase in vividness (Siegel and Jarvik 1975, 125–132). They stop using similes to describe their experiences and insist that the images are indeed exactly what they appear to be. They seem to "lose insight into the differences between literal and analogous meanings" (Siegel and Jarvik 1975). Lewis-

Williams describes certain images that combine anthropomorphic forms with phosphene elements and interprets them as a shaman's close identification with his own hallucinations: "In the end, they are what they see and what they feel" (Lewis-Williams 1986, 174).

Clearly, the transformations of consciousness induced by hallucinogenic substances involve perceptual alterations of a subject's mental and physical states (Ripinsky-Naxon 1993, 147). Not coincidentally, the perceptions tend to closely parallel common shamanistic themes such as death and rebirth; the presence of, or the shaman's transformation into, supernatural helpers or allies; celestial journey or descent to the underworld; and magical flight.

Death and Rebirth, Metamorphosis, and Magical Flight

A number of ethnographers (Benedict 1923, 15; Blackburn 1975, 43, 188; Gayton 1948, 34, 44, 48; Kroeber 1907, 23; Schultes 1972, 35; Zigmond 1977, 65) have observed that death is a commonly used metaphor for entry into trance states. This ritual death and rebirth that shamans and shaman-initiates experienced while in altered states of consciousness (what Von Winning [1969] referred to as the "life emerging from death" motif) was intense and far more convincing than any rites of passage that did not involve trance. This was due, at least in part, to the close neurophysiological analogy between altered states and real death. Both may involve such symptoms as physical collapse, weakening of vital signs, and bleeding from the nose and mouth. (Whitley 1998e). Furthermore, the maiden voyage to the Otherworld is the most crucial journey a shaman-initiate will ever make. He must overcome obstacles along the way and his very life is threatened by the ever-present possibility that his dream state will be interrupted so suddenly that his wandering soul will not have enough time to return to his body. "A novice suffering this fate will never get to practice and will soon die" (Wilbert 1972, 63). We now know that such perceptions are heavily influenced by the action of psychoactive chemicals on the brain. Scientific research tells us that alkaloids like hyoscyamine, harmine, and hyosine often create symptoms of physical discomfort that may include slowing of the pulse, numbness, and blurring of sensory stimuli from the external world: a kind of amnesiac state that heightens the death and rebirth experience (Dobkin de Rios 1996, 222; Lamb 1985).

Another common drug-linked theme is the metamorphosis of humans into animals (or, less frequently, plants) that were considered to be spirit familiars or supernatural helpers. Species of the family *Solanaceae* are implicated in a large number of these transformations. Hesse informs us that "[a] characteristic feature of solanaceae psychosis is that the intoxicated person imagines himself to have been changed into some animal, and the hallucinosis is completed by the sensation of growing feathers and hair" (Hesse 1946, 103–4). Harner (1973d, 140–45) provides ample evidence that solanaceous ointments were used in medieval times to facilitate metamorphosis of humans into werewolves. Giovanni Batista Porta, a colleague of Galileo, wrote that "[to] make a man believe he was changed into a Bird or Beast," he drank a potion that was made of henbane, mandrake, stramonium or Solanum manicum, and belladonna (Porta 1658 [original 1589], 219). Barber, summarizing clinical studies of hallucinogens, observed that nearly all subjects stated that their bodies "feel strange or funny. More bizarre feelings are registered at higher doses, such as the body melting into the background or floating in space" (Barber 1970, 22).

This phenomenon, often referred to in modern times as an "out-of-body experience," is a commonly reported subjective state, especially during peak hallucinatory periods (Hofmann 1959; Masters and Houston 1966; Siegel 1977, 136; Siegel and Jarvik 1975, 128; Tart 1975). Episodes frequently involve the perception of seeing one's body in objective space, but without a body-like container for the hallucinating mind. Reports of such experiences often stress the otherworldly, mystical nature of the perception and are often associated with profound, drug-induced altered states of consciousness (Dobkin de Rios 1996, 77).

Claudio Naranjo writes about one of his test subjects who reported that, during trance, one of his hands "seemed to lose weight, it rose, rose . . . and then I felt that it was no longer a hand but the tip of a wing. I was turning into a winged being" (Naranjo 1973, 180). Perceptions like this express a fundamental feature of shamanism referred to as "magical flight" or the "shaman's journey." As Eliade (1958, 480) observed, "Siberian and North American shamans fly. All over the world, the same magical power is credited to sorcerers and medicine men." This theme of bodily transport is quite common, and, although the details may differ, there was no doubt in the minds of the ancients that their shamans could, during an altered state of consciousness, launch themselves into the company of spirits in order to gain knowledge and power.

When we encounter an obviously ancient and very widely distributed belief such as the shamanic journey, it seems logical to wonder whether there might be some kind of biochemical reinforcement for the concept. We know that hallucinogenic compounds disrupt the normal state of consciousness in various ways and that one of the most common effects is the sensation of transcendence or flight. Studies show that the alkaloids of Datura, a plant frequently associated with shamanistic rituals and the performance of the shaman's essential functions, including magical flight and soul journey to the Otherworlds, probably affect the vestibular system, regulating balance (Dugan, Gumbmann, and Friedman 1989).

Topical activity is typical of the Solanaceae family. Zuni rain priests, for example, applied the powdered roots of Datura meteloides to their eyes in order to commune with their Feathered Kingdom (Schultes and Hofmann 1972, 1980). Yaqui sorcerers of northern Mexico were known to rub crushed *Datura* leaves on their genitals, legs, and feet to experience the sensation of flight (Davis 1998, 161–62; Harner 1973d, 140). Scopolamine, atropine, and the related tropanes present in *Datura* are also found in belladonna, mandrake, and henbane. Historians tell us that witches throughout medieval Europe rubbed their bodies with hallucinogenic ointments made from these plants. A particularly efficient means of application was through the moist tissue of the vaginal labia, and the witch's broomstick was considered a most effective applicator (Davis 1998, 162; Harner 1973d, 129). Apparently the witches' midnight flight to the sabbat was not through space, but across the hallucinatory landscape of the mind.

Clearly, the hallucinogenic experience is a transcultural phenomenon that is influenced by the biochemical effects of psychoactive drugs on the brain. This is not to suggest, however, that some simple biochemical reductionism is the end of the story. While both the Zuni and Yaqui use *Datura* "to fly," they do not have the exact same experience. Cultural factors play a significant role; indeed, there is evidence that they are extremely important for determining both the content and structure of supernatural ideology (Harner 1973a, 152). Powerful cultural stimuli interact with the chemistry of the plants to produce learned, expected results. In other words, while some elements of the experience may be similar because of the biochemical properties of plants used to induce altered states, each society interprets the experience in terms of its own beliefs and values (Tart 1975).

Shamanism, Hallucinogens, and Culture

For various reasons, we tread very lightly when discussing hallucinogens in any context. The use of drugs in a shamanistic setting is clearly a case in point: we can read entire books on shamanism or primitive religions without finding any reference to hallucinogens. This certainly holds true for archaeology, where the literature has largely overlooked not only the use of mind-altering drugs among traditional cultures but the entire phenomenon of shamanistic practices as well. Nevertheless, a number of scholars (many of them anthropologists) have provided ample evidence for the link between hallucinogens and shamanism and, more importantly, their impact on cultural development (e.g., Furst 1982, 1990; Furst and Coe 1977; Harner 1981; Hultkrantz 1987; La Barre 1970, 1972, 1989; Ripinsky-Naxon 1989, 1993). Marlene Dobkin de Rios (1968, 1972, 1974, 1977, 1982, 1996) has spent more than thirty years studying the specific relationship between hallucinogens and culture. She is firmly convinced that psychoactive substances have played more than just a minor role in structuring the lives, beliefs, and values of large numbers of people and that the economic behavior, social organization, and belief systems of many societies have been deeply affected by the use of mind-altering plants (Dobkin de Rios 1996, 3).

For most traditional societies, the heightened suggestibility induced by these plants forged in memory the values, beliefs, and knowledge that was considered indispensable for success in life. The various techniques employed by shamans, including the ability to see the causes of disease and augur the future were, in turn, prescribed by cultural norms. Experience gained during drug-induced visions and integrated through socially approved cognitive channels was a dynamic factor in the cultural process (Ripinsky-Naxon 1993, 9). We can no longer overlook the fact that these hallucinogenic experiences were deeply integrated into the supernatural life and total culture of many societies (Harner 1973a). When the shaman enters a trance and becomes a powerful animal or bird capable of traveling to the spirit realm, the transformation is—in his mind and in the belief of his people—literal. The visual and sensory imagery of an altered state, especially when induced by hallucinogens, is taken as proof that the supernatural world has truly been attained (Hedges 1992, 71).

Thus, from the viewpoint of the indigenous culture, a drug-induced vision is not regarded as a hallucination or illusion but instead as another form of reality—often the ultimate reality. Some would no doubt consider this another instance of Western culture conferring a "primitive" connotation on shamanistic societies. Kehoe, for example, refers to the "Western assumption that if you aren't a literate, city-dwelling citizen of a major nation, then you are an unsophisticated, emotional primitive, and unable to figure out the difference between dreams, hallucinations, and reality" (Kehoe 2000, 70). I submit that it is just as difficult for a modern "civilized" individual, spaced out on LSD or high on some synthetic designer drug, to make those distinctions as it was for "primitive" people.

We also need to make a fundamental distinction between the use of hallucinogens within a religious-ritualistic context in an aboriginal society and their recreational use in the West. For traditional cultures, drug use was not intended to provide some temporary kind of escape, but rather to validate culturally prescribed behavior, social values, and worldview (Ripinsky-Naxon 1993, 131). Because of the religious connotations, access to hallucinogens was usually restricted (Dobkin de Rios and Smith 1977). We know, for example, that, throughout prehistory, tobacco was rarely viewed as a secular plant (Dobkin de Rios 1996, 38); its use was, in most cases, strictly ritualistic (Wilbert 1972, 55).

Kehoe states that no psychedelic plant other than tobacco was used in North America and that "tobacco smoked there in ceremonies is stronger that commercial cigarette tobaccos and can have a stimulant effect, but it is primarily incense, its smoke enveloping participants in the ritual and rising to the Above" (Kehoe 2000, 65). To the contrary, North American Natives used other hallucinogenic substances, including *Datura* and peyote. And to suggest that tobacco smoke was "primarily incense" is akin to saying that Native Americans were unaware of its psychoactive properties and therefore did not inhale. Whatever the circumstances, the focus of shamanistic practice is clearly not on the mere experience of ecstasy, but rather on the goals to be derived from it.

Once we understand that traditional cultures perceive hallucinogens as sacred substances that facilitate entry into valuable altered states where visions essential for the continued existence of a society can be acquired, then the role of the shaman becomes quite obvious. As specialists responsible for managing all social, physical and biotic environments, they alone have the facility for entering into trance, and their effectiveness is measured by this ability (Grim 1983, 50).

There are other factors that specifically link shamans with altered states of consciousness. While all people apparently have a natural potential for the trance experience, it seems that some may have a greater biological and/or psychological predisposition toward achieving it (Bean and Vane 1992, 14). A person's mental state, the makeup of his or her personality, the physical setting, or cultural factors may act as determinants (Ripinsky-Naxon 1993, 86). Differences in a person's ability to experience or manipulate mental imagery can be an important element; studies show that in many traditional societies, individuals who have spontaneous visions or experience enhanced visual imagery are much more likely to be singled out as candidates for shamanic training (Eliade 1964, 84; Harner 1972, 224; Noll 1985). Robert Lowie, noting individual differences among the Crow Indians that allowed some to see visions more readily than others, wrote that "we must assume that some people experience visions because of temperamental disposition, which their envious copyists lack" (Lowie 1925, 12).

Apparently, the achievement of an altered state, whether drug-induced or otherwise, can be learned, and a shaman may be able to control the experience, adjusting the various levels of trance to suit some particular circumstance (Bean and Vane 1992, 14). Dobkin de Rios (1996, x) believes that traditional societies intentionally chose to introduce cultural values by managing these drug-induced altered states of consciousness, and the pivotal figure was the shaman. During a long apprenticeship, the shaman-neophyte received insights into all things vital to his people, including knowledge of all flora and fauna, traditions and origin myths, genealogies and appropriate rituals—not to mention the acquisition and perfection of skills with hallucinogens that were thought to be intrinsic channels of communication with the supernatural.

Prior to Western contact, the idea of a "calling" (or "vocation") was generally acknowledged for a shaman or priest. In those drug-using societies for which we have sufficient data, the shaman is usually seen as a special individual whose nervous system and mental aptitude permit him to deal more competently with those areas of activity generated by hallucinogenic plant use (Dobkin de Rios 1996, 133). The psychological and neurophysiological elements that enter into play in determining the future shaman are often manifest as a so-called shamanic illness. The occurrence of mental crises associated with the shamanic calling is a transcultural phenomenon witnessed wherever shamanism is practiced. These crises may exhibit the outward appearance of a mental imbalance or a nervous breakdown, and the characteristics are frequently described in psychopathological terms (Kalweit 1984, xiv).

Shamanic States and Psychopathology

Scientists recognize that the occurrence of phosphene images and other manifestations of altered states of consciousness are often associated with certain brain disorders. This is especially true for those maladies that affect the central nervous system, such as mental anxiety, depression, migraine headaches, or schizophrenia. Some type of chemical imbalance or deficiency in chemical transmission is often implicated and, of all the chemical neurotransmitters that may be responsible, serotonin is the one most frequently mentioned (Borne 1994). Insufficient levels of serotonin in specific regions of the brain can bring about catatonic and depressive states, while excessive levels cause hallucinations and excitability (Barron, Jarvik, and Bunnell 1965). Thus, we should not be surprised when we learn that high concentrations of serotonin are often present in the brains of schizophrenics (Ripinsky-Naxon 1993, 144). Little wonder, then, that many members of the scientific community still equate drug intoxication with psychotic states found in mental illnesses such as schizophrenia (Holland 1997).

Those who recognize the significant role of hallucinogens in the history and process of shamanism reject this idea in favor of more objective assessments. They make a basic distinction between the schizophrenic or psychopathological personality and that of a true shaman. The schizophrenic personality sees the environment as disparate and fragmented, without structural unity; his or her world is disintegrated and idiosyncratic. The world of the shaman, on the other hand, is quite the opposite; it is characterized by an intrinsic unity, with all the elements integrated into a cohesive structure. The shamanic state of consciousness is not a condition limited exclusively to the idiosyncratic experience of a single person; instead, the structural elements manifest recurrent themes across transcendental borders (Ripinsky-Naxon 1993, 104).

Shamanism is not, in itself, a pathological indication. Rather, we should consider it as a normal state for exceptional individuals within their own respective cultural frameworks. In the real world, mental disorders are defined by each culture's notion of what constitutes mentally deviant or extraordinary behavior. The role of an indigenous society in creating and recognizing its shamans is expressed through cultural dynamics that affect the designation (rather than the definition) of what constitutes a mental or physical anomaly. A shaman exhibits symptoms of a mental disorder precisely because he works in borderline territory, replete with all kinds of hazards emanating from the worlds that make up his reality (Ripinsky-Naxon 1993, 102–3).

Western cultures are simply not in a position to pass value judgments on phenomena that have proven to be functionally adaptive within their respective cultural contexts, particularly when they are neither completely understood nor adequately experienced in the West. This is especially true for those who reject any shamanistic interpretation of the material record. Paul Bahn, as an example, addressing the issue of altered states and entoptic phenomena, argues (correctly) that it does not require a shamanic trance to see entoptics (Bahn 1998, 240). He also believes that "for a profoundly creative mind, drugs are unnecessary to have a hyper-reality experience. Trance is merely a biological ability at which some people excel—a state of focused awareness, when one feels defocused from the outside world and often experiences a sense of falling, flying or whirling" (241). Again, Bahn is technically correct. But he is seriously mistaken, in my view, when he maintains that, "even if one accepts fully the possibility that the creators (of rock art) may have been influenced by hallucinations, that does not prove that they were medicine men—unless one calls everyone who experiences an altered state of consciousness a shaman, in which case we are all shamans, and the word loses all meaning, becoming synonymous with human being" (245).

Bahn quite obviously does not understand what shamanism is all about; nor does he seem to comprehend the pervasive and multidimensional social role played by the shaman in prehistoric societies. Most of us accept the idea that all human beings have the potential to shift, voluntarily or involuntarily, between different states of consciousness. Most also realize that this capability is a fundamental feature of the human nervous system. But to infer, as Bahn does, that the shaman in a drug-induced trance is no different than any other member of his community is misguided. This way of thinking belies an extremely ethnocentric Western viewpoint—one that demonstrates a complete lack of knowledge concerning the worldview of prehistoric hunter-gatherers.

In a similar vein, Alice Kehoe labels anyone who uses terms like "primitive" as a racist. Those who "perpetuate the classic myth that out beyond civilization roam noble savages preserving a primordial religion more pure and true than any in the West" are accused of "dehumanizing non-Western cultures" (Kehoe 2000, 2). In her opinion, using one simple word (shaman) for all non-Western religious practitioners "brings us back to that millennia-old division between civilized Us and primitive, far-away Others" (45). She is convinced that those who maintain that rock art is an attempt by shamans in trance to depict beliefs in spirit animals—religious beliefs that contrast with our Western religions—are promoting cultural primitivism (72). In an egregious affront, Kehoe accuses Clottes and Lewis-Williams of "armchair racism." She cleverly twists a passage from their book, *The Shamans of Prehistory* (1998, 63), to make it appear that they condone the nineteenth-century notion that the ancients were "less evolved" than "civilized" people (94). Kehoe's accusation is unwarranted. Clottes and Lewis-Williams were simply tracing the development of interpretive hypotheses for the creation of Paleolithic rock art, pointing out that these theories are influenced by the major trends of thought at any given time (Clottes and Lewis-Williams 1998, 64).

Cognitive scholars recognize the need to consciously identify and relinquish their own ethnocentric views in their efforts to interpret the past as objectively as possible. With this perspective they have made remarkable progress in elucidating the shamanic world. By integrating neuroscientific data, ethnographic accounts, and current anthropological studies, these researchers have lifted the veil that shrouds the phenomenon of shamanism—not completely, but certainly enough to give us a firmer empirical footing and to encourage additional investigation. This enlightened understanding of shamanism also offers a unique opportunity for examining the material remains of ancient cultures from a very different perspective.

Those who choose to pursue this approach must begin by realizing that, for the ancients, the sacred is very different from the routine or mundane, that the supernatural brings humans into contact with an order of reality that is different from their ordinary world. For traditional non-Western societies the sacred is not an epiphenomenon nor a secondary expression of reality. It is, instead, the deepest aspect of reality, one that can be attained only through direct human experience. Recognizing that this direct human experience refers specifically to the activities of the shaman and, assuming that the shaman must have related his experience in some material way, it seems reasonable to argue that evidence of these activities must be present in the archaeological record. If we examine the material remains from this perspective, the evidence for shamanism is, as the next chapter demonstrates, quite extensive.

The Archaeological Evidence for Shamanism   10

THE SHAMANIC EXPERIENCE reflects a psychological metaphor of incredible proportions—life, death, rebirth, and transformation. It provides the well-trained shaman with a heightened capacity for understanding the world and all its problems. The experience is so remarkable, so dramatic, that in order to convey its meaning to the community shamans have had to improvise new and highly innovative techniques of communication—methods that have given birth to and encouraged various art forms. Only these can carry ineffable messages; thus, the laymen of a society can hear and see realities in a way that enforces social cohesion, promotes the mental health of the community at large, and reinforces the symbolic representation of their world (Bean and Vane 1992, 13–14).

Cognitive scholars hold that such messages are reflected archaeologically. They believe that the shamanic experience, and therefore the worldview of the people served by the shaman, is preserved in the material record—not only in rock art, but in ceramics, textiles, tools, and other types of artifacts. Viewing the phenomenon of shamanism in a much wider archaeological context, including recently acquired knowledge concerning the chemical and neurological events that influence the trance experience, allows us to more clearly delineate the temporal and spatial dimensions of shamanism.

The Antiquity and Universality of Shamanism

Some researchers view the traces of ancient pollen in the so-called flower burial at Shanidar Cave as an early indication of symbolic behavior. Others, particularly those who refuse to acknowledge evidence for any form of ritual behavior in Middle Paleolithic times, reject this idea. Robert Gargett, for example, argues that the wind was responsible for the deposition of the flowers at Shanidar (Gargett 1989,

176). Turner and Hannon (1988) believe that the pollen grains percolated through the soil sediments or were deposited by burrowing animals. Researchers who were directly involved with the excavations have, however, brushed aside these arguments. Ralph Solecki, the principle investigator, said, "It would have taken a hurricane wind to blow bouquets of flowers . . . and very accurately pinpoint the site of Shanidar IV" (Solecki 1989, 324). Arlette Leroi-Gourhan, the scientist who did the palynological work on the floral remains, concluded that at least seven species of complete flowers had been introduced into the cave—all at the same time. The samples were found more than fifteen meters from the cave entrance, and Leroi-Gourhan is convinced that neither birds nor rodents nor the presence of mammalian coprolites can account for the unique assemblage of flowers (Leroi-Gourhan 1975, 1989).

Shanidar Cave (as well as other Middle Paleolithic burial sites) provides other intriguing clues about the behavior of its inhabitants. Evidence of injury or disease in some form or another is present in almost all reasonably complete adult Neanderthals (Trinkaus 1986). The remains at Shanidar represent the largest sample of Neanderthals found in the Middle East: nine individuals ranging in age from very young infants to relatively old men. Trinkaus's study of this sample revealed a whole catalogue of injuries and degenerative disease in the heads, arms, ribs, legs, and feet (Trinkaus 1983). The male called Shanidar I, for example, apparently suffered head injuries and extensive crushing of the right side of his body; there is also evidence of infection and partial paralysis. He was probably blinded in his left eye and would have been considerably disabled; yet he must have lived with these injuries for several years. The evidence suggests that these people *did* care for older, infirm individuals (Stringer and Gamble 1993).

While it is certainly not conclusive, the evidence for intentional burial and a concern for the sick and disabled does allow us to make some cautious inferences about the presence of a ritual specialist or curer, someone who possessed the capability and had the responsibility for treating the injured and the infirm, and a person who could also preside at the death of a member of the community and assure the well-being of the soul during its journey through the afterlife. If we keep in mind that other mammals, especially chimpanzees, are aware of the healing qualities of some plants (Calvin 1992, 194; Wrangham and Goodall 1989) and that the medicinal properties of the plants found at Shanidar are still actively recognized throughout Southwest Asia (Ripinsky-Naxon 1993, 206), we can certainly infer this knowledge must have been available to Neanderthals as well as other species of the genus *Homo.* Furthermore, we know that baboons, chimpanzees, monkeys, cats, dogs, and other animals experience hallucinations (Siegel and Jarvik 1975, 81–104). This suggests that the capacity for trance states and the ability to hallucinate are a function of the mammalian (not just the human) nervous system. Can we deny then, that Neanderthals, along with their modern human counterparts, had access to the same hallucinogenic plants as well as the same capability for entering into altered states of consciousness?

Less contentious is the idea that Neanderthals and their contemporaries were hunters and gatherers. Most Middle Paleolithic sites, whether inhabited by modern humans or Neanderthals, show evidence of generalized hunter/gatherer adaptations (Hayden 1993, 139). This is a critical point because researchers have established an explicit connection between shamanism and hunting and gathering cultures. Winkelman (1989), for example, using a cross-cultural study of a large sample of societies from around the world, discovered a definite correlation between shamanistic practices and nonsedentary cultures that employ some combination of hunting, foraging, or fishing as their principal subsistence strategy. Evidence like this, combined with historical accounts and ethnographic data that reach back for hundreds of years, has led Eliade (1964) and others (e.g., Clottes and Lewis-Williams 1998; Furst 1982; Grim 1983; Krupp 1997; Ripinsky-Naxon 1993) to conclude that shamanism, in one form or another, has flourished in all hunter-gatherer societies, contemporary and ancient alike, for many millennia and on all the inhabited continents. If we accept the fact that shamanism is a worldwide phenomenon, practiced by hunter-gatherer societies for thousands of years, then it is reasonable to infer that shamanic practices must, in some way, be reflected in the material record. The only question is, where exactly should we look? Rock art, having been the focus of recent shamanic interpretations in both the Old and New Worlds, is an obvious place to begin.

Shamanism and Rock Art

Until recently, North American archaeologists usually considered rock art to be a minor aspect of the material record and one that did not lend itself to the type of analysis applied to more conventional cultural remains such as architecture, ceramics, or lithics. Seldom was it viewed as an activity in itself, or recognized as evidence of primitive belief in important supernatural forces. Throughout the history of rock art research, few have attempted to develop a broad interpretive framework for the study of rock art. This is no longer the case. Many researchers (Blackburn 1977; Boyd 1998; Clottes and Lewis-Williams 1998; Hedges 1983, 1992; Krupp 1997; Lewis-Williams 1980, 1981, 1983a, 1983b; Lewis-Williams and Dowson 1988; Noll 1985; Ripinsky-Naxon 1993; Ritter and Ritter 1977; Shafer 1986; Whitley 1992a, 1992b, 1994a, 1994b, 1996, 1998a, 1998b, 1998c, 1998d, 2000) now agree that much of the rock art created by hunting and gathering societies is associated in some way with shamanistic activity, including representations of phenomena experienced by shamans in their quest for the spirit world.

The following analysis of rock art as a reflection of shamanic experiences deals primarily with the rock art in western North America and especially that of the Coso Range in east-central California. However, since the effects of altered states of consciousness are broadly similar, regardless of the means used to enter into trance, the themes expressed in the motifs comprise a kind of shamanistic symbolic repertoire that is found in much of the art around the world. But before discussing the actual images, I will briefly consider the "canvas"—the caves and rock walls where the art appears.

Caves and Rock Surfaces

Caves (and rocks more generally) were viewed as entrances or portals to the supernatural world. The rock face had its own special significance, for the shaman considered it was a veil suspended between this world and the spiritual realm (Lewis-Williams and Dowson 1990). Rocks were also thought to be numinous, that is, inhabited (and also protected) by supernatural beings (Blackburn 1975, 116–17; Kroeber 1925, 514; Zigmond 1977, 70, 71, 127, 175–79). When the shaman was in an altered state, cracks in the rock surface opened, allowing entry to the sacred realm. Rock surfaces, then, were not simply convenient places for painting or engraving or some sort of neutral "blackboard" where artists could place any images they wished. What lay behind the rock surface gave spiritual significance to, and in some ways governed, whatever was placed on it. Power was acquired from the rock by association—putting a hand on it, carrying a small fragment, or pecking or painting on it. Rock art on the surface of the rock added to its power.

Handprints are found in rock art from the Paleolithic caves of Europe to the rockshelters of Patagonia in southern Argentina. These images were created not to make pictures of hands, but rather to establish a bond between the person, the rock veil, and the supernatural world that seethed beneath it. "Negative" images were stencils made by placing a hand on the rock face and then spraying paint, possibly out of the mouth, over and around the hand. When the hand was removed, a negative outline remained (figure 1). Clottes and Lewis-Williams (1998, 95) believe that it was the act of covering the hand and the immediately adjacent surface that was important. The shaman was, in effect, sealing his hands into the walls, causing them to disappear; those moments when the hands were "invisible" were what mattered most. The hands thus reached into the supernatural realm behind the membrane of the rock. In the case of positive hands (figure 2), whether painted or engraved, the meaning was the same; the shaman established a relationship between himself and the hidden world of the spirits.

Figure 1 "Negative" handprints at Canyon de Chelly in northern Arizona. Photo © Fred Hirschmann

Figure 2   Engraved handprints at Comanche Springs, New Mexico.

Footprints or tracks are also common in the rock art of the Far West (as well as at hunter-gatherer sites worldwide) but are interpreted differently. Supernatural be-ings reside on cliff faces and at permanent water sources such as springs, lakes, and ponds—points on the landscape where supernatural power was considered to be clos-est to the surface of the mundane world (Whitley 1998b, 145). Creatures inhabiting these places are often referred to as giants or small humanoid beings, like the dwarves and "water babies" that are found in myth and legend throughout the world. This can probably be explained, at least in part, by the physiological phenomena known as *macropsia* and *micropsia* (seeing things larger or smaller) that often occur during drug-induced altered states (Dobkin de Rios 1996, 132). Barber (1970) believes that this universal reporting of small or large images in the wake of drug use may result from physiological changes that alter pupil activity in complex ways.

In the Great Basin, the creation of rock art was often attributed to these spirit beings, which were sometimes described as having infantile human features (Whitley 1996, 78). In this part of the world, small human footprints (figure 3) were often associated with "water babies"—diminutive humanlike spirits who lived in

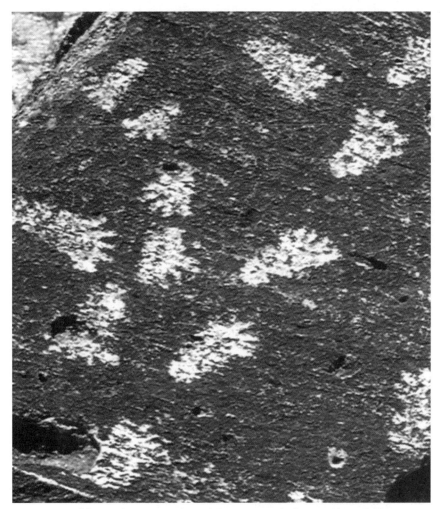

Figure 3   Small human footprints at the Red Canyon petroglyph site, Bishop, California.

rocks, springs, and pools and served as particularly powerful spirit helpers (Driver 1937, 86; Kelly 1932, 137; Park 1938, 15; Voegelin 1938, 61; Zigmond 1977, 710). Thus, the sight of the water baby's tracks was thought to represent a supernatural experience. Cognitive researchers hold that specific elements of these supernatural encounters, including phenomena experienced by shamans during altered states of consciousness, are also reflected in the rock art.

Rock Art and the Stages of Trance

We know that, during the first stage of trance, subjects experience entoptic phenomena, most often in the form of flecks, meandering lines, zigzags, nested curves, grids, checkerboards, dots, and spirals. Oster (1970, 83, 87) was one of the first to notice that these patterns closely resemble design elements in various kinds of aboriginal art, and examples of basic entoptics are common in the rock art of the Far West (figure 4). At least 25 percent of the petroglyphs found in the Coso Range, for example, are geometric motifs (Grant, Baird, and Pringle 1968). Some individual sites have more; at Little Lake, on the western edge of the Coso Range, over 75 percent of the rock art consists of geometric images (Whitley 1998b, 127).

Kroeber (1925, 938) observed that the polychrome painted styles of the Chumash and Yokuts coincided with areas of intensive use of *toalache* (*Datura*) in shamanistic rituals. Other researchers (Blackburn 1977; Lee 1979; Wellmann 1978) have elaborated on this theme, and the rock art of these cultures provides prime examples of parallels between aboriginal art and known characteristics of hallucinatory images. Chumash rock art is especially rich in phosphene imagery; in some cases the designs are outlined with white dots that duplicate one attribute of *Datura* visions (figure 5). Chumash and Yokuts rock art represent only two of the many styles where the art meets all of the basic requirements to be described as visionary imagery (Hedges 1992, 81).

As individuals progress through the second stage of trance, they begin to construe these entoptic forms into meaningful representational images based on cultural beliefs and expectations (Reichel-Dolmatoff 1972). Little wonder, then, that a shaman traveling to the Coso Range to acquire or increase rainmaking power would interpret geometric patterns, such as meandering lines or nested curves, as the body or horns of a bighorn sheep, the supernatural helper of the rain shaman (figure 6). The body is often portrayed as a more complex form of an entoptic boat shape to which head, legs, and tail have been added. Placing an animal's legs on the arc of the navicular body suggests that the flickering margin of the entoptic arc may have been construed as the flashing legs of the running animal (Lewis-Williams and Dowson 1988, 210).

Figure 4   Entoptic motifs at the Chidago site, Bishop, California.

Similarly, shimmering zigzags may be construed as a writhing or moving snake (Clottes and Lewis-Williams 1998, 16). We know that after bighorn sheep, the most common identifiable animal figures in the Coso Range are rattlesnakes (Whitley 1998b, 124). Most depictions of rattlesnakes conform to graphic conventions used throughout western North America: zigzags and diamond chains (figure 7). In typical Native American fashion, the zigzag or diamond chain was

Figure 5   Entoptics seen in first stage of trance. Painted Cave, Santa Barbara, California.

connected with the appearance and behavior of the species they were intended to portray. Zigzags mimicked the pattern made in the sand by the sidewinder rattlesnake; a diamond chain depicted the scale pattern of the diamondback rattler or a related species (Whitley 1998b, 124). Snakes were the supernatural helpers of rattlesnake shamans (Whitley 2000) and were also believed to protect rock art sites; along with grizzly bears and mountain lions, they acted as guardians of the entrances to the supernatural realm.

Spirals and concentric circles are found at rock art sites around the world and may appear alone or blended with iconic figures (figure 8). Klüver provides us with a link to an altered states experience when he refers to a subject who reported

Figure 6   Bighorn sheep engravings, Big Petroglyph Canyon, Coso Range, California.

"one of my legs assumed spiral form" (Klüver 1966, 24). These geometric images are especially common in the Great Basin where they represent the whirlwind and may also symbolize the shaman's ability to concentrate supernatural power (Whitley 1996, 1998c, 2000). This motif can also signify a path or passageway to the spiritual world (Ripinsky-Naxon 1993, 112) and is associated with the final trance stage.

The third stage of trance is reached via a rotating tunnel or a vortex (Horowitz 1975, 178). On the sides of the vortex is a lattice of concentric squares derived

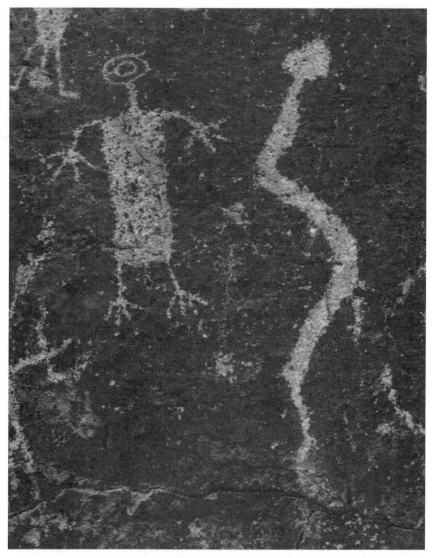

Figure 7   Zigzag line depicting a snake. Coso Range, California.

from the geometric imagery of the first stage, and in the compartments of this lattice are the first true hallucinations of people and animals (Clottes and Lewis-Williams 1998, 17). During peak hallucinatory periods, subjects begin to feel dissociated from their bodies and often become part of their own imagery (Siegel 1977, 136; Siegel and Jarvik 1975, 128). A major aspect of drug-induced alteration of visual perceptions is that images frequently remain present, even as new

Figure 8   Spirals, animals, and human figures. Canyon del Muerto, northern Arizona.

ones are superimposed (Dobkin de Rios 1996, 132). Thus, representational forms (like bighorn sheep or human figures) may be seen alone or projected against entoptic patterns (figure 9).

Klüver provides an example of the blending of anthropomorphic forms with geometric motifs. While in a hallucinogen-induced altered state, one of his laboratory subjects reported that "he saw fretwork before his eyes, that his arms, hands, and fingers turned into fretwork and that he became identical with fretwork. There was no difference between the fretwork and himself" (Klüver 1966, 71–72). Images of patterned body anthropomorphs are found at rock art sites throughout western North America and the designs often consist of entoptic forms. On one rock face in the Upper Renegade Canyon in the Coso Range, for example, there is an anthropomorph with a dot pattern on the torso (figure 10). The dot motif suggests that the shaman identified himself with an entoptic form seen in the first stage of trance. There are many anthropomorphs in the Coso Range with complex body patterns comprising familiar form constants: wavy and zigzag lines, dots, grids, lozenges, and so forth (figure 11). Each design is unique, and Whitley (1998b, 157) interprets them as the individual shaman's "patterns of power," that result from, and are influenced by, entoptic images seen in trance states. Somatic hallucinations portrayed in the rock art may also include the sensation of an elongated body (figure 12), enlarged extremities, and extra digits or limbs (figure 13).

A frequently reported experience during stage three is transformation not into some geometric form but into an animal (Clottes and Lewis-Williams 1998, 17). A particularly vivid example comes from a Western subject in a trance state who reported, "I thought of a fox, and instantly I was transformed into that animal. I could distinctly feel myself a fox, could see my long ears and bushy tail . . . my complete anatomy was that of a fox. My eyes seemed to be located in the back of my mouth. I looked out between parted lips, saw two rows of teeth" (Siegel and Jarvik 1975, 105). Lewis-Williams (1986) describes the

Figure 9   Bighorn sheep emerging from entoptic forms. Inscription Canyon, Barstow, California.

Figure 10   Anthropomorph with dot pattern torso. Upper Renegade Canyon, Coso Range.

Figure 11   Patterned body anthropomorphs at Little Petroglyph Canyon, Coso Range.

Figure 12   Anthropomorph with elongated body. Little Petroglyph Canyon, Coso Range.

Figure 13   Anthropomorph with enlarged feet and extra digits. Little Petroglyph Canyon, Coso Range.

hallucinatory elements of southern San rock art compositions that combine phosphenes with images of men and animals when shamans turned into antelopes rather than foxes (figure 14).

In the Far West there are dramatic examples of the blending of human and animal forms. Patterned body humans, for example, are occasionally shown with bird claw feet (figure 11); stick figure humans may have torsos or legs that appear to transform into the zigzags of the rattlesnake, sometimes depicted as emerging from

Figure 14   Human figure with antelope head and shoulders. Drakensberg Mountains, South Africa.

cracks in rocks (figure 15); mountain sheep may have flat, plantigrade humanlike feet instead of hooves; and humans sometimes have exaggerated limbs or elongated bodies and heads (figure 13). These combinations of geometric entoptic forms with hallucinatory figures simply demonstrate a continuum that has been observed in both medical and ethnographic contexts. Cognitive archaeologists interpret them as metaphors for the supernatural experience.

Shamanic Themes in Rock Art

As discussed earlier, the first and perhaps most common metaphor for a shaman's entry into the supernatural was death or killing. The acquisition of an altered state was in some sense thought to be a kind of autosacrifice: a shaman "killed himself" in order to enter the supernatural world. Similarly, when he stole another person's soul and took it to the spirit realm, this too was described as "killing." As metaphors for entry into the supernatural, death and killing are depicted in the rock art in a variety of ways. Most typical are the so-called hunting scenes with a human shooting an animal (figure 16) or the rendering of a bighorn sheep impaled by a spear or arrow. We know from the ethnography that, in the Coso

Figure 15   Rattlesnake shaman emerging from crack in rock. McCoy Springs, Blythe, California.

Range, the bighorn sheep was the supernatural helper of the rain shaman. And because a shaman in an altered state was himself a bighorn spirit helper (note that the stick figures in the hunting scenes have horned heads), whenever he "killed" himself in order to make rain fall, he also killed his spirit helper and alter ego, the bighorn sheep (Whitley 1998b, 155). Depictions of hunting scenes and killed sheep, then, have nothing to do with the hunting of food animals in the mundane

Figure 16   Humans "killing" bighorn sheep. Sheep Canyon, Coso Range, California.

world. They are, instead, graphic metaphors expressing the same concepts and beliefs as the verbal metaphors found in the ethnography.

A universal feature of shamanism is the "magical flight" (Eliade 1964) or "shamanic journey" (Harner 1981) of the shaman's soul that takes place while in trance. During an altered state of consciousness the shaman "can safely abandon his body and roam at vast distances, can penetrate the underworld and rise to the sky" (Eliade 1964, 182). Knowing that the harmine alkaloids in many psychoactive plants produce changes in visual acuity, a sense of weightlessness, and disassociated mental states that contribute to an out-of-body experience, it is not surprising that mystical flight is a commonly used metaphor for an altered state of consciousness.

These allusions to the flight metaphor and the shaman's ability to fly are depicted in the rock art in a variety of ways. The use of avian imagery, such as birds, combinations of birds and humans, and bird costumery was rather common (see figures 2 and 8). In the Great Basin the mountain quail had a strong supernatural connotation among Numic speakers. The Master of the Game, one of the primary spirit beings visited by the shaman, was often clothed in a quail feather cape. The quail was also said to play the flute that opened the door to the supernatural realm (Whitley 1994c, 26–27). A quail topknot feather headdress was thought to be the exclusive ritual headgear of the rain shaman (Kelly 1932, 202), and the patterned body anthropomorph in figure 11 is wearing just such a headdress (note also the birdclaw-like feet). As noted previously, many patterned body figures are portrayed with concentric circles or spirals for heads. Since concentric circles and spirals are graphic conventions for the whirlwind—a motif synonymous with a shaman's flying power—these images are another allusion to magical flight.

The later stages of trance also have significant sexual overtones. Writing about Desana shamanic initiation, Reichel-Dolmatoff (1979a, 42) says that "[t]he entire transformative sequence is . . . comparable to a succession of neurological sensations perceived during an advanced state of drug-induced trance, and many of these states and conditions have a strong sexual resonance." Desana shamans perceive, during the preparation of the narcotic *yagé*, explicit allusions to the sexual act, not in the sense of ordinary mechanical eroticism but instead linked to the process of creation. The container in which the plant is processed is analogous to the vagina and uterus; the stirring rod signifies the penis.

In western North America (as in other parts of the world) sexual potency was equated with supernatural power. Shamans were considered unusually virile; in some cases, they were thought to be so sexually predatory that young girls were kept away from them (Whitley 2000). Moreover, certain hallucinogens, such as jimson weed, are aphrodisiacs that can cause sexual arousal (La Barre 1980, 63). Intercourse was a specific metaphor for the shaman's entry into the supernatural world, and rock art reflected a strong sexual symbolism. Although human stick figures are sometimes depicted as phallic or priapic, actual intercourse is rarely portrayed in the art. Instead, this metaphor is often expressed by vulva-shaped motifs, indicating the rock art site itself symbolizes the vagina. The shaman's entry through a portal to the spiritual realm was thus a kind of ritual intercourse with his rock art site, a metaphorical vagina (Whitley 1996, 24–25).

Before we move away from rock art, it would be well to note that the oldest documented use of hallucinogens is found in the art of the central Sahara, especially southern Algeria. Here we find compelling archaeological evidence of a de-

veloped ethnomycological ritual complex that came into existence sometime before the African Later Stone Age, around 9,000 to 6,000 years ago (Ripinsky-
Naxon 1993, 153). The rock art depicts mushroom-men, with heads resembling
fungi. Each person has a mushroom in his hand, and interrupted lines suggest a
connection, a route, between the head of the man and the mushroom being held.
While it is difficult to identify specific categories of mycoflora (the mushroom
family of plants) shown in the rock drawings, Giorgio Samorini (1992) noted the
striking similarities between the images depicted in the art and two of the most
widespread hallucinogens: the *Psilocybe* species and a variety of *Amanita spp.*

This kind of evidence tends to reinforce Reichel-Dolmatoff's (1972, 104)
view that "[e]verything we would designate as *art* is inspired and based upon the
hallucinatory experience." This observation is supported by detailed studies conducted among the Tukano Indians of the Amazon, where design elements in ritual art with hallucinatory origins show a close correlation with basic phosphene
patterns (Reichel-Dolmatoff 1978, 15–34). For the Tukanoan shaman, the designs are a storeroom that supplies the basis for nearly all their art motifs. They
depict these entoptic precepts on their house walls, ceramics, bark cloth, basket-
work, and rattles. Because the Tukanoan art has a biochemical and neurological basis, we can look for similar foundations in the universality of certain basic patterns
and motifs as expressions of common biochemical and neurophysiological
processes (Ripinsky-Naxon 1993, 149).

Other Archaeological Evidence for Shamanism

What Westerners are inclined to call art and enjoy as an aesthetic expression is, for
the Native Americans, a more sober means of communication, one in which each
color, each sound, each combination and sequence expresses a deeply held truth
that needs to be propagated and perpetuated (Reichel-Dolmatoff 1987, 14). If
we accept the notion that images perceived during altered states exert a profound
influence on iconography, we should expect to find evidence of this not only in
rock art but in other aspects of the material record as well. The following sections
will consider some of these other archaeological manifestations of shamanism.

Stone and Ceramics

Archaeologists have found frescoes in central Mexico dating to around 1700 B.P.
The designs in these paintings place mushroom worship in this part of the New
World back at least to that period (Schultes 1972, 7). Far more ancient are the remarkable artifacts known as "mushroom stones." Stefan de Borhegyi (1961,
1965) has written extensively concerning the corpus of over a hundred mushroom
stones and ceramics found in Mesoamerica and has documented the presence of

this motif in both stone and pottery throughout the Guatemalan highlands and in other parts of the central region.

De Borhegyi believes the association of mushrooms with their gods and the Underworld induced the Maya to produce diverse and numerous effigies of this plant. As an example, nine tiny stone mushroom figurines discovered in a 2,200-year-old burial site in Kaminaljúyu near Guatemala City clearly suggest a correlation with the nine lords of *Xibalbá*, the rulers of the Maya Underworld (de Borhegyi 1961). A late-seventeenth-century manuscript, *Vocabulario de la lengua Cakchiquel*, provides a link between these stone mushroom figures and the ritual use of sacred hallucinogenic mushrooms. The author, Fray Tomás Coto, mentions a Cakchiquel-Maya name for a hallucinogenic mushroom, *xibalbalbaj okox*, which means "underworld mushroom" (Wasson 1957). To bolster the argument that mushroom stones and ceramics denote use of the psychotropic mushrooms themselves, de Borhegyi points to a connection between mushroom intoxication and the ritual use of aromatic pine resins. In many parts of the ancient world where similar hallucinogens are used, odiferous plants play a major role in heightening sensory responses during trance states (Dobkin de Rios 1996, 120). Interestingly, de Borhegyi notes that, when the mushroom motif disappears from the material record, so too does the three-pronged *incensario* container in which pine resins were burned.

We also have evidence for the use of hallucinogenic mushrooms and other psychoactive plants in art from the north coast of Peru. Moche ceramics depict human figures adorned with mushrooms of not only different species but also different genera. A stirrup-spout vessel in the Peabody Museum collection at Harvard University offers a fine example of this type of Moche iconography. The vessel is in the form of a human head. The headdress has delicate curvilinear waves that turn into bird-head motifs; a large naturalistic mushroom protrudes from the figure's forehead, and there is no doubt that it represents the hallucinogenic *Amanita muscaria* (Ripinsky-Naxon 1993, 179). Another stirrup-spout pot depicts a person kneeling on one leg; two large mushrooms surmount his headdress and his right hand holds another.

As noted earlier, a strong sexual tenor permeates all aspects of the trance state, and this too is reflected in ceramic iconography. The preparation of *ayahuasca* by Tukanoan shamans is filled with a wide array of sexual symbolisms; the process of mixing the psychotropic ingredients connotes intercourse between the *yagé* vessel, a metaphor for the female body, and the mixing rod, a metaphor for the male principle (Reichel-Dolmatoff 1979a, 53–54). Pottery making itself is modeled on the transitions of life (Ripinsky-Naxon 1993, 135). Metaphorically, the finished vessel represents a woman, decorated with motifs such as a Y-shaped ideogram to signify the clitoris (and probably the labias) as portals to the vaginal opening. Similarly, the Barasana Indians of the Pira-paraña river region decorate their hallucinogen-containing vessels with a U-shaped design, signifying a tunnel or vaginal passage that the participants in the shamanic trance must enter so that they may undergo the transformation of rebirth (Reichel-Dolmatoff 1987, 16).

Moche pottery is well known in art circles for its erotic themes, but the presence of sexual motifs in the ceramics may indicate more than merely a lusty interest in life: specifically, a link to shamanistic activity. Most experts who deal with Moche art and iconography (e.g., Benson 1972; Donnan 1976) believe that sexual representations found in this art are almost always of a magico-religious character. Researchers have described shamanistic activities from the north coast of Peru, where a certain herb turns a man into a "sexual beast" who cannot satisfy his sexual appetite or instincts—a theme that would correspond with many of the representations of enlarged male phalli found in the art of this region (Dobkin de Rios 1996, 109). Other images depict copulation with four-footed creatures as well as animal-animal copulation. These motifs relate to the issue of shamanic power since one function of the shaman is to ensure the reproduction and increase of animals that the community depends on for its subsistence (Dobkin de Rios 1996, 107). Elizabeth Benson (1972, 51) argues that death haunts almost all Moche art and iconography, and, as a result, sexual motifs may be associated with the common hallucinogen-linked theme of death and rebirth.

The use of plant hallucinogens to achieve contact with the supernatural realm in order to serve social goals is extremely important in traditional Moche culture (Dobkin de Rios 1996, 91–92), and this theme is clearly demonstrated in ceramic iconography. Moche stirrup-spout vessels dating back 1,500 years or more (Sharon 1972, 117) are molded in the shape of a hallucinogenic San Pedro cactus. Other ceramics depict what appear to be shamans holding stumps of cacti in their hands as well as transformation of shamans into animals in association with a thornless cactus.

In Mesoamerica, peyote is represented in tombs that are more than 2,000 years old. Based on calibrated radiocarbon dates, a culture called Colima flourished in western Mexico between 2200–1500 B.P. A Colima figurine vessel of a person holding a cactus in each hand (identifiable as the hallucinogen *Lophophora williamsii*) verifies the use of this plant, as does a Colima redware pot, decorated with four peyote cacti images in raised relief. The preponderance of the peyote motif in Colima art is a significant index of the ritual behavior of the inhabitants of the region (Ripinsky-Naxon 1993, 169).

Another important genus represented is *Datura*, a plant that plays a critical role in the religious life not only among the Indians of western Mexico but also in the American Southwest. Small pre-Columbian Colima sculptures portraying scenes of people and mushrooms allude to an ancient hallucinogenic ritual complex in West Mexico, comparable to the one we find in Oaxaca today (Ripinsky-Naxon

1993, 169). It is quite likely that Colima spheroid vessels in the shape of spiny seedpots represent the particularly dangerous hallucinogen *Datura meteloides*, much like their analogs that depict peyote and sacred mushrooms.

The Colima artifacts also include dog figurines wearing human masks. The ritual function of masks extends back for untold millennia; evidence from the Paleolithic caves of southwestern Europe indicates that such practices were in vogue for more than 30,000 years. The shamanistic custom of putting on animal and bird masks probably survives from ancient times when humans used a variety of devices to establish a bond with supernatural beings and create interchangeability between animal and human forms; the mask, then, became a metaphor for transference of the spirit or soul. While the exact meaning of the Colima iconography is unknown, we can speculate that a masked dog was meant to act as a guide or psychopomp, leading the soul of the deceased on the journey to the Underworld. We can also assume that the mask was intended to transform the dog into a human; perhaps what we see is a representation of the shaman's avatar or alter ego (Ripinsky-Naxon 1993, 43). In this context, it is interesting to note that, for the Jívaro Indians of South America, the encounter with the supernatural realm is so significant that they sometimes offer a special hallucinogenic admixture to their dogs so that these animals, too, may validate their souls by experiencing realities from another plane of existence (Harner 1972, 134).

Ethnographers have observed that, in many traditional societies, the use of rattles, drums, or other percussive instruments is part and parcel of ritual, creating conditions of "sonic driving" that may help to entrain brainwaves and thus act as a transporting technique. Musical sound seems to be a fundamental phenomenon in every shamanic culture, serving as a sacred ceremonial function rather than as ordinary entertainment (Ripinsky-Naxon 1993, 49). In addition to instrumentally created sounds, whistling is a practice commonly used by shamans to summon ancestral spirits; it is also employed in the retrieval of strayed souls (Ripinsky 1975, 45).

In a short article published in 1971, Fred Katz and Marlene Dobkin de Rios reported on this important acoustical component in Peruvian *ayahuasca* ceremonies. They noted that one of the most significant types of music performed by the shaman was whistling; it included the use of specific tones at various parts of the ritual. Dobkin de Rios linked an ancient Pythagorean belief concerning the effects of music on consciousness (where musical progressions are associated with certain states of mind) to the connection that some hallucinogen users make between musical tones and visual imagery, color perceptions in particular. The shaman whistled in order to assist his clients at transitional points during altered states; certain tonal progressions coincided precisely with those transitions. Dobkin de Rios speculated that this might influence the activation of *ayahuasca* alkaloids. The musical component of the *ayahuasca* ritual (the need to generate specific whistling tones) may provide an insight into some mysterious Peruvian ceramics—the so-called whistling bottles.

Whistling bottles were manufactured as early as 3,000 B.P. in Peru and appear to be a continuation of an established ceramic tradition that began a few centuries earlier in Ecuador (Donnan 1992, 23). Moche craftsmen were responsible for most of these vessels, but they were also made by Chimu and other cultures. Peruvian potters created single and double-chambered whistling bottles; both can be made to whistle by blowing directly into the spout, but the dual-chambered vessels can also produce whistling sounds through the manipulation of liquid from one chamber to the other. Although most archaeologists assume they were drinking vessels, there is evidence that suggests these curious artifacts may have been used for more than just imbibing beverages. Daniel Statnekov, an amateur collector, reported that when he blew into one of these bottles it generated a strange, high-pitched tone; he began to perceive himself as a kind of moving luminescence rushing through space until he confronted an inky black cloud that chilled him "like death" and he was forced to snap out of his vision. He had not used drugs prior to this experience, but it was remarkably similar to that reported by *ayahuasca* users (Statnekov 1987).

Statnekov set out to prove scientifically that the whistling bottles were not used primarily for drinking. He and acoustical physicist Steven Garrett tested about seventy of the vessels, from different cultures and time periods, by sending pressurized air through the bottles in an anechoic chamber. The sounds that were emitted passed through a spectrum analyzer that recorded the average frequencies for all the bottles. Based on a relatively small octave range, Statnekov and Garrett decided the bottles were not used as musical instruments. To the contrary, the clustering of frequencies in the range of the ear's greatest sensitivity, and the higher sound levels produced when the vessels were blown orally, suggested they were created for a special use—whistling (Garrett and Statnekov 1977). These findings lend credence to the idea that Peruvian shamans may have used these whistling bottles to generate specific tonal sequences that synergistically amplified the hallucinatory experience.

Hallucinogenic snuffs have been used in the Americas for the last three thousand years or more (Ripinsky-Naxon 1993, 178). A widespread pre-Hispanic snuffing complex has been identified in Mesoamerica where none had previously been reported. The evidence consists of a number of ceramic snuffing pipes, some more than two thousand years old, as well as clay figurines from Colima, in western Mexico, dating from about 2200–1900 B.P. Researchers are not certain what substances were used, but *Nicotiana rustica* (tobacco), as well as relatives of some South American sources of hallucinogenic snuff (*Anadenanthera peregrina*), are prime candidates

(Furst 1990, xxiii). The earliest clay pipes found in Mexico date to Olmec times, ca. 3200–2900 B.P. (Wilbert 1972, 80). The archaeological evidence from South America is in the form of snuffing paraphernalia found at the pre-ceramic site of Huaca Prieta in the Chicama Valley of Peru (Benson 1972, 58–59).

One of the active hallucinogenic compounds in *Anadenanthera peregrina* (a tree found in northern South America from which a powerful narcotic snuff is derived) is bufotenine, a drug that is also present in the skin of poisonous toads like *Bufo marinus*. Such toads have long played an important role in mythology and ritual art, not only in Mesoamerica (especially for the Maya) but also in other parts of Central and South America. Furst (in Schultes 1972, 28) speculates that while the large quantities of Bufo remains found in the Olmec ceremonial site of San Lorenzo, Veracruz, might have served as food, it is also possible that the Olmec used the poisonous toads as additives or "fortifiers" for fermented ritual beverages. This proposition leads to another form of evidence relating to the use of hallucinogenic plants and, by derivation, shamanism: the floral remains found in many archaeological sites.

Floral Remains

Some of the oldest archaeological evidence for early drug use in the New World involves the so-called mescal bean—a red seed from the shrub *Sophora secundiflora* indigenous to northern Mexico and Texas. There are at least a dozen caves and rockshelters in southwestern Texas where these *Sophora* beans have been recorded (Campbell 1958). Based on radiocarbon dates provided by the Smithsonian Institution, it seems that Paleo-Indian hunters were familiar with and used these red beans for more than ten thousand years (Adovasio and Fry 1976). Radiocarbon assays from the Bonfire Shelter site in Texas yielded dates of 10,440–10,120 B.P. for the earliest human occupation levels. Excavations at this site uncovered *Sophora* seeds, together with Folsom points and Plainview-type projectiles, as well as the remains of extinct Pleistocene bison (*Bison antiquus*). Studies conducted at the Fate Bell Shelter site in Trans-Pecos Texas revealed seeds of the narcotic *S. secundiflora* in all stratigraphic levels, representing a time span of 9000–1000 B.P. (Ripinsky-Naxon 1993, 168).

Although the presence of mescal beans in caves and rockshelters—even when found in containers holding nonutilitarian objects—does not necessarily prove they were used to induce altered states of consciousness, there is some additional archaeological evidence that does suggest the shamanistic use of these beans (Campbell 1958). *Sophora* seeds have been found at several sites that also contain shamanistic rock art. Harry Shafer (1986), for example, has noted that many of the Pecos River paintings include representations of shamanic flight, power animals, visionary imagery, and a host of other elements that are perfectly understandable in light of a shamanistic interpretation. Other varieties of hallucinogenic plants are also found at these sites. The oldest remains of peyote (*Lophophora williamsii*) from a prehistoric rockshelter near the Pecos River have been radiocarbon dated at ca. 7000 B.P. (Furst 1990, xiii). Carolyn Boyd (1998), using several lines of evidence, argues that the well-known "White Shaman" site on the Lower Pecos River is a pictographic representation of a peyote ceremony. Similar graphic representations are also found in other types of media, such as textiles.

Textiles

For the ancient people of South America's Andean region, textiles played a paramount role in society. Textiles were a portable medium that could convey vast quantities of information, including cultural identity, regional affiliation, social status, and, most significantly, worldview (Gundrum 2000, 46). In northern Peru the ritual and symbolic importance of the hallucinogenic San Pedro cactus (*Trichocereus pachanoi*) dates back at least three thousand years; it is often found in association with jaguars and spirit beings on textiles of the Chavín horizon. The rich heritage of textiles among the ancient Nazca fishermen of south coastal Peru allows us to reconstruct the role of San Pedro cactus and the *wilka* shrub in their culture (Dobkin de Rios 1996, 16).

According to Dobkin de Rios (1996, 63), the worldview, beliefs, and values of the Nazca are depicted in their iconography, which illustrates a complex world full of magico-religious ideas. They are expressed by means of a combination of simple and known elements, such as birds, men, plants, and fish, mixed with other symbolic images like trophy heads, plumes, and other appendages. One well-known entity that combines human and magical attributes is often referred to as the "mythological masked being" (Roark 1965) and the "occulate being" (Rowe 1961) or a personage directly related to the "flying god of Paracas" (Kaufmann 1976). Based on a personal examination of more than 750 artifacts at museums in Lima, Peru, Dobkin de Rios (1996, 63) believes that these various masked mythical beings, found on many embroidered textiles and in ceramic iconography, represent powerful shamanic leaders.

In an article about a two-thousand-year-old mantle from the Paracas Peninsula of Peru, Darrell Gundrum (2000, 48) discusses an anthropomorphic figure that combines the distinct images of a feline and a serpent. He identifies this figure as a shaman by the presence of ritual paraphernalia in his hands. The left hand holds a feathered fan believed to imbue magical powers of flight or enlightenment upon its holder; in the right hand there are several small darts representing the mystical projectiles shamans use to "shoot" into their enemies to inflict illness. The concept of shooting or injecting foreign objects into a person's body is a common shamanic theme, and one of the materials often mentioned in this context is quartz crystal.

Quartz Crystals

For the Cubeo Indians of the Northwest Amazon, one of the most crucial processes in the transitional passage from layman to shaman is the insertion of quartz crystals into the neophyte's stomach. Later, these crystals will be used as shamanic weapons (Goldman 1963, 264). Quartz crystals represent shamanistic, transformational power objects and spirit helpers, highly valued for their potency and considered as vitally essential among peoples throughout the world. In many cultures, ranging from the California Yuman Indians to the Australian aborigines, quartz crystal is considered "living" or a "live rock" (Ripinsky-Naxon 1993, 123–24). Eliade refers to these rock crystals as "solid light" associated with shamanic enlightenment. When Eliade notes that shamans "feel a relationship between the condition of a supernatural being and a superabundance of light" (1964, 138), he also engages, consciously or not, a relationship between the visionary experience and the production of phosphenes.

Among western Tukanoan shamans, quartz crystal is their most important power object, engulfed in rich lore. Crystals are passed down from father to son, and these valuable items are stored in special woven boxes (Reichel-Dolmatoff 1979b, 17–18). Tukanoan speakers from the northwestern region of the Amazon use rattles containing small particles of quartz crystals. When shaken against the interior walls of the gourd, the crystals become energized and ignite the gourd's soft inner lining, producing smoke and sometimes sparks that can be seen escaping through slits and holes in the rattle. These sparks become a metaphor for procreation *in utero* (Reichel-Dolmatoff 1979b, 33–34, 1987, 10). Wilbert (1972, 65; 1977, 92) has also observed this practice among the Warao Indians of Venezuela; they believe the shaman's rattle holds additional spirit helpers in the form of quartz crystals.

In far western North America, quartz and other crystals commonly served as shaman's talismans and were used as ritual objects in curing, rainmaking, and other ceremonies (Whitley 1998d). Some archaeological sites in California have yielded quartz crystals, along with other objects of material culture, that date to around 8,000 B.P. (Ripinsky-Naxon 1993, 91). At a rock art site known as Sally's Rockshelter, in the north-central Mojave Desert, Whitley discovered a series of quartz cobbles that had been deliberately placed in cracks in rocks around an engraved panel, along with a scatter of small broken pieces of quartz and quartz hammerstones (Whitley et al. 1999). Intrigued by the association of petroglyphs with the white quartz rocks at Sally's Rockshelter, Whitley and his colleagues began an investigation of this phenomenon at other sites. Foreign material analyses of thirty-five petroglyphs from three different rock art localities in the Mojave Desert demonstrated that the association between quartz and rock art was quite common—almost 65 percent contained remnants of quartz hammerstones used to peck the images. The analyses and chronometric dating suggest that this association was not only common but also very ancient; quartz or quartzite hammerstones appear to have been used for petroglyph manufacture for thousands of years in the Mojave Desert.

It seems appropriate to end this review of the archaeological evidence for shamanism with rock art; it was, after all, a closer examination of rock art that initiated this examination of the cognitive realm. The evidence discussed in this chapter is not, by any means, complete—it is simply a part of a much larger picture. These cumulative data—the archaeological evidence for manifestations of this phenomenon combined with our ever-increasing understanding of how the human mind works, the propensity for altered states of consciousness through time—now make it possible to draw some informed conclusions about the cognitive approach and the shamanic interpretation of prehistoric art.

Approaching the Final Frontier 11

> *No one sensible of the dynamics of history would wish to deny that there exists a level of causation at which the ideas of individuals make a difference to what happens. Therefore, the critical question is the extent to which that level of causation is accessible to prehistorians, who depend on archaeological evidence as their sources. The problem is that past ideas are represented as such through symbols, which are by definition arbitrary with respect to their referents. The more plausible interpretations of material culture meanings developed by post-processualists involve cases in which ethnographic or historical sources permit the symbols to be decoded. For prehistory, where no such bilinguals exist, how are the symbols in the archaeological text to be read?*

—ANTONIO GILMAN

DURING THE 1980s, when many American archaeologists were expressing their concerns about the basic assumptions of the New Archaeology, questions like this loomed large. Some archaeologists continued to defend the processualist way of thinking and castigated those who found fault with the existing paradigm. Earle and Preucel, for example, in an effort to appraise the validity of alternative approaches, wrote that, "[w]hile the work of the radicals is undeniably provocative, we remain unconvinced of their ability to penetrate the mind of a prehistoric individual. Particularly troubling to us are their apparent rejection of theory and disregard for a replicable and verifiable methodology" (Earle and Preucel 1987, 509).

The so-called radicals were not members of some fringe group bent on over-throwing all existing archaeological method and theory. They were, instead, ar-chaeologists who were simply expressing their disillusionment with the positivist paradigm as a means for explaining variation in the material record. While the processualists continued to admonish their adversaries for failing to put forward any viable theory or methodology for interpreting the past (Yoffee and Sherratt 1993, 8), a few scholars, particularly those who held stronger convictions about human agency and the importance of examining culture-specific ideology and be-liefs, had already started to develop an explicit approach that would afford access to the ancient mind.

Previous chapters considered the theoretical orientation of these cognitive scholars and examined some of the ways they employed their tools, particularly the use of ethnographic analogy and the neuropsychological model. While much of this was concerned with a shamanic interpretation of rock art, I also discussed the nonarchaeological evidence for shamanism that derives from recent neurosci-entific studies concerning altered states of consciousness and brain chemistry. I am now in a position to argue that these combined data provide substantive and compelling support for shamanism as an explanatory hypothesis, and one that can account for much of the symbolism expressed in the archaeological record. There are still, as one might imagine, a few naysayers who do not (and probably never will) accept any form of shamanistic interpretation or the methodology of a cog-nitive approach. Their main objections will be addressed in this final summary, but first I will critically examine some of the alternative explanations for the creation of prehistoric art.

Other Interpretations of the Art

In an earlier chapter I discussed the major themes that have been used over the years to explain the Upper Paleolithic art, such as totemism, art for art's sake, and structuralism. The majority of these theories have been effectively discredited (or at least found inadequate) and are seldom mentioned in today's literature. There is, however, one exception: hunting magic. We will therefore begin our discussion of some of the other interpretations by once again revisiting this long-lived hy-pothesis.

Hunting Magic

As mentioned earlier, some guides still talk about sympathetic hunting magic as the impetus for Upper Paleolithic cave art. This has been one of the most popu-lar, and persistent, alternative hypotheses advanced for the rock art found in far western North America. One of the main reasons for its popularity was Heizer and Baumhoff's (1962) book *Prehistoric Rock Art of Nevada and Eastern California*. After this work was published, hunting magic became the explanation of choice for Great Basin rock art. Most archaeologists (e.g., Lee 1997; Miller 1983; Ricks 1996; Whitley 1992a, 1992b, 1994a, 1998b) have put aside a hunting magic interpretation for Great Basin rock art and for a primary reason: the lack of empirical evidence. Whitley, for example, notes that in the Coso Range there is very little archaeological evidence for intensive or even systematic bighorn sheep hunting, despite the immense number of bighorn petroglyphs (Whitley 1998b, 136). Whitley spent four years excavating a major village site at the western edge of the Coso Range that was occupied during the height of the putative sheep-hunting cult. This work was partly designed to test the hypothesis having to do with a relationship between rock art and subsistence practices. Analysis of faunal remains recovered from the site revealed thousands of rabbit bones, dozens of pack-rat bones, a few deer bones, and an occasional bird or reptile bone. There was only one mountain sheep bone, representing less than one-tenth of one percent of animal remains from the site. Other sites in the area produced similar results. Whitley concluded that if, in fact, Coso artists had been concerned with relating the art to their subsistence practices, as the hunting magic hypothesis assumes, the Coso canyons would be filled with engravings of rabbits instead of bighorn sheep (Whitley 1998b, 136).

Despite arguing against hunting magic in California and Great Basin rock art, Whitley does not deny that hunting magic was present in the Far West (1999). The practice of antelope hunting magic by Numic shamans is, for example, especially well documented (e.g., Park 1938). Nonetheless, this kind of hunting magic is not represented in the rock art. This lack of empirical evidence, then, combined with the fact that any connection between rock art and hunting magic was categorically denied by ethnographic informants, led Whitley to conclude that the art derived from other kinds of shamanistic practices.

One more aspect that deserves attention is the relationship between shamans, animals, and plant hallucinogens. We know that hunter-gatherers the world over have, for thousands of years, forged strong ties with the animals. To this day, the Mundari hunter in the White Nile area of Africa draws his intended prey on the ground before setting out on the hunt. He returns later in the day to pour the blood and place the hair of the killed animal on the image. On the following morning, he erases the drawing in the belief that the creature he killed made a successful soul-journey to the Otherworld (Ripinsky-Naxon 1993, 23–24). Rituals like this have been performed for untold millennia. For our Paleolithic ancestors, death was the first teacher—the edge beyond which life, as they knew it, ended and wonder began. Religion may be nursed by mystery, but it was born of the hunt, from the need on the part of humans to rationalize the fact that to live they had to kill the animals that gave them life (Davis 1998, 144). Little wonder, then, that, of the group activities that can be said to best illustrate shamanism, hunting magic undeniably comes first; for it was the shaman who was identified metaphorically with the creatures that provided the community with food, clothing, and shelter. And there is evidence that this mystical relationship between man and animals was, in some cases, reinforced by hallucinogens.

People living in the Amazonian rain forests use *ayahuasca* to help in the hunt. Taking advantage of this hallucinogen, the adult men of the community re-create in their visions the most minute, difficult movements and activities of the animals they stalked and hunted. Their visions enable them to learn, once again in the conscious mind, the aspects of animal behavior that they know almost at a subliminal level, so that, in the future, they can be at one with their prey and thus hasten their victory. The substances that increase and heighten the hunter's perceptive capacities also act to strengthen the mystical bond that exists between the hunter and the animals he hunts (Dobkin de Rios 1996, 196).

In northeastern Siberia, the tribesmen lived in intimacy with their great herds of reindeer. Fly-agaric inebriation was common among these animals; when they ate these mushrooms, they behaved as if they were intoxicated (Wasson and Wasson 1957). The inebriating properties of the fly-agaric pass quickly through the urinary system and the reindeer were, it appears, addicted to drinking urine—especially human urine (Wasson 1968, 239–40). Ethnographic accounts tell us that the Siberian shamans practiced urine drinking as part of their mushroom rituals (Jochelson 1905, 365–72), and Dobkin de Rios argues that the animal's fondness for fly-agaric mushrooms may have caused humans to experiment with this plant (Dobkin de Rios 1996, 195).

Among the Huichol of western Mexico, the relationship of man, animals, and plants is well documented (Furst 1972; Lumholtz 1900; Meyerhoff 1968; Ripinsky-Naxon 1993). The Huichol currently live in Durango, Zacatecas, and the neighboring states of Jalisco and Nayarít, but their peyote pilgrimages require that they journey to *Wirikúta*, their traditional homeland in the high desert of San Luis Potosí. It is their place of creation, a place where the First People, the first Huichol, once lived. The First Shaman led these divine ancestors on their first peyote quest back to *Wirikúta*, the sacred center of the world, in order to renew their spiritual health. Although the Huichol now are settled maize farmers, they still recall the nomadic hunting traditions of their ancestors in *Wirikúta*. During their pilgrimage, they stalk the peyote cactus as if it were a deer. When they come upon the plant, they ritually "kill" it with ceremonial arrows. Every shaman-led hunt for peyote is a return to primordial beginnings. Reentering Paradise with the help of a plant that induces altered states of consciousness and guided by a shaman who is adept at negotiating the landscape of space and time, those who make this pilgrimage are spiritually renewed (Krupp 1997, 57).

Siegel (1973) has documented over three hundred cases of animals ingesting plant hallucinogens and suggests, on the basis of these data, that the use of these plants could be set back at least forty thousand years before the present. Dobkin de Rios (1996) believes that this close bond between humans and animals over so many millennia, as well as the possibility that the ancients learned about drug plants from observing animals, signifies great antiquity for the use of hallucinogens in the human record.

Archaeoastronomy

During the 1970s, archaeoastronomical studies in western North America attempted to connect portions of the rock art with native astronomical beliefs and practices. According to the hypothesis developed from these studies, many sites were solstice observatories, and many of the motifs depicted celestial phenomena such as stars and constellations. One of the better known examples concerns the astronomical significance of some art-shadowline combinations found at Fajada Butte, situated at the southern entrance to Chaco Canyon in New Mexico. High up one side of this freestanding butte are some fallen slabs of rocks. Crawling beneath them, you can watch midday shadows—narrowed to leave only a slit of light—moving slowly across a spiral pecked on an underlying rock. The image is known as the Sun Dagger, and it purportedly marks the summer solstice; but one sees about the same thing for weeks. Nothing at this site uniquely marks the exact day of the solstice. The illuminated spiral on the side of Fajada Butte may have been made to celebrate the summer solstice, but it does not *mark* it in the sense of specifying the day of turnaround (Calvin 1992, 51).

Whitley (1998b, 137) believes that such putative alignments between sites and light and shadow effects or depictions of celestial phenomena like star charts are based upon questionable evidence. He argues that the means of data collection are often anecdotal rather than systematic and scientific; data are selected because they seem to fit the archaeoastronomical interpretation. Whitley also thinks that this hypothesis was, like hunting magic, predicated on the belief that there were little if any ethnographic data on rock art. In light of extensive ethnographic analyses made by Whitley in the 1980s, any link between archaeoastronomy and rock art is very dubious. The existing ethnographic record concerning the creation of far western rock art makes no mention of astronomical beliefs or practices.

This is not to say that there was no connection between astronomical beliefs and religion; cosmology, after all, includes knowledge of the planets and stars, and, in some instances, celestial phenomena were personified as supernatural spirits and mythological beings. Among the Numic-speaking peoples of the Great Basin, for example, the constellation we call Orion was known as Bighorn Sheep (Whitley 1998b, 2000). So too, Old Stone Age eyes may have viewed the stars as mighty hunters, just as the !Kung do to this day. They may have marked time according to the phases of the moon and sensed power in the rising sun, but when they searched for a metaphor of their cosmos, they found it in the animals, whose behavior conformed to the rhythms of the rest of nature. They tied themselves to the universe by forging a mystical rapport with animals, one that was negotiated by their shamans and cemented by their art. Edwin Krupp correctly points out that what people do with the sky is related to the scale and complexity of their political organization. Kings and emperors can afford a cadre of professional astronomers, but a nomadic hunter does not need one (Krupp 1997, 124).

Literal Readings and Everyday Activities

Some who reject the idea of a shamanistic origin for rock art continue to insist that the art could have depicted mundane events. Alice Kehoe, for example, argues that "[t]here's no room in these grand theories for children making pictures to pass the time while their mamas are picking berries." She also accuses Lewis-Williams of discounting the "obvious notion" that the eland might have been painted by San bushman "simply because it is so striking a creature on the veld landscape" (Kehoe 2000, 72).

In Paul Bahn's opinion, certain researchers appear to have adopted "a rather patronizing view of the 'empiricist perspective' (that is, the literal interpretation of representations) as being somehow naïve, trivializing, simplistic or old-fashioned." He believes that such views can be just as valid or well founded as the more symbolic or mystical interpretations. Bahn is convinced that, "literal interpretations of prehistoric art are far safer—and at worst may be incomplete rather that wrong" (Bahn 1998, 221). From Bahn's safe perspective, "prehistoric artists, like those of more recent times, were people like ourselves and their art can therefore be expected to reflect every facet of life" (246).

Peter Furst, arguing from a different perspective, notes that people who hold to this view tend to see all spherical objects as "balls." A figurine holding a "ball" must, then, be a ballplayer, even when it depicts a seated, bare-breasted female. Because they bear a fancied resemblance to European-style court jesters, some Colima figures are arbitrarily labeled as "clowns." Joined pairs are always viewed as "wedding couples," and hunchbacks with enormously enlarged phalli are considered to be "erotic." A figure holding a staff or club or some other weaponry is a "warrior," and so on, ad infinitum. Furst is careful to state that this does not imply that ballplayers, warriors, dancers, married couples, or other secular subjects were not portrayed. On the contrary, many of these images at least seem to depict everyday life rather than recognizable ritualistic or religious activities and spirit beings (Furst 1973, 102).

He points out, however, that while such explanations may be comforting, they do not tax our powers of analysis and imagination, nor do they require any familiarity with the wide range of cultural facts which, when used with care, offer alternative (albeit more complex) interpretations. Furst, challenging the "literal" readings of the art, observes that "a great many Colima figures . . . have horns growing from their foreheads. By what criteria is this an 'everyday activity'? Or the wearing of human masks by dogs? Are these hallucinogenic plants, known ethnographically and historically as sacred or even divine all over Mesoamerica, 'secular subjects'?" (Furst 1973, 102–3).

Furst is suggesting, of course, that the shamanic hypothesis provides a much more viable interpretive framework for a corpus of art and iconography that otherwise resists interpretation. Knowing that the study of shamanism is an integral part of the cognitive approach, critics attack not only the theory but also the methods used in its development. Bahn (1998, 243), for example, referring specifically to the way that cognitive researchers use the ethnographic record, insists that "a large number of cumulative assumptions have been made in order to link ethnographic evidence with rock art and to link both of them with shamans and trance."

In Defense of Ethnoarchaeology and Analogy

Researchers have used ethnographic data in archaeological interpretation for a long time. In the late nineteenth and early twentieth centuries, New World archaeologists used ethnographic information from elderly living informants, as well as ethnohistoric records, to interpret finds from archaeological sites being excavated. In the 1930s, William Strong stressed the interdependence of archaeology and ethnology and argued that archaeologists would be well served if they looked to ethnologists for theoretical leads as well as factual information (Strong 1936). Even Lewis Binford believed that archaeologists should be trained as ethnologists if they wanted to establish correlations among living cultures and the past (Trigger 1989, 300). Most processualists insisted, nevertheless, that the archaeological record could only be understood on its own terms, and they rejected what others considered useful methods for studying prehistory.

One of their arguments was that many native cultures were considerably changed as a result of European contact some time before the earliest descriptions were recorded and that all hunter-gatherer societies around the world were probably influenced to some degree by more advanced civilizations prior to ethnographic studies (e.g., Fried 1975; Kehoe 2000; Monks 1981; Trigger 1981; Wobst 1978). Others maintain that it is not possible to learn anything about the mental activities of prehistoric people because their minds are gone and the mental contents are not recoverable (Hill 1994). Some believe that since we are not participants in the cultures that produced the images, we will never have the ability to understand their meaning (Douglass 1997). Furthermore, even for those traditional societies that trace their ancestry to prehistoric cultures and often maintain a rich oral tradition about the art and symbolism, the possibility always exists that the meanings have changed over time and space (Bahn 1998, 247).

Cognitive scholars recognize that meanings may have changed but insist that such changes can be perceived in the archaeological record if it is properly interrogated. For these researchers, "proper interrogation" means not only a thorough assessment of the ethnography as it relates to material remains but also a clear understanding of how and why the record was created. They point out that archaeological analyses of ideology have traditionally relied on historical and protohistorical sources. In American anthropology (and archaeology) a number of early studies of New World religions were often based, directly or indirectly, on available written records (Demarest 1987). Inquiries concerning the religious practices of cultures such as the Aztec, Inca, and Post-Classic Maya often made use of pre-Columbian codices, conquistador chronicles, church and government surveys, and archives of various legal records (Demarest 1989, 89).

Flannery and Marcus (1976), for example, made one of the earliest efforts to more fully understand the ancient Zapotec Indians by combining cosmological beliefs with a more traditional analysis of the subsistence and settlement systems. They attempted to demonstrate that a higher proportion of ancient Zapotec subsistence behavior could be more fully explained if, instead of restricting their investigations to a study of agricultural products and irrigation canals, they took into account what was known about Zapotec ideas concerning the relationship of lightning, rain, and blood sacrifice. They stressed, however, that they could only do so because of the sixteenth-century Spanish eyewitness accounts of the Zapotec. The problem here is that the reports, chronicles, surveys, and eyewitness accounts expressed the viewpoint of the Spanish conquerors, a perspective that was, more often than not, biased and ethnocentric.

In a similar vein, interpretations that depend heavily on local ethnographic or ethnohistoric information are also suspect. Bahn, for example, referring to nonliteral interpretations of rock art, argues that this kind of testimony is most often derived from one or two informants and an investigator can easily get conflicting comments about the same motifs from different individuals (Bahn 1998, 221). He also writes, "It is also a well-known phenomenon that some informants will say what they imagine the investigator wants to hear, or will say something, any-thing, rather than admit . . . ignorance. Informants may be self-contradictory, change their minds, or tell untruths." A few pages later, however, Bahn appears to contradict himself. He castigates those who believe that "ethnographic testimony cannot be taken at face value (except where it fits the hypothesis) and needs to be analyzed and interpreted." He accuses such researchers of claiming

> somewhat patronizingly, that most informants were not capable of ar-ticulating—or perhaps did not know—the deeper meanings of their beliefs, but that they (the researchers themselves) are fully capable of re-trieving the metaphors and hidden meanings in this stunted testimony. This attitude smacks of neocolonialism and seems to continue the eighteenth-century practice whereby Western scholars defined and ana-lyzed alien religious beliefs. (243–44)

Cognitive researchers make no such claims. Bahn does a great disservice to all modern students of prehistory and indicates that he is completely unaware of present-day methods of interpreting the ethnographic data. The type of thinking he alludes to reflects an earlier archaeological approach to anthropology—one that assumed that the ethnographic record reflected a complete elucidation of the ethnographic past, that ethnographic statements were observations whose mean-ings were straightforward, and that understanding them required no further inter-pretation. Thus, when researchers approached the ethnographic record (or an ethnographic informant) and asked who made the art and for what reasons, their expectations were for explicit and final explanations (Whitley 1994b, 81).

Today, cognitive archaeologists (and most anthropologists) recognize that this is simply not the way in which much of the ethnographic data are expressed, par-ticularly data pertaining to topics like religion, belief systems, and symbolism. This is especially true when these data are filtered through a process that involves an ethnographer, translator, and informant. These researchers understand that the problem of translation is more than just a technical issue that can be resolved by a linguist, fully fluent in both languages, who is capable of providing an exact lit-eral translation. They also realize that this complexity results because all cultures and languages, including our own, rely heavily on the use of metaphor in both ver-bal and written expressions. In other words, most literal translations of the ethno-graphic record do not provide the real sense of meaning of an informant's com-ments precisely because they were transcribed and translated as "objectively" as possible. We can overcome these difficulties only if we become familiar with the linguistic metaphors that are commonly used in a particular society (Whitley 1994b, 81–82).

Bahn argues that even if we were to accept the accuracy and validity of ethnographic or ethnohistoric information, it is still of limited use. He believes that while "such information is undoubtedly invaluable for art of the historical periods and the periods immediately preceding them, it is not applicable to any truly prehistoric art, even in those same areas" (Bahn 1998, 222). Referring specifically to the work of Lewis-Williams and his colleagues in southern Africa, Bahn insists the case for a shamanic interpretation of Bushman art relies very heavily on a "tortuous interpretation of ethnography," with much of it derived from present-day Kalahari bushmen who "have no knowledge of any painting tradition" (245). Bahn also claims that, "[t]he Bleek and Lloyd records used by proponents of shamanism as the foundation stone of the whole theory contain no mention of trance, nor of any practices, dreams or beliefs involving it" (244).

Bahn is wrong on this score. The Bleek and Lloyd records referred to are the work of Wilhelm Bleek, a German linguist, his daughter, Dorothea Bleek and his sister-in-law, Lucy Lloyd. Over a period of several decades, beginning in the 1870s, the Bleek family became acquainted with southern /Xam Bushmen, collected many of their traditions and stories and recorded them for the rest of the world. In addition to the Bleek material, Lewis-Williams also relied on a smaller, but no less significant, collection of myths and commentary concerning the rock paintings obtained in 1873 by Joseph Orpen (1874) from a San guide in the southeastern mountains. While neither Orpen's nor Bleek's informants were themselves artists, they did concede that the art was the work of their own people (Lewis-Williams 1984, 225). In addition, Lewis-Williams used a second major ethnographic source: the San who currently live in the Kalahari Desert. These twentieth-century ethnographies, in his opinion, clarify much that is obscure in the nineteenth-century works. He believes that, notwithstanding a wide separation in space and time and the fact that the Kalahari people speak different languages from the now extinct southern groups and do not paint, it is "increasingly clear that they all shared a great many beliefs and rituals, albeit with minor local variations" (Lewis-Williams 1984, 226).

In a series of books and articles, Lewis-Williams describes in detail how an analysis of San ethnography strongly suggests that many parietal paintings were closely associated with shamans (Lewis-Williams 1980, 1981, 1982, 1983b, 1984, 1987). He also tackles the question of stylistic differences. Admitting that the paintings of such widely separated areas as the southwestern Cape and the Natal Drakensberg are generally distinguishable, Lewis-Williams notes that we must not confuse style with meaning and that the depiction and combination of significant details in all areas demonstrates a conceptual unity of the art (Lewis-Williams 1984, 227). To support his argument concerning the spatial relevance of the trance hypothesis, he refers to Tanzanian rock paintings that portray the same dancing postures, phosphenes, nasal hemorrhage, attenuation of human figures, and therianthropes (half-human and half-animal forms) that are found throughout southern Africa. He argues that the similarities are so detailed that it is legitimate to hypothesize that the northern art was also linked with hunter-gatherer trance performance. A repetition of diagnostic details and key metaphors indicates that we are dealing with the same fundamental belief systems (229).

Lewis-Williams was certain that the "fundamental beliefs" expressed in the San rock art were shamanistic, and this fact was a basic premise in the formulation of the neuropsychological model. While recognizing that Upper Paleolithic art has, in an absolute sense, no real counterpart in any present-day primitive society he insisted, nevertheless, that "a neurological bridge affords some access to the Upper Paleolithic" (Lewis-Williams and Dowson 1988, 202). Some scholars are, as one might expect, a bit skeptical. Bahn, for example, believes any effort to link universal symbols or symbolic intent over thousands of years, even in a single region, to create a historical link between various cultures is a "typical misuse of ethnographic analogy" (Bahn 1998, 249).

Those who rail against the misuse (or any use) of ethnographic analogy miss an extremely important point concerning the neuropsychological model and the use of analogy. When Lewis-Williams and Dowson (1988, 201) noted that their model for addressing the Upper Paleolithic art "avoids simplistic ethnographic analogy," they were not referring to the way they had used the San ethnographic records. Their detailed analysis of the nineteenth and twentieth-century accounts simply led them to conclude that San beliefs, rituals, and symbolism were notably similar over a wide geographic territory and that they were shamanistic. They did not, contrary to what some critics contend, imply that the ethnographic data could be used analogously to infer that Upper Paleolithic art was shamanistic. Their conclusions, derived from ethnographic analysis, about the shamanistic nature of the San painted art served only to direct their attention to altered states of consciousness.

Analogy and Neuropsychology

It was not the ethnography, then, that led to the construction of the neuropsychological model, but the universality of entoptic phenomena. Research clearly demonstrates that the *kinds* of hallucinations experienced while in altered states of consciousness are cross-culturally uniform. Although all of the senses can be affected during trance states, cognitive scholars are most often concerned with visual hallucinations and, as discussed earlier, laboratory experiments have shown that these hallucinations are experienced in three stages: Subjects see only entoptic phenomena during the first stage of trance; in the second, they attempt to make sense of these images by construing them into familiar objects; and in the third, the subject's attention focuses almost exclusively on the iconic hallucinations that involve animals, people, monsters, and emotionally charged events in which they actively participate. Thus, two elements become intertwined: the geometric entoptic images derived from the universal human nervous system (the neurologically controlled elements) and those iconic images that derive from the subject's specific culture (the psychological elements). Because both kinds of images are processed according to neurologically based principles like rotation, fragmentation, or combination, iconic hallucinations blend with entoptic images and various images combine to produce composite animals and therianthropes (Lewis-Williams 1991, 152).

Lewis-Williams and Dowson gauged the usefulness of their model by first applying it to southern African San art. They used ethnography to show that the San shaman-artists depicted animal symbols of the supernatural power they harnessed to gain trance states, metaphors of trance experience, and hallucinations of the spiritual dimensions they believed they had entered (Lewis-Williams 1980, 1981, 1982, 1986; Lewis-Williams and Dowson 1989). The depictions included geometric motifs that appeared to be entoptic in origin, construals of entoptic forms and therianthropes, "realistic" animals, and the tumultuous events experienced in deep trance (Lewis-Williams 1980, 1982; Lewis-Williams and Dowson 1989). The way in which the model fit and made sense of San art in general increased their confidence in its usefulness and encouraged them to apply it to other arts that were not known to be derived from altered states of consciousness (Lewis-Williams 1991, 154).

As Lewis-Williams points out, the application of the model to Upper Paleolithic art was not a comparison of hallucinations experienced under laboratory conditions with hallucinations experienced in the Upper Paleolithic. It was, instead, a comparison of a range of motifs that are known to be *depictions* of certain hallucinations experienced by Westerners with *depictions* of Upper Paleolithic art (Lewis-Williams 1991, 154). The Upper Paleolithic images include zigzags, dots, grids, catenary curves, and the other geometric "signs" that fall within the range of entoptic elements determined through laboratory research. Sometimes the motifs are actually placed on animals, but others occur in isolation. In addition, the Upper Paleolithic art includes a range of images equivalent to third-stage hallucinations. Lewis-Williams and Dowson concluded that their model orders and fits Upper Paleolithic art as well as it does the San rock art (Lewis-Williams 1991; Lewis-Williams and Dowson 1988).

This is not an analogical argument from San art to Upper Paleolithic art. The genesis of the analogy is a neuropsychological model of altered states of consciousness that derives from laboratory research that has nothing to do with rock art. The source of analogy is neuropsychological rather than ethnographic.

In Defense of the Neuropsychological Model

Not surprisingly, some critics have chosen to discredit the model itself—with its emphasis on altered states and the association with shamanic trance—as the origin of virtually all motifs and images in all periods and cultures (Bahn 1998, 240). Bahn, although he is, by his own admission, "totally ignorant of the nonarchaeological literature on the subject," continues to rail against the "phosphene theory" because it "appears that the theory cannot fail simply because there are very few basic shapes that one can draw, whether they come from the mind's eye, hallucinations, or idle doodling." He believes that "in any collection of nonfigurative art there are bound to be lots of marks that look like some or all of the six entoptic categories" (217). In his opinion, "A zigzag motif could easily be inspired by lightning, just as circles can be inspired by ripples in water" (241). He refuses to accept the notion that a portrayal of what he interprets as a "hunting net" could be a geometric image perceived during trance. He derides any approach where "[e]very other conceivable motif . . . becomes a metaphor of trance," where "fish, for example, are metaphors for underwater journeying." As far as he is concerned, images that portray sexual intercourse, fighting, or flight are "all interpreted in oblique ways even when more prosaic explanations are available" (242).

Cognitive researchers point out that explanations that take into account hallucinatory imagery and entoptics provide an economical interpretation of many design combinations and modes of representation that are not easily explained by other means. The neuropsychological model succeeds in accounting for the variety in motifs, stylistic practices, and modes of rendering found in much of the rock art around the world. Moreover, since the model was developed from laboratory subjects' descriptions, it provides an independent scientific test of the veracity of the ethnographic interpretation of the rock art; the origin of paintings and engravings in visionary imagery is confirmed by a comparison between the motif assemblages and the model.

As Lewis-Williams and Dowson (1988) noted, the model is simply an analytical tool for addressing the complexity of the art. It only considers the nature of the motif forms that originate in the mental imagery of altered states of consciousness; nowhere in the model is there any implication about or clue concerning the meaning of the images.

Neuropsychology and Meaning

Even though the model provides us only with an understanding of the form of the mental images, the neuropsychological universals that result from altered states experiences do afford some insights into the content and meaning of the visions and therefore of the art that was created to portray the shamanic dream experience.

Bodily reactions and hallucinations reflect common themes or events described in the recorded verbal descriptions of visionary experiences. We now know that many of these themes and events are cross-cultural reactions to altered states because the same reactions, hallucinations, and experiences are described by informants from a variety of cultures throughout the world and across different time periods. Thus, the ethnography (where it exists) explains, for example, the relationship and meaning of bighorn sheep in the rock art of the Coso Range or the relationship of the shaman and the eland in San rock art. The fact that images perceived and events putatively occurring during trance states are grossly similar from culture to culture affords a bridge that allows us to understand aspects of visionary art that would otherwise (especially in the absence of any confirming ethnography) be lost in the depths of the past.

Bahn seems to favor more functional interpretations not only because he is unwilling to accept the neuropsychological model but also because he would have us believe that such "strict adherence to a single theory is a prophylactic against thought." Bahn (1998, 243) is convinced that this type of approach "limits potential explanations and imposes a bogus, reductionist, utterly hypothetical homogeneity on a vast array of different motifs." Kehoe mimics this line of thinking, stating that to claim "that rock art most likely was done by 'shamans' coming out of trance and representing 'inside the eye' patterns is reductionist" (Kehoe 2000, 80). Bahn characterizes the shamanic interpretation as a "shaky edifice," which has been built on an "inverted pyramid" that "has risen so high that many have lost sight of its tiny and very wobbly foundation" (Bahn 1998, 245).

Wobbly foundation indeed! Considering the enlightened methods used by cognitive scholars to interpret the ethnographic data, the meticulous research involved in the development of the neuropsychological model and the greatly enhanced knowledge of the shamanistic nature of the practices and belief systems of hunters-gatherers over space and time, it seems quite absurd to characterize the shamanic hypothesis, and, by derivation, the cognitive approach that led to it, as a "shaky edifice."

In Defense of the Cognitive Approach and a Shamanic Hypothesis

In the early days of the New Archaeology, processualists advocated the application of a nomothetic-deductive methodology for uncovering general laws that governed human behavior. The basis for this approach was a philosophy known as "logical positivism," which considers the world to be comprised of observable phenomena that act in an orderly way—a world ruled by covering laws that can be identified by rigorous research methods. Processualists believed that this approach would allow them to use archaeological data to formulate and test hypotheses that identify general and universal laws that govern cultural processes (Fagan 1991, 470). Since their goal was to become more scientific, they ignored all aspects of intellectual and symbolic behavior that are the product of the human mind; these were not archaeological data and therefore could not be used to develop testable hypotheses.

I argue not only that the approach was flawed but also that researchers who used this methodology to search for "universal laws" were looking in the wrong place. The highly specific deductive methods employed by the "hard" sciences like physics are far less applicable to archaeological data. As Fagan (1991, 470) so succinctly argues, "Archaeology is just not that sort of science." When Fagan (471) suggested that the scientific discipline closest to archaeology was biology, he was alluding to a research direction that was anathema for most processualists. A few intrepid scholars had, however, already begun to look to biology and related disciplines in their attempt to understand human cognition and to determine how it might be reflected in the archaeological record. And since they were dealing with the human mind, these researchers turned to biochemistry, neuroscience, psychology, and similar fields of study.

This approach uncovered a universal and irrefutable fact: all human beings have equivalent neuropsychological systems. This tenet became the cornerstone for a neuropsychological model which, in turn, provided cognitive scholars with a significant tool for connecting archaeological remains with ancient mental states. Keep in mind, however, that the neuropsychological studies leading to the development of this model were triggered by a more traditional form of research: the analyses of ethnographic data that confirmed the shamanic nature of southern San and Great Basin Numic rock art. These scholars also had empirical evidence that preagricultural societies throughout the world were hunters and gatherers and that most hunter-gatherer cultures, both ancient and modern, were shamanistic. Combining these data with the idea that all humans, regardless of culture, use similar cognitive processes, they were able to argue that modern-day hunter-gatherers could legitimately be compared with their prehistoric counterparts.

Thus, although hunter-gatherer shamanism might take many forms, there are remarkable similarities through space and time. And while cognitive researchers realized that this was due to neurologically generated commonalities resulting from the way the human nervous system behaves in altered states, they also knew that similar cognitive processes could produce different results. Once again, they looked to neuropsychological research for enlightenment. The model tells us that, even though the stages of trance are universal and hard-wired into the human nervous system, the meanings given to the entoptics experienced in stage one of trance, the objects into which they are transformed in the second stage, and the hallucinations of stage three are all culture-specific. In other words, the images, hallucinations, and construals experienced in altered states are similar in that they derive from equivalent neurological systems but are interpreted according to culturally defined beliefs and worldview.

For cognitive scholars, the implications were quite astonishing. Using multiple lines of evidence and arguments that incorporated strong relations of relevance, they had developed an approach that gave them access to prehistoric cognition and an understanding of the way in which it was expressed in the art. Furthermore, they had a method for interpreting variations in the archaeological record—a tool for explaining the extensive "diversity" that had confounded the processualists— that could account for much more than any ecosystemic approach.

This is not to say that the shamanic interpretation implies a single origin and purpose for all prehistoric art. Clottes and Lewis-Williams (1998, 112), for example, do not argue that each and every Upper Paleolithic image, portable or on walls of caves, was the product of shamanistic practices and beliefs. Whitley also believes that the ethnographic record suggests considerable variability in the origin and meaning of Native California rock art. Even though the paintings and engravings clearly depict visionary images of the supernatural world, these images may represent mythological events, spirit beings, curing, rainmaking, and a variety of other kinds of shamanistic practices or specialties, depending upon region, context, and artist. Similarly, the motifs may have been made by shamans acting as ritual specialists, by female or male puberty initiates involved in group or private ceremonies, or, in some instances, by adult nonshamans experiencing important events in their lives (Whitley 1994b, 92). In all cases, however, the art is fundamentally shamanistic, in that it was based on beliefs and practices having to do with the supernatural world and depicted images experienced during altered states of consciousness (Whitley 2000, 49).

Some critics do not believe that a single hypothesis can account for all of the diversity in the art. Bahn (1998, 247) suggests that "[to] cram even a single corpus into one explanation like shamanism is to impose a spurious uniformity on a vast and diverse phenomenon." Furthermore, when Bahn (246) states that "such blanket explanations . . . cannot be tested or proven wrong," he continues to defend the positivist approach to science and explicitly rejects the notion of "best fit" hypotheses. Bahn misses the point entirely. Lewis-Williams and Dowson said from the very beginning, "We do not claim to prove anything; we merely offer a hypothesis that we believe explains more, and more varied, data than the competing hypotheses" (Lewis-Williams and Dowson 1988, 237). They stressed the concept that a hypothesis does not have to explain *all* data instantly before it can be adopted. In the absence of a "misleading notion of proof," it simply has to account for more data better than the competing hypotheses (238). With this in mind, they argued that their explanation for the signs and other features of Upper Paleolithic art was, at that stage of their research, the "best fit."

This way of thinking is sanctioned by many modern scholars, including those who deal in the so-called "hard" sciences. As physicist Stephen Hawking points out, any physical theory is always provisional in the sense that it is only a hypothesis—something that cannot be "proved." However, "each time new experiments are observed to agree with the predictions the theory survives, and our confidence in it is increased" (Hawking 1988, 10). From Hawking's point of view, the ultimate goal of physics is to develop a single theory that will explain the entire universe. Physicists currently define the universe in terms of two basic partial theories—the general theory of relativity and quantum mechanics. Scientists recognize, however, that these two theories are inconsistent with each other; it is impossible for both to be correct. And this is why one of the major ventures in physics today is the search for a new theory that will incorporate them both.

Scientists also acknowledge that the partial theories we already have are sufficient to make accurate predictions in all but the most extreme situations. Hawking freely admits that the search for the ultimate theory seems difficult to justify on practical grounds and that the discovery of a complete unified theory may not promote the survival of our species or even affect our lifestyle. Hawking believes we continue our pursuit of knowledge for other reasons: "ever since the dawn of civilization, people have not been content to see events as unconnected and inexplicable. They have craved an understanding of the underlying order in the world" (Hawking 1988, 11–13).

The question is which path to follow in our search for understanding. The easier route is rather narrow and clings to the idea that "[s]uch grand schemes . . . are products of their own time and culture," ones that will "inevitably collapse, to be replaced by more realistic theories based on more modest hypotheses fitted to more limited data" (Bahn 1998, 221). Or should we be more adventurous and blaze a wider trail, a trail that might afford a broader, more exploratory route? Avoiding a well-worn track does not mean that we are headed in the wrong direction. Nor do a few missteps imply that we have lost our way. As Clottes and Lewis-Williams suggest, "For all we know, there may well have been other conceptual currents and practices of which we know nothing. Yet despite all the diversity of the dirt, there is a long-term unity that testifies to some sort of common framework" (Clottes and Lewis-Williams 1998, 112). Cognitive scholars have tried to uncover that broader structure. Those elements that are not yet understood (the temporal and regional differences, the nonshamanistic components) represent opportunities for further investigation. While Clottes and Lewis-Williams were referring specifically to a shamanic interpretation of Upper Paleolithic art, it is clear that a better understanding of shamanism affords an avenue of inquiry that goes far beyond the rock art.

A Cognitive Approach to Major Themes in Archaeology

Whether or not a shamanic hypothesis can explain all or even a large part of pre-historic drawings and engravings is really not the issue, for in the end it is not just about rock art. More importantly, the search for an interpretive approach that could explain the art led to investigations of human cognition and shamanism, and this is a key with the potential to unlock the doorways to the past. If one accepts the premise that most preagricultural societies made their living by hunting and gathering, that shamanism comprised the basic religion of hunter-gatherers the world over, and that human cognition was expressed in shamanistic practices and symbols, prehistoric processes can be interpreted from a very different perspective. By way of illustration, I will consider, from a cognitive point of view, a few of the major issues that have been the focus of archaeological research for several years.

Trade

Many researchers believe that as far back as 2300 B.P., the Chichimecas, the original Aztec group, as well as the Toltecs, were acquainted with a variety of drugs, including peyote. Peyote came from the far northern deserts of present-day Texas and Mexico. The Aztecs knew this plant only in its preserved state, and therefore we can assume that it was dried and transported several hundred miles to the south (Safford 1916). Similarly, since wild ancestors of the tobacco plant are not indigenous to North America, one must assume that tobacco use on this continent diffused from contact with South America (Dobkin de Rios 1996, 38).

One of the most prominent items of exchange in central Australia was the narcotic *pituri* (Mulvaney and Kamminga 1999, 97). Dieri men (members of one of the tribes that controlled the pituri trade) traveled more than 450 kilometers along the Dreaming pathways to collect *Duboisia* leaves. Pituri was traded along with other exotic goods including the sanctified ochre from their Dreaming quarries (98). Various groups who lacked this valuable plant in their own territory exchanged items such as spears, boomerangs, nets, shields, fish, and yams for pituri (Basedow 1925). Roth (1901) observed that the Aboriginal men would offer any of their possessions, including their women, to replenish their supply.

The Origins of Agriculture

The processual approach has clearly shown that we can no longer seek an explanation for agricultural beginnings in a single cause. It appears, instead, that a variety of underlying factors may have been involved, and one of them might have been religion. Shamanism is arguably the oldest of human spiritual endeavors, born at the dawn of our species' awareness. As healers, shamans typically recognize an entire range of ailments that can be treated symptomatically, much as is done in Western medicine, and to this end they use medicinal plants and folk preparations, many of which are pharmacologically active. From the shaman's perspective, however, purely physical ailments that are treatable with herbal remedies are not as serious as the problems that arise when an individual's spiritual harmony is disturbed. Invariably, then, it is intervention on a spiritual plane that ultimately determines the patient's fate, and for this the healer uses specific techniques to achieve an altered state of consciousness.

For many primitive cultures the psychic effect of pharmacologically active substances is often far more important than the purely physical ones. For this reason, hallucinogens, more than any other plants, are closely linked with the treatment of disease and the struggle against death, and with all related rituals (Schultes 1972, 5). It follows, then, that the shaman, as the religious and medical specialist of his community, would consciously explore the environment not only for plants with therapeutic value but also for those whose properties assisted the journey of the soul.

Consider, for a moment, that lysergic acid diethylamide (LSD) is the active ingredient in the ergot *Claviceps purpurea* and *C. paspali*. These are fungal parasites that grow on rye, barley, and other cereals. Both species contain small quantities of the hallucinogenic alkaloids ergonovine and ergine, and they were much desired for their psychoactive properties. There is little doubt that the hallucinogenic effect of the water-soluble alkaloids in the ergot of *Claviceps spp.* was recognized and exploited for many centuries before the present (Ripinsky-Naxon 1993, 186). Evidence like this suggests that it may be more rewarding to entertain the notion that plants with pharmacological and psychoactive properties were among the first to be subjected to manipulation by humans.

Food sources, after all, comprise merely abstract constructs. What counts is not so much which plants might be potentially exploited, but the recognition of their usefulness to society. In a wild state, wheat, barley, and rye are just grasses, useful neither to the dietary demands of humans nor to the everyday economy. Despite the processual fondness for optimal foraging theory, diet breadth models and so on, it seems unlikely that hunter-gatherers could anticipate the nutritional benefits locked in the genetic potential of these plants. We may assume, instead, that these people, and especially their shamans, would be more inclined to experiment with potential foodstuffs and narcotic plants that gave them special power to heal the spirit and facilitated transport to the supernatural realm.

The shaman who treated illness and looked after the general well-being of his community was often also responsible for ceremonies aimed at promoting the fecundity of natural resources, and we can speculate that acquired experience with these plants was subsequently transferred to subsistence crops. While experiential knowledge was transmitted with guarded jealousy within the specialists' circles, the shamans must have imparted some of this knowledge to the earliest cultivators, enhancing at the same time the complexity of ritual life. Thus, the domestication of cereal might well have been simply an ancillary outcome—a by-product—that was the result of manipulation of ergot-infested grasses that had been gathered and tended because of a fungal parasite. This is only conjecture, of course, but it does afford some food for thought. Whatever the underlying cause, agrarian transformation and the advent of sedentary village-based lifeways led inevitably to sociopolitical stratification and the earliest religious hierarchies. Cultural changes were set in motion, and shamanism was an integral part of the process.

Culture Change

Ritual knowledge was highly esteemed in traditional societies, especially those where hunting and gathering were the basic economic activities. We also know that revealed knowledge was the purview of the shaman, for he alone functioned as an intermediary between his community and the supernatural world; by interacting with the spirit realm, he strengthened the bond that existed between his people and the bearers of knowledge. Although we usually think of shamans as healers and ritual specialists, their role in society was also often a secular one. The ethnographic record tells us that, in many parts of the world, shamans were chiefs and headmen as well as religious leaders. The Eskimo terms for "shaman," *angakok*, and for "leader," *angajkok*, share the same root (Ripinsky-Naxon 1993, 63). Similarly, we know the generic Numic words for "headman" and "shaman" were exactly the same (Whitley 1994a). Even though the headman/shaman ruled by consensus rather than through an outright exercise of authority, control of subsistence activities and revealed knowledge did afford a certain level of prestige or influence within the community. Thus, as egalitarian as hunter-gatherer bands might appear, a degree of social differentiation existed among them.

As societies grow in complexity, the value placed on direct knowledge of the supernatural, as well as the means of obtaining it, also changes. Global studies show that, with the advent of intensive agriculture and the social stratification that follows, elite segments of society usurp and manipulate revealed knowledge and access to power (Winkelman 1989). Even though the control of ideology and the ability to direct resources provide organizational advantages, they are not free of costs. Centralized power leads to a higher level of sociopolitical complexity and the uneven distribution of wealth, and this generally means the end of shamanic traditions.

Access to altered states of consciousness is, after all, as much a part of sumptuary laws as is access to material goods (Dobkin de Rios 1996, 201). The concept of a state society includes the complete control over ideology and legitimized power, and any attempts to circumvent such control are subject to regulation and punishment. In more traditional societies, those who gained knowledge through drug-induced altered states of consciousness believed that knowledge and power were proprietary. In a state-level society, however, the power to bewitch through access to drugs would be perceived as a threat to legitimate power, and drug-using shamans would be dangerous. Consider, as an example, that prior to Inca consolidation of sedentary agricultural villages, the use of coca appears to have been widespread. After the inhabitants were subjugated, the Inca forbade the use of this substance to any but the Inca and his own court, and myths were promulgated telling how the gods gave coca to the Inca as the source of his power (Taylor 1966).

The maintenance of ideology also requires an investment in visible emblems of its validity. Donnan (1992, 123–24) writes about the trend toward increasing secularization of iconographic content during the span of development of ancient Peruvian ceramics. Pottery produced in the Formative Period emphasized the depiction of supernatural creatures such as anthropomorphic animals, birds, plants, and the Occulate Being, as well as a variety of supernatural symbols and activities. In the later Moche, Nazca, and Vicús styles, more secular activities are portrayed. This increasing secularization continues during the time of the Inca Empire, and Donnan suggests this trend may reflect the degree to which the production and use of ceramics were tied to religion. Presumably, this link was quite strong in earlier times and less so in later periods when a more secular, administrative elite began to develop.

Roberte Hamayon, a French ethnologist and expert on Asian shamanism, sees a difference between hunting shamanism, with its emphasis on supernatural exchange with animal spirits, and pastoral shamanism, where the spirits are more like humans. Ancestors, supernatural beings, and mythical founders converge as sources of transcendental power (Hamayon 1994). But as people become anchored more firmly in one place, as village-based foragers, seasonally migrating herders or landbound farmers, their concept of the universe evolves. And yet, if one looks carefully, vestiges of shamanic practices can still be found in cultures far removed from their hunting origins—in pastoral communities, in agriculturally based chiefdoms, in sacred kingships, and even in agrarian empires. We know, for example, that by about 2250 B.P., rice technology had transformed the economy of Japan into one of intensive agriculture, and yet Shinto, the religious basis of Japan's imperial tradition, still adopts the world perspective of the shaman and interacts with the spiritual realm according to ancient shamanic procedures (Krupp 1997, 196).

The Peopling of the Americas

Whitley (1998b, 162) has made a compelling argument for a shamanic origin of the earliest rock art in the Coso Range. We also have evidence for early shamanism in many other parts of the New World. The archaeological record tells us that Clovis people buried caches of precious materials like crystalline quartz, decorated ivory and bone, and high quality stone for toolmaking (Frison and Bradley 1999). At a site known as Fenn Cache, spearpoints have a thin coating of red ocher and are found with quartz crystals. Surely we can assume, based on current knowledge of the importance of quartz crystals in shamanistic ritual, that they must have had something to do with belief systems. We have even older evidence in the form of twenty-two species of known medicinal plants (identical to those used today by local native peoples for curing) recovered from the pre-Clovis site of Monte Verde in Chile (Dillehay 1997). The site has a feature known as the "Wishbone Structure" on account of its unique shape and is sometimes referred to as a medicine hut. This recalls the discussion in chapter 10 of Y- or U-shaped designs commonly found on ritual vessels; they are the motifs that represent a portal that must be entered to undergo the transformation of death and rebirth.

While the accumulated evidence supports and strengthens the contention that even the earliest New World cultures were shamanistic, it reveals virtually nothing about their origins. There are, however, some intriguing, albeit tenuous, clues. A number of symbols on Olmec jade, stone, and ceramics, for example, bear a close resemblance to inscriptions from the Shang Dynasty in China. The artistic styles are so much alike as to suggest that the two cultures followed similar religious practices. Both used red cinnabar to decorate ceremonial objects, and both placed jade beads in the mouths of their dead to ward off evil (Selim 2000). This is not to imply that Olmec ancestors came from China. Cognitive research does show, however, that shamanistic practices and beliefs are culture-specific—and resistant to change. It is possible, then, that these similarities reflect some cultural affinity that has survived through time and space.

The cognitive approach, then, can offer different insights and ways of addressing some of the major issues in archaeology. Indeed, this type of research may well prove to be one of the most powerful weapons at our disposal for investigating the greatest puzzle of all: human evolution. The development of the human brain is, after all, one of the most provocative and least understood of all the evolutionary processes, and the consequences are arguably more profound and far-reaching than for any other mammalian species.

Some Thoughts on Future Research

We can no longer deny that a large portion of the archaeological record is a product of human cognition. Nor can we insist that ideology, cosmology, and beliefs had no role in shaping human societies, or that they are epiphenomena that cannot be studied. Cognitive scholars have, in fact, been studying them for over twenty years, and this research has been remarkably productive. The most important findings have to do with shamanism: its connection with hunter-gatherer societies; altered states of consciousness; the stages of trance and the way the human neurological system works; the special role of the shaman in his society; and finally, the way that all of these are expressed in the archaeological record.

Cognitive researchers have also shown that the study of shamanic practices, supernatural belief systems and related matters can benefit from an investigation of the use of hallucinogens in ancient societies. Researchers may discover, for example, that drug-related experiences were not only the bases for the complex belief systems and ideology that comprised a community's worldview, but also played a role in the deep-seated belief in the reality of a supernatural world. Anthropologists, like the missionaries and explorers who came before them, all too often passed over the importance of the unidentified noxious herbs that the people they were studying used to access altered states. While recognizing that the divinity attributed to these hallucinogenic plants is chemical in nature, we should never lose sight of the native's own interpretation of these "magical" or "sacred" plants.

To ignore or deprecate these views may doom the most carefully planned scientific inquiry to failure; certainly our prehistoric ancestors did not have our modern attitudes about how good a scientific explanation should be in order to be judged successful. The theoretical repertoire for cognitive research comes, in the main, from a new scientific orientation, one that is losing its specifically Western character. It gives more attention to beliefs and worldviews of other cultures and attempts to bring them into harmony with modern knowledge. Scholars now have at their disposal a different way of looking at the material record and a unique set of tools for plying their trade. Whether or not they elect to use them is another matter.

Those who search for explanations of past human behavior at least in part through explicit reference to the human mind have already chosen this path. As a result, they are in a position to take advantage of an array of new insights and approaches having to do with the workings of the human mind. At present, molecular biologists study events within the neuron, neurophysiologists determine how the neurons interact, and psychologists and psychiatrists examine the pathology and behavior of the human brain as a whole. When all this research is finally brought together and human cognition is more fully understood, the borders that separate these various disciplines will no doubt fade under the light of a more powerful synthesis.

An anthropologically oriented archaeology can (and should) be part of this grand scheme. The emerging insights of the combined sciences can help in shaping the way archaeologists practice their craft in the future. This does not mean

Bibliography

Adovasio, J. M., and G. S. Fry. 1976. Prehistoric Psychotropic Drug Use in Northeastern Mexico and Trans-Peco Texas. *Economic Botany* 30 (1).

Agenbroad, L. 1994. Paleo-Indian Rock Art on the Colorado Plateau: 11,000 years of Petroglyphs. Paper presented at the 1994 International Rock Art Congress, Flagstaff, Ariz.

Alexander, J. C. 1982. *Positivism, Presuppositions and Current Controversies: Theoretical Logic in Society.* Vol. I. Berkeley: University of California Press.

Applegate, R. B. 1978. *Atishwin: The Dream Helper in South-Central California.* Socorro, N.Mex.: Ballena Press.

Arbousset, T., and F. Daumas. 1846. *Narrative of an Exploratory Tour to the North-East to the Colony of the Cape of Good Hope.* Cape Town: A.-S. Robertson.

Asaad, G., and B. Shapiro. 1986. Hallucinations: Theoretical and Clinical Overview. *American Journal of Psychiatry* 143:1088–97.

Bahn, P. G. 1988. Comment on "The Sign of All Times: Entoptic Phenomena in Upper Paleolithic Art," by J. D. Lewis-Williams and T. A. Dowson. *Current Anthropology* 29:217–18.

———. 1998. *The Cambridge Illustrated History of Prehistoric Art.* Cambridge, England: Cambridge University Press.

Barber, T. X. 1970. *LSD, Marihuana, Yoga and Hypnosis.* Chicago: Aldine.

Bard, J. C. 1979. *The Development of a Patination Dating Technique for Great Basin Petroglyphs Utilizing Neutron Activation and X-Ray Fluorescence.* Ph.D. diss. University of California, Berkeley.

Barron, F., M. E. Jarvik, and S. Bunnell. 1965. The Hallucinogenic Drugs. *Scientific American* 210 (4): 29–37.

Bartusiak, M. 1997. Giving Birth to Galaxies. *Discovery* (February): 58–65.

Basedow, H. 1925. *The Australian Aborigines.* Adelaide: Preece and Sons.

Basgall, M. E., W. R. Hildebrandt, and M. C. Hall. 1987. *The Late Holocene Archaeology of Drinkwater Basin, Fort Irwin, San Bernardino County, California.* Report on file, U.S. Army Corps of Engineers, Los Angeles District.

Baumhoff, M. A., R. F. Heizer, and A. B. Elsasser. 1958. *The Largomarsino Petroglyph Group (Site 26-St-1) near Virginia City, Nevada.* Reports of the University of California (Berkeley) Archaeological Survey 43, Part II.

Bean, L. J. 1975. Power and Its Application in Native California. *Journal of California Anthropology* 2 (1):25–33.

———. 1992a. Introduction. In *California Indian Shamanism*, edited by L. J. Bean, 1–6. Menlo Park, Calif.: Ballena Press.

———. 1992b. Power and Its Applications in Native California. In *California Indian Shamanism*, edited by L. J. Bean, 21–32. Menlo Park, Calif.: Ballena Press.

Bean, L. J., and S. B. Vane. 1992. The Shamanic Experience. In *California Indian Shamanism*, edited by L. J. Bean, 7–19. Menlo Park, Calif.: Ballena Press.

Bell, J. A. 1994. Interpretation and Testability in Theories about Prehistoric Thinking. In *The Ancient Mind: Elements of Cognitive Archaeology*, edited by C. Renfrew and E. B. W. Zubrov, 15–21. Cambridge, England: Cambridge University Press.

Benedict, R. F. 1923. *The Concept of the Guardian Spirit in North America.* Memoir No. 29. American Anthropological Association.

Bennett, J. W. 1943. Recent Developments in the Functional Interpretation of Archaeological Data. *American Antiquity* 9:208–19.

Benson, E. P. 1972. *The Mochica. A Culture of Peru.* New York: Praeger.

Benton, J. S. 1978. Dating a Pictograph. *American Indian Rock Art* 4:21–25.

Bernstein, R. J. 1983. *Beyond Objectivism and Relativism: Science, Hermeneutics, and Praxis.* Philadelphia: University of Pennsylvania Press.

Bettinger, R. L. 1982. Archaeology East of the Range of Light: Aboriginal Human Ecology of the Inyo-Mono Region, California. *Monographs in California and Great Basin Anthropology* No. 1. Davis, Calif.: University of California, Davis.

Bettinger, R. L., and M. A. Baumhoff. 1982. The Numic Spread: Great Basin Cultures in Competition. *American Antiquity* 47:485–503.

Binford, L. R. 1962. Archaeology as Anthropology. *American Antiquity* 28:217–25.

———. 1964. A Consideration of Archaeological Research Design. *American Antiquity* 29:425–41.

———. 1965. Archaeological Systematics and the Study of Cultural Process. *American Antiquity* 31:203–10.

———. 1967 Smudge Pits and Hide Smoking: The Use of Analogy in Archaeological Reasoning. *American Antiquity* 32:1–12.

———. 1968. Archaeological Perspectives. In *New Perspectives in Archaeology*, edited by S. R. Binford and L. R. Binford, 5–32. Chicago: Aldine.

———. 1983. *Working at Archaeology.* New York: Academic Press.

———. 1986. In Pursuit of the Future. In *American Archaeology Past and Future: A Celebration of the Society for American Archaeology 1935–1985*, edited by D. J. Meltzer, D. D. Fowler, and J. A. Sabloff, 459–79. Washington, D.C.: Smithsonian Institution.

———. 1987. Data, Relativism and Archaeological Science. *Man* 22:391–404.

Blackburn, T. C. 1975. *December's Child: A Book of Chumash Oral Narratives.* Berkeley: University of California Press.

———. 1977. Biopsychological Aspects of Chumash Rock Art. *Journal of California Anthropology* 4:88–94.

Blacker, H. 1998. Maybe Angels: A Confluence of Imagination and Rational Inquiry. Interview with Rupert Sheldrake. *What is Enlightenment?* 6 (1).

Blanton, R. E. 1976. The Role of Symbiosis in Adaptation and Sociocultural Change in the Valley of Mexico. In *The Valley of Mexico*, edited by E. R. Wolf, 181–202. Albuquerque: University of New Mexico Press.

———. 1978. *Monte Albán: Settlement Patterns at the Ancient Zapotec Capital*. New York: Academic Press.

Bloch, M. 1977. The Past and the Present in the Present. *Man* 12:278–92.

Boas, F. 1927. *Primitive Art*. New York: Dover Publications.

Boas, F., ed. 1938. *General Anthropology*. New York: D. C. Heath and Company.

Bogoras, W. 1902. The Folklore of Northeastern Asia, as Compared with That of Northeastern America. *American Anthropologist*, n.s. 4:577–683.

———. 1904. *The Chukchee*. American Museum of Natural History Memoirs, no. 11. New York: American Museum of Natural History.

Borne, R. F. 1994. Serotonin: The Neurotransmitter for the '90s. *Drug Topics*, 10 October, 108.

Bourguignon, E. 1968. World Distribution and Patterns of Possession States. In *Trance and Possession States*, edited by R. Prince. Montreal: R. M. Bucke Memorial Society.

Boyd, C. E. 1998. Pictographic Evidence of Peyotism in the Lower Pecos, Texas Archaic. In *The Archaeology of Rock-Art*, edited by C. Chippindale and P. S. C. Taçon, pp. 229–46. Cambridge, England: Cambridge University Press.

Bradley, R. 1991. Ritual, Time and History. *World Archaeology* 23:209–19.

Burton, T. M. 1998. Drug Makers' Goal: Prozac without the Lag. *Wall Street Journal*, 27 April.

Caldwell, J. R. 1959. The New American Archaeology. *Science* 129:303–07.

Calvin, W. H. 1992. *How the Shaman Stole the Moon: In Search of Ancient Prophet-Scientists from Stonehenge to the Grand Canyon*. New York: Bantam.

Campbell, T. N. 1958. Origin of the Mescal Bean Cult. *American Anthropologist* 60:156–60.

Carnap, R. 1936. Testability and Meaning. *Philosophy of Science* 3:419–71.

———. 1937. Testability and Meaning. *Philosophy of Science* 4:1–40.

Childe, V. G. 1949. *Social Worlds of Knowledge*. London: Oxford University Press.

Chippindale, C. 1993. Ambition, Deference, Discrepancy, Consumption: The Intellectual Background to a Post-Processual Archaeology. In *Archaeological Theory: Who Sets the Agenda?* edited by N. Yoffee and A. Sherratt, 27–36. Cambridge: Cambridge University Press.

Chippindale, C., and P. S. C. Taçon, eds. 1998. *The Archaeology of Rock-Art*. Cambridge, England: Cambridge University Press.

Claus, E. P., and V. E. Tyler. 1965. *Pharmacognosy*. Philadelphia: Lea and Febiger.

Clendinnen, Inga. 1991. *Aztecs*. Cambridge, England: Cambridge University Press.

Clewlow, C. W., Jr. 1998. The History of California Rock Art Studies: A View from the Coso Range. In *Coso Rock Art: A New Perspective*, edited by E. Younkin, (publication no. 12) 11–26. Ridgecrest, Calif.: Maturango Press.

Clottes, J. 1994. Who Painted What in Upper Paleolithic Caves. In *New Light on Old Art: Recent Advances in Hunter-Gatherer Rock Art Research*, edited by D. S. Whitley and L. L. Loendorf, 1–8. Los Angeles: Institute of Archaeology, University of California.

———. 1996. Epilogue. In *Dawn of Art: The Chauvet Cave*, edited by J.-M. Chauvet, E. B. Deschamps and C. Hillaire, 89–127. New York: Harry N. Abrams.

———. 1998. The 'Three Cs': Fresh Avenues towards European Paleolithic Art. In *The Archaeology of Rock-Art*, edited by C. Chippindale and P. S. C. Taçon, 112–29. Cambridge, England: Cambridge University Press.

Clottes, J., and J. D. Lewis-Williams. 1998. *The Shamans of Prehistory: Trance and Magic in the Painted Caves*. New York: Harry N. Abrams.

Conkey, M. W. 1989. The Structural Analysis of Paleolithic Art. In *Archaeological Thought in America*, edited by C. C. Lamberg-Karlovsky, 135–54. Cambridge, England: Cambridge University Press.

Cook, T. D., and D. T. Campbell. 1986. The Causal Assumptions of Quasi-Experimental Practice. *Synthese* 8:141–80.

Cooper, J. M. 1949. A Cross-Cultural Survey of South American Indian Tribes: Stimulants and Narcotics. In *Handbook of South American Indians*, edited by J. Steward, vol. 5. Washington, D.C.: Smithsonian Institution.

Copi, I. M. 1968. *Introduction to Logic*. New York: MacMillan.

Czaplicka, M. A. 1914. *Aboriginal Siberia*. Oxford: Clarendon Press.

D'Andrade, R. G. 1984. Cultural Meaning Systems. In *Culture Theory: Essays on Mind, Self and Emotion*, edited by R. A. Shweder and R. G. D'Andrade. Cambridge, England: Cambridge University Press.

Davis, W. 1998. *Shadows in the Sun: Travels to Landscapes of Spirit and Desire*. Washington, D.C.: Island Press.

d'Azevedo, W. L., W. A. Davis, D. D. Fowler, and W. Settles, eds. 1966. *The Current Status of Anthropological Research in the Great Basin: 1964*. Desert Research Publications in the Social Sciences and Humanities No. 1. Reno: University of Nevada.

de Borhegyi, S. A. 1961. Miniature Mushroom Stones from Guatemala. *American Antiquity* 26:498–504.

———. 1965. Archaeological Synthesis of the Guatemala Highlands. In *The Handbook of Middle American Indians*, edited by R. Wauchope, vol. 2. Austin: University of Texas Press.

Demarest, A. A. 1987. The Archaeology of Religion. In *The Encyclopedia of Religion*, edited by M. Eliade. New York: MacMillan.

———. 1989. Ideology and Evolution in American Archaeology: Looking beyond the Economic Base. In *Archaeological Thought in America*, edited by C. C. Lamberg-Karlovsky, 89–120. Cambridge: Cambridge University Press.

de Sahugún, Bernadino. 1950. *Florentine Codex: General History of the Things of New Spain*. English translation (1970) by A. J. O. Anderson and C. E. Dibble. Santa Fe, N.Mex.: University of Utah and School of American Research.

Dillehay, T. D., ed. 1997. *Monte Verde, a Late Pleistocene Settlement in Chile: The Archaeological Context and Interpretation*, vol. II. Washington, D.C.: Smithsonian Institution.

Dobkin de Rios, M. 1968. Folk Curing with a Psychedelic Cactus in Northern Peru. *International Journal of Social Psychiatry* 15:23–32.

———. 1972. *Visionary Vine: Psychedelic Healing in the Peruvian Amazon*. San Francisco: Chandler.

———. 1974. The Influence of Psychoactive Flora and Fauna on Maya Religion. *Current Anthropology* 15:147–64.

———. 1977. Plant Hallucinogens and the Religion of the Mochica—An Ancient Peruvian People. *Economic Botany* 31:189–203.

———. 1982. Plant Hallucinogens, Sexuality and Shamanism in the Ceramic Art of Peru. *Journal of Psychoactive Drugs* 14:81–90.

———. 1996. *Hallucinogens: Cross-Cultural Perspectives*. Prospect Heights, Ill.: Waveland Press.

Dobkin de Rios, M., and D. E. Smith. 1977. Drug Use and Abuse Cross-Cultural Perspective. *Human Organization* 36:15–21.

Donnan, C. B. 1976. *Moche Art and Iconography.* UCLA Latin American Series, vol. 33. Los Angeles: University of California, Los Angeles.

————. 1992. *Ceramics of Ancient Peru.* Fowler Museum of Cultural History, University of California. Los Angeles: University of California.

Dorn, R. I. 1986. Rock Varnish as an Indicator of Aeolian Environmental Change. In *Aeolian Geomorphology,* edited by W. G. Nickling, 291–307. London: Allen & Unwin.

————. 1994. Dating Petroglyphs with a Three-Tier Rock Varnish Approach. In *New Light on Old Art: Recent Advances in Hunter-Gatherer Rock Art Research,* edited by D. S. Whitley and L. L. Loendorf, 13–36. Los Angeles: Institute of Archaeology, University of California.

————. 1998. Age Determination of the Coso Rock Art. In *Coso Rock Art: A New Perspective,* edited by E. Younkin, 69–96. Ridgecrest, Calif.: Maturango Press.

Dorn, R. I., and D. S. Whitley. 1983. Cation-Ratio Dating of Petroglyphs from the Western Great Basin. *Nature* 302:816–18.

————. 1984. Chronometric and Relative Age Determination of Petroglyphs in the Western United States. *Annals of the Association of American Geographers* 74(2):308–22.

Douglass, A. A. 1997. *Cracking the Secret Code: Deciphering Rock Art.* Archaeology and Public Education. Vol. 7, no. 3. Los Angeles: University of California.

Driver, H. E. 1937. Cultural Element Distributions, VI. Southern Sierra Nevada. *University of California Anthropological Records* 1:35–154.

Duffield, W. A., and G. I. Smith. 1978. Pleistocene History of Volcanism and the Owens River near Little Lake, California. *Journal of Research, U. S. Geological Survey* 6:395–408.

Dugan, G. M., M. R. Gumbmann, and M. Friedman. 1989. Toxicological Evaluation of Jimson Weed (*Datura stramonium*) Seed. *Food and Chemical Toxicology* 27:501–10.

Dunnell, R. C. 1982. Science, Social Science and Common Sense: The Agonizing Dilemma of Modern Archaeology. *Journal of Anthropological Research* 38:1–25.

Eagleton, T. 1983. *Literary Theory.* Minneapolis: University of Minnesota Press.

Earle, T. K. 1994. Preface. In *New Light on Old Art: Recent Advances in Hunter-Gatherer Rock Art Research,* edited by D. S. Whitley and L. L. Loendorf, vii–viii. Los Angeles: Institute of Archaeology, University of California.

Earle, T. K., and R. W. Preucel. 1987. Archaeology and the Radical Critique. *Current Anthropology* 28:501–38.

Eliade, M. 1958. *Rites and Symbols of Initiation: The Mysteries of Birth and Rebirth.* New York: Harper Colophon.

————. 1964. *Shamanism: Archaic Techniques of Ecstasy.* Princeton: Princeton University Press.

Fagan, B. M. 1991. *In the Beginning: An Introduction to Archaeology.* New York: HarperCollins.

Farmer, M. F. 1955. Awoti Bows. *Plateau* 28 (1). Flagstaff: Museum of Northern Arizona.

Farnsworth, N. R. 1968. Hallucinogenic Plants. *Science* 162:1086–92.

Flannery, K. V. 1973. The Origins of Agriculture. *Annual Review of Anthropology* 2:271–310.

Flannery, K. V., and J. Marcus. 1976. Oaxaca and the Zapotec Cosmos. *American Scientist* 64:374–83.

————. 1993. Cognitive Archaeology. *Cambridge Archaeological Journal* 3:260–67.

Fowler, D. D. 1980. History of Great Basin Anthropological Research, 1776–1979. *Journal of California and Great Basin Anthropology* 2 (1): 8–36.

Fried, M. H. 1975. *The Notion of Tribe.* Menlo Park, Calif.: Cummings.

Freidel, D. A., and L. Schele. 1988. Kingship and the Late Preclassic Lowlands: The Instruments and Places of Ritual Power. *American Anthropologist* 90:547–67.

Frison, G., and B. Bradley. 1999. *The Fenn Cache: Clovis Weapons and Tools*. Santa Fe, N.Mex.: One Horse Land and Cattle Company.

Furst, P. T. 1972. To Find Our Life: Peyote among the Huichol Indians of Mexico. In *Flesh of the Gods: The Ritual Use of Hallucinogens*, edited by P. T. Furst, 136–84. London: Allen and Unwin.

———. 1973. West Mexican Art: Secular or Sacred? In *The Iconography of Middle American Sculpture*, 98–133. New York: The Metropolitan Museum of Art.

———. 1977. The Roots and Continuities of Shamanism. In *Stones, Bones and Skin: Ritual and Shamanic Art*, edited by A. T. Brodzy, R. Daneswich, and N. Johnson, 1–28. Toronto: The Society for Art Publications.

———. 1982. *Hallucinogens and Culture*. Novato, Calif.: Chandler and Sharp.

———. 1990. Introduction. In *The Flesh of the Gods: The Ritual Use of Hallucinogens* (1972 reissue), edited by P. T. Furst, vii–xxviii. Prospect Heights, Ill.: Waveland Press.

Furst, P. T., and M. D. Coe. 1977. Ritual Enemas. *Natural History* 86:88–91.

Gardner, H. 1985. *The Mind's New Science: A History of the Cognitive Revolution*. 2nd ed. New York: Basic Books.

Garfinkel, A. P. 1978. "Coso" Style Pictographs of the Southern Sierra Nevada. *Journal of California Anthropology* 5:95–101.

Gargett, R. H. 1989. Grave Shortcomings: The Evidence for Neanderthal Burial. *Current Anthropology* 30:157–90.

Garrett, S., and D. K. Statnekov. 1977. Peruvian Whistling Bottles. *Journal of the Acoustical Society of America* 62:449–55.

Gayton, A. H. 1930. Yokuts—Mono Chiefs and Shamans. *University of California Publications in American Archaeology and Ethnology* (Berkeley) 24:361–420.

———. 1948. Yokuts and Western Mono Ethnography. *Anthropological Records* 10:1–290.

Giddens, A., and J. H. Turner. 1987. Introduction, In *Social Theory Today*, edited by A. Giddens and J. H. Turner. Stanford: Stanford University Press.

Gifford, E. W. 1932. The Northfork Mono. *University of California Publications in American Archaeology and Ethnology* (Berkeley) 31(2):15–65.

Gilman, A. 1987. Comment on "Archaeology and the Radical Critique" by T. K. Earle and R. W. Preucel. *Current Anthropology* 28:501–38.

Gilreath, A. J., M. E. Basgall, and M. C. Hall. 1987. Compendium of Chronologically Indicative Data from Fort Irwin Archaeological Sites. Draft report on file, U.S. Army Corps of Engineers, Los Angeles.

Goldman, I. 1963. *The Cubeo Indians of the Northwest Amazon*. Illinois Studies in Anthropology 2. Urbana: University of Illinois Press.

Goodspeed, T. 1954. *The Genus Nicotiana*. Waltham, Mass.: Chronica Botanica.

Goss, J. A. 1977. Linguistic Tools for the Great Basin Historian. *University of Nevada Publications in the Social Sciences* 12:49–70. Reno: University of Nevada Press.

Grant, C. 1965. *The Rock Paintings of the Chumash*. Berkeley: University of California Press.

———. 1967. *Rock Art of the American Indian*. New York: Promontory Press.

Grant, C., J. W. Baird, and J. K. Pringle. 1968. *Rock Drawings of the Coso Range, Inyo County, California*. No. 4. Ridgecrest, Calif.: Maturango Press.

Grim, J. A. 1983. *The Shaman: Patterns of Religious Healing among the Ojibway Indians*. Norman: University of Oklahoma Press.

Grosscup, G. L. 1960. The Cultural History of Lovelock Cave, Nevada. *University of California Archaeological Survey* no. 52. Berkeley: University of California.

Gundrum, D. S. 2000. Fabric of Time. *Archaeology*, March/April, 46–51.

Halifax, J. 1982. *Shamanism: The Wounded Healer*. New York: Crossroad.

Hamayon, R. N. 1994. Shamanism in Siberia: From Partnership in Supernature to Counter-Power in Society. In *Shamanism, History, and the State*, edited by N. Thomas and C. Humphrey, 76–89. Ann Arbor: University of Michigan Press.

Harner, M. J. 1972. *The Jivaro: People of the Sacred Waterfall*. New York: Anchor.

———. 1973a. Preface. In *Hallucinogens and Shamanism*, edited by M. J. Harner, vii–viii. New York: Oxford University Press.

———. 1973b. In Cultures Undergoing Westernization. In *Hallucinogens and Shamanism*, edited by M. J. Harner, 49–52. New York: Oxford University Press.

———. 1973c. In the Primitive World: The Upper Amazon. In *Hallucinogens and Shamanism*, edited by M. J. Harner, 1–7. New York: Oxford University Press.

———. 1973d. The Role of Hallucinogenic Plants in European Witchcraft. In *Hallucinogens and Shamanism*, edited by M. J. Harner, 125–50. New York: Oxford University Press.

———. 1981. *The Way of the Shaman: A Guide to Power and Healing*. New York: Harper and Row.

Harrington, M. R. 1957. A Pinto Site at Little Lake, California. *Southwest Museum Papers*, no. 17. Highland Park, Calif.: Anderson, Ritchie & Simon.

Harris, M. 1964. *The Nature of Cultural Things*. New York: Random House.

———. 1968. *The Rise of Anthropological Theory*. New York: Crowell.

———. 1974. *Cows, Pigs, Wars and Witches: The Riddles of Culture*. New York: Random House.

———. 1977. *Cannibals and Kings: The Origins of Cultures*. New York: Random House.

———. 1979. *Cultural Materialism: The Struggle for a Science of Culture*. New York: Random House.

Hawking, S. W. 1988. *A Brief History of Time: From the Big Bang to Black Holes*. New York: Bantam Books.

Hawkins, M. 1997. *Hunting Down the Universe: The Missing Mass, Primordial Black Holes, and Other Dark Matters*. New York: Addison-Wesley.

Hayden, B. 1993. The Cultural Capacity of Neanderthals: A Review and Re-evaluation. *Journal of Human Evolution* 24:113–46.

Hedges, K. 1976. Southern California Rock Art as Shamanic Art. *American Indian Rock Art* 2:126–38. El Paso, Tex.: El Paso Archaeological Society.

———. 1982. Phosphenes in the Context of Native American Rock Art. In *American Indian Rock Art* vols. 7–8, edited by F. G. Bock, 1–10. El Toro, Calif.: American Rock Art Research Association.

———. 1983. The Shamanic Origins of Rock Art. In *Ancient Images on Stone: Rock Art in the Californians*, edited by J. A. Van Tilburg, 46–61. Los Angeles: UCLA Institute of Archaeology, Rock Art Archive.

———. 1992. Shamanistic Aspects of California Rock Art. In *California Indian Shamanism*, edited by L. J. Bean, 67–88. Menlo Park, Calif.: Ballena Press.

Heinze, R-I. 1986. More on Mental Imagery and Shamanism. *Current Anthropology* 27:154.

Heizer, R. F., and M. A. Baumhoff. 1959. Great Basin Petroglyphs and Game Trails. *Science* 129:904–5.

———. 1962. *Prehistoric Rock Art of Nevada and Eastern California*. Berkeley: University of California Press.

Heizer, R. F., and C. W. Clewlow, Jr. 1973. *Prehistoric Rock Art of California*. Socorro, N.Mex.: Ballena Press.

Hempel, C. G. 1962. Deductive-Nomological vs. Statistical Explanation. In *Scientific Explanation, Space, and Time*, edited by H. Feigl and G. Maxwell, 98–169. Minneapolis: University of Minnesota Press.

———. 1965. *Aspects of Scientific Explanation*. New York: Free Press.

———. 1966. *Philosophy of Natural Science*. New York: Prentice-Hall.

Hempel, C. G., and P. Oppenheim. 1948. Studies in the Logic of Explanation. *Philosophy of Science* 15:135–75.

Henry, T. A. 1949. *The Plant Alkaloids*. London: J. & A. Churchill.

Hesse, E. 1946. *Narcotics and Drug Addiction*. New York: Philosophical Library.

Hill, J. N. 1972. The Methodological Debate in Contemporary Archaeology. In *Models in Archaeology*, edited by D. L. Clarke, 61–107. London: Methuen and Company.

———. 1977. Systems Theory and the Explanation of Change. In *Explanation of Prehistoric Change*, edited by J. N. Hill, 59–103. Albuquerque: University of New Mexico Press.

———. 1994. Prehistoric Cognition and the Science of Archaeology. In *The Ancient Mind: Elements of Cognitive Archaeology*, edited by C. Renfrew and E. B. W. Zubrov, 83–92. Cambridge: Cambridge University Press.

Hodder, I. 1982. Theoretical Archaeology: A Reactionary View. In *Symbolic and Structural Archaeology*, edited by I. Hodder, 162–67. Cambridge: Cambridge University Press.

———. 1983. *The Present Past: An Introduction to Anthropology for Archaeologists*. New York: Pica Press.

———. 1984. Archaeology in 1984. *Antiquity* 58:25–32.

———. 1985. Postprocessual Archaeology. In *Advances in Archaeological Method and Theory*, vol. 8, edited by M. Schiffer, 1–26. Orlando, Fla.: Academic Press.

———. 1986. *Reading the Past: Current Approaches to Interpretation in Archaeology*. Cambridge: Cambridge University Press.

———. 1987. Foreword. In *Re-constructing Archaeology: Theory and Practice*, edited by M. Shanks and C. Tilley. Cambridge: Cambridge University Press.

———. 1991. Postprocessual Archaeology and the Current Debate. In *Processual and Postprocessual Archaeologies: Multiple Ways of Knowing the Past*, edited by R. Preucel, 30–41. Occasional Paper No. 10. Carbondale: Center for Archaeological Investigations, Southern Illinois University.

Hoffer, A., and H. Osmund. 1967. *The Hallucinogens*. New York: Academic Press.

Hofmann, A. 1959. Psychotomimetic Drugs, Chemical and Pharmacological Aspects. *Acta Physiol. Pharmachol Neerl.* 8:240–58.

———. 1963 The Active Principles of the Seeds of *Rivea corymbosa* and *Ipomoea violacea*. *Botanical Museum Leaflets* XX:194–212. Cambridge, Mass.: Harvard University.

Holland, J. 1997. Conference Highlights: Hallucinogenic Drugs in Experimental Psychiatric Research.Vaals, Netherlands. March 13–15.

Horowitz, M. J. 1964. The Imagery of Visual Hallucinations. *Journal of Nervous and Mental Disease* 138:513–23.

———. 1975. Hallucinations: An Information-Processing Approach. In *Hallucinations: Behaviour, Experience and Theory*, edited by R. K. Siegel and L. J. West, 163–95. New York: Wiley.

Hotz, R. L. 1998. Seeking the Biology of Spirituality. *Los Angeles Times* 26 April, A1, 32.

Hubble, E. P. 1936. *The Realm of the Nebulae*. New Haven, Conn.: Yale University Press.

Huffman, T. N. 1986. Cognitive Studies of the Iron Age in South Africa. *World Archaeology* 18: 84–95.

Hulkrantz, A. 1979. *The Religions of the American Indian.* Berkeley: University of California Press.

———. 1987. *Native Religions of North America: The Power of Visions and Fertility.* San Francisco: Harper and Row.

Hunt, S. D. 1990. Truth in Marketing Theory and Research. *Journal of Marketing* 54:1–15.

Ingold, T. 1984. Timescales, Social Relationships and the Exploitation of Animals: Anthropological Reflections on Prehistory. In *Animals and Archaeology: 3, Early Herders and Their Flocks*, edited by J. Clutton-Brock and C. Grigson, 3–12. Oxford: British Archaeological Reports.

Irwin, C. N., ed. 1980. *The Shoshone Indians of Inyo County, California: The Kerr Manuscript.* Ballena Press Publications in Archaeology, Ethnography, and History 15. Socorro, N.Mex.: Ballena Press.

Jacobs, B. L. 1987. How Hallucinogenic Drugs Work. *American Scientist* 75:387–90.

Jenkins, D. L. and C. N. Warren. 1984. Obsidian Hydration and the Pinto Chronology in the Mojave Desert. *Journal of California and Great Basin Anthropology* 6(1): 44–60.

Jennings, J. D. 1964. The Desert West. In *Prehistoric Man in the New World*, edited by J. D. Jennings and E. Norbeck, 149–74. Chicago: University of Chicago Press.

Jennings, J. D., and E. Norbeck. 1955. Great Basin Prehistory: A Review. *American Antiquity* 21:1–11.

Jochelson, W. 1905. *The Koryak.* American Museum of Natural History Memoirs, no. 10. New York: American Museum of Natural History.

———. 1924. *The Yukaghir and Yukaghirized Tungus.* American Museum of Natural History Memoirs, no. 13. New York: American Museum of Natural History.

Johnston, P. 1933. Prehistoric Pageantry in Stone. *Touring Topics* 28 (11).

Kalweit, H. 1984. *Dreamtime and Inner Space: The World of the Shaman.* Boston: Shambhala.

Katz, F., and M. Dobkin de Rios. 1971. Hallucinogenic Music: An Analysis of the Role of Whistling in Peruvian Ayahuasca Healing Sessions. *Journal of American Folklore* 84:333–36.

Katz, R. 1982. *Boiling Energy: Community Healing among the Kalahari !Kung.* Cambridge, England: Cambridge University Press.

Kaufmann, F. 1976. *El Peru Arqueológico.* Lima, Peru: Ediciones Kompaktos.

Kehoe, A. B. 2000. *Shamans and Religion: An Anthropological Exploration in Critical Thinking.* Prospect Heights, Ill.: Waveland Press.

Kelly, I. T. 1932. Ethnography of the Surprise Valley Paiutes. *University of California Papers in American Archaeology and Ethnology* (Berkeley) 31(3):67–210.

———. 1936. Chemehuevi Shamanism. In *Essays in Anthropology, Presented to A. L. Kroeber in Celebration of His Sixtieth Birthday*, (no editor), 129–42. Berkeley: University of California Press.

———. 1939. Southern Paiute Shamanism. *University of California Anthropological Records* 2(4):151–167.

Kelley, J. C. 1950. Atlatls, Bows and Arrows, Pictographs and the Pecos River Focus. *American Antiquity* 16:71–74.

Kelley, J. H., and M. P. Hanen. 1988. *Archaeology and the Methodology of Science.* Albuquerque: University of New Mexico Press.

Kidder, A. V. 1924. *An Introduction to the Study of Southwestern Archaeology.* Papers of the Southwestern Expedition, Phillips Academy, no. 1. New Haven, Conn.: Yale University Press.

Kirchner, H. 1952. An Archaeological Contribution to the Early History of Shamanism. *Anthropos* 47:244–86.

Kirkland, F., and W. W. Newcomb, Jr. 1967. *The Rock Art of Texas Indians.* Austin: University of Texas Press.

Kluckhohn, C. 1940. The Conceptual Structure in Middle American Studies. In *The Maya and Their Neighbors,* edited by C. L. Hay et al., 41–51. New York: Appleton-Century.

Klüver, H. 1926. Mescal Visions and Eidetic Vision. *American Journal of Psychology* 37:502–15.

———. 1942. Mechanisms of Hallucinations. In *Studies in Personality,* edited by Q. McNemar and M. A. Merrill, 175–207. New York: McGraw-Hill.

———. 1966 *Mescal and Mechanisms of Hallucination.* Chicago: University of Chicago Press.

Knoll, M., J. Kruger, O. Höfer, and S. D. Lawder. 1963. Effects of Chemical Stimulation of Electrically Induced Phosphenes on Their Bandwidth, Shape, Number, and Intensity. *Confinia Neurologica* 23:201–26.

Kohl, P. L. 1993. Limits of a Post-processual Archaeology (or, The Dangers of a New Scholasticism). In *Archaeological Theory: Who Sets the Agenda?* edited by N. Yoffee and A. Sherratt, 13–19. Cambridge: Cambridge University Press.

Kroeber, A. L. 1907. Indian Myths of South Central California. *University of California Publications in American Archaeology and Ethnology* (Berkeley) 4(4):169–250.

———. 1925. Handbook of the Indians of California. *Bureau of American Ethnology, Bulletin* 78. Washington, D.C.: Smithsonian Institution.

Krupp, E. C. 1997. *Skywatchers, Shamans and Kings: Astronomy and the Archaeology of Power.* New York: John Wiley & Sons.

La Barre, W. 1970. Old and New World Narcotics: A Statistical Question and an Ethnological Reply. *Economic Botany* 24:368–72.

———. 1972. Hallucinogens and the Shamanic Origins of Religion. In *Flesh of the Gods: The Ritual Use of Hallucinogens,* edited by P. T. Furst, 261–78. London: Allen and Unwin.

———. 1980. *Culture in Context.* Durham, N.C.: Duke University Press.

———. 1989. *The Peyote Cult.* Norman: University of Oklahoma Press.

Lakatos, I. 1969. Criticism and the Logic of Scientific Research Programmes. *Proceedings of the Aristotelian Society* 69:149–86.

Lamb, F. B. 1985. *Rio Tigre and Beyond: The Amazon Jungle Medicine of Manuel Cordova.* Berkeley: North Atlantic Books.

Lamb, S. M. 1958. Linguistic Prehistory in the Great Basin. *International Journal of American Linguistics* 24:95–100.

Lamberg-Karlovsky, C. C. 1989. Introduction. In *Archaeological Thought in America,* edited by C. C. Lamberg-Karlovsky, 1–16. Cambridge: Cambridge University Press.

Landau, L. 1984. *Science and Values.* Berkeley: University of California Press.

Laufer, B. 1913. Remarks. *American Anthropologist* 15:573–77.

———. 1917. Origin of the Word "Shaman." *American Anthropologist* 19:362–63.

Leach, E. R. 1973. Concluding Address. In *The Explanation of Culture Change: Models in Prehistory,* edited by A. C. Renfrew, 761–71. London: Duckworth.

Lee, G. 1979. The San Emigdio Rock Art Site. *Journal of California and Great Basin Anthropology* I (2):295–305.

———. 1997. Review of "A Survey and Analysis of Prehistoric Rock Art of the Warner Valley Region, Lake County, Oregon" by M. Ricks. *Journal of California and Great Basin Anthropology* 19(2):297–300.

Leone, M. 1982. Some Opinions about Recovering Mind. *American Antiquity* 47:742–60.

Leroi-Gourhan, André. 1965. *Treasures of Paleolithic Art.* New York: Abrams.

———. 1982. *The Dawn of European Art.* Cambridge, England: Cambridge University Press.

———. 1986. The Religion of the Caves: Magic or Metaphysic? Translated from the French by A. Michelson. *October* 37:7–17.

Leroi-Gourhan, Arlette. 1975. The Flowers Found with Shanidar IV, a Neanderthal Burial in Iraq. *Science* 190:562–64.

———. 1989. Comment on Grave Shortcomings: The Evidence for Neanderthal Burial. *Current Anthropology* 30:157–90.

LeVine, R. A. 1984. Properties of Culture: An Ethnographic View. In *Culture Theory: Essays on Mind, Self and Emotion,* edited by R. A. Shweder and R. A. LeVine, 67–87. Cambridge: Cambridge University Press.

Lewin, L. 1964. *Phantastica, Narcotic and Stimulating Drugs: Their Use and Abuse.* Translated from the 2nd German edition by P. H. A. Wirth. New York: E. P. Dutton.

Lewis-Williams, J. D. 1980. Ethnography and Iconography: Aspects of Southern San Thought and Art. *Man,* n.s. 15:467–82.

———. 1981. *Believing and Seeing: Symbolic Meaning in Southern San Rock Paintings.* London: Academic Press.

———. 1982. The Economic and Social Context of Southern San Art. *Current Anthropology* 23:429–48.

———. 1983a. Introductory Essay: Science and Rock Art. In *New Approaches to Southern African Rock Art,* edited by J. D. Lewis-Williams, 3–13. Goodwin Series, no. 4. Cape Town: South African Archaeological Society.

———. 1983b. *Rock Art of Southern Africa.* Cambridge, England: Cambridge University Press.

———. 1984. Ideological Continuities in Prehistoric Southern Africa: The Evidence of Rock Art. In *Past and Present in Hunter Gatherer Studies,* edited by C. Schrire, 225–51. New York: Academic Press.

———. 1985. The San Artistic Achievement. *African Arts* 18(3):54–59.

———. 1986. Cognitive and Optical Illusions in San Rock Art. *Current Anthropology* 27:171–78.

———. 1987. A Dream of Eland: An Unexplored Component of San Shamanism and Rock Art. *World Archaeology* 19:165–76.

———. 1991. Wrestling with Analogy: A Methodological Dilemma in Upper Paleolithic Art Research. *Proceedings of the Prehistoric Society* 57(1):149–62.

Lewis-Williams, J. D., and T. A. Dowson. 1988. The Signs of All Times: Entoptic Phenomena and Upper Paleolithic Art. *Current Anthropology* 29:201–45.

———. 1989. *Images of Power: Understanding Bushman Rock Art.* Johannesburg: Southern Book Publishers.

———. 1990. Through the Veil: San Rock Paintings and the Rock Face. *South African Archaeological Bulletin* 45:5–16.

Lewis-Williams, J. D., and J. H. N. Loubser. 1986. Deceptive Appearances: A Critique of Southern African Rock Art Studies. *Advances in World Archaeology* 5:253–89.

Lincoln, Y. S., and E. G. Guba. 1985. *Naturalistic Inquiry.* Newbury Park, Calif.: Sage.

Liu, T., and R. I. Dorn. 1996. Understanding the Spatial Variability of Environmental Change in Drylands with Rock Varnish Laminations. *Annals of the Association of American Geographers* 86(2):187–212.

Liversidge, A. F. 1995. The Limits of Science. *The Cultural Studies Times*, Fall.

Lommel, A. 1967. *Shamanism: The Beginnings of Art*. New York: McGraw-Hill.

Lowie, R. 1924. Notes on Shoshonean Ethnography. *Anthropological Papers, American Museum of Natural History* (New York) 20:185–314.

———. 1925. *The Crow Indians*. New York: Farrar & Rinehart.

———. 1948. *Primitive Religion*. New York: Liveright.

Lumholtz, C. 1900. *Symbolism of the Huichol Indians*. American Museum of Natural History Memoirs I, no. 2. New York: American Museum of Natural History.

Mallery, G. 1893. *Picture-Writing of the American Indians*. Tenth Annual Report of the Bureau of American Ethnology, Washington, D.C.

Marcus, J. 1983. A Synthesis of the Cultural Evolution of the Zapotec and Mixtec. In *The Cloud People*, edited by K. V. Flannery and J. Marcus, 355–60. New York: Academic Press.

Martin, P. S., C. Lloyd, and A. Spoehr. 1938. Archaeological Work in the Ackmen-Lowry Area, Southwestern Colorado, 1937. *Field Museum of Natural History, Anthropological Series* 23:217–304. Chicago: Field Museum of Natural History.

Martin, P. S., and J. Rinaldo. 1939. Modified Basketmaker Sites, Ackmen-Lowry Area, Southwestern Colorado, 1938. *Field Museum of Natural History, Anthropological Series* 23:305–499. Chicago: Field Museum of Natural History.

Masters, R. E. L., and J. Houston. 1966. *The Varieties of Psychedelic Experience*. New York: Dell.

McGuire, R. H., and B. J. Saitta. 1963. Although They Have Petty Captains, They Obey Them Badly: The Dialectics of Prehispanic Western Pueblo Social Organization. *American Antiquity* 61:197–213.

Meyerhoff, B. G. 1968. *The Deer-Maize-Peyote Complex among the Huichol Indians of Mexico*. Ph.D. diss. University of California, Los Angeles.

Michelson, A. 1986. In Praise of Horizontality: André Leroi-Gourhan 1911–1986. *October* 37:3–5.

Miller, D., and C. Tilley, eds. 1984. *Ideology, Power, and Prehistory*. Cambridge: Cambridge University Press.

Miller, J. 1983. Basin Religion and Theology: A Comparative Study of Power (*Puha*). *Journal of California and Great Basin Anthropology* 5:66–86.

Mithen, S. 1994. From Domain Specific to Generalized Intelligence: A Cognitive Interpretation of the Middle/Upper Paleolithic. In *The Ancient Mind: Elements of Cognitive Archaeology*, edited by C. Renfrew and E. B. W. Zubrow, 29–39. Cambridge: Cambridge University Press.

Molyneaux, B. L. 1977. Formalism and Contextualism: An Historiography of Rock Art Research in the New World. M.A. thesis, Department of Anthropology, Trent University, Petersborough, Ontario, Canada.

Monks, G. G. 1981. Seasonality Studies. *Advances in Archaeological Method and Theory* 4:177–240.

Morris, E. H. 1936. *Archaeological Background of Dates in Early Arizona Chronology*. The Ring Bulletin, vol. 2, no. 4, 34–36. Tucson: University of Arizona.

Morwood, M. J., and C. E. Smith. 1996. Contemporary Approaches to World Rock Art. <http://www.unc.edu.au/Arch/RockArt/MMRockArt.html>

Mulvaney, J., and J. Kamminga. 1999. *Prehistory of Australia*. Washington, D.C.: Smithsonian Institution.

Munz, P. A., and D. D. Keck. 1959. *A California Floral and Supplement*. Berkeley: University of California Press.

Naranjo, C. 1973. Psychological Aspects of the Yage Experience in an Experimental Setting. In *Hallucinogens and Shamanism*, edited by M. J. Harner, 176–90. New York: Oxford University Press.

Newberg, A. B., E. G. d'Aquili, and V. Rause. 2001. *God Won't Go Away: Brain Science and the Biology of Religion*. New York: Ballantine.

Nietzsche, F. W. 1966. *Beyond Good and Evil: Prelude to a Philosophy of the Future*. Translated by W. Kaufmann. New York: Vintage Books.

Noll, R. 1985. Mental Imagery Cultivation as a Cultural Phenomenon: The Role of Visions in Shamanism. *Current Anthropology* 26:443–61.

Orpen, J. M. 1874. A Glimpse into the Mythology of the Maluti Bushmen. *Cape Monthly Magazine* (n.s.) 9(49):1–13.

Ortner, S. B. 1984. Theory in Anthropology since the Sixties. *Comparative Studies of Society and History* 26:126–66.

Osgood, C. B. 1951. Culture: Its Empirical and Non-Empirical Character. *Southwestern Journal of Anthropology* 7:202–14.

Oster, G. 1970. Phosphenes. *Scientific American* 222(2):82–87.

Ouzman, S. 1998. Toward a Mindscape of Landscape: Rock-Art as Expression of World Understanding. In *The Archaeology of Rock-Art*, edited by C. Chippindale and P. S. C. Taçon, 30–41. Cambridge, England: Cambridge University Press.

Park, W. Z. 1938. *Shamanism in Western North America: A Study in Cultural Relationships*. Northwestern University Studies in the Social Sciences, no. 2. Evanston, Ill.: Northwestern University Press.

Phillips, P. 1955. American Archaeology and General Anthropological Theory. *Southwestern Journal of Anthropology* 11:246–50.

Porta, G. B. 1957. *Naturall Magick*. Translated from the expurgated 1589 Italian edition. Reproduction of the 1658 English edition. New York: Basic Books.

Porush, D. 1993. Finding God. *Omni*, October: 27–29.

Radin, P. 1914. Religion of the North American Indians. *Journal of American Folklore* 27:335–73.

Ramachandran, V. S., and S. Blakeslee. 1999. *Phantoms in the Brain: Probing the Mysteries of the Human Mind*. New York: Quill.

Raphaël, M. 1945. *Prehistoric Cave Paintings*. New York: Pantheon.

Read, G. W., and R. Gaines eds. 1949. *Gold Rush: The Journals, Drawings and Other Papers of J. Goldsborough Bruff*. New York: Columbia University Press.

Redman, C. L. 1991. Distinguished Lecture in Archaeology: In Defense of the Seventies—The Adolescence of New Archaeology. *American Anthropologist* 93:295–307.

Reichel-Dolmatoff, G. 1972. The Cultural Context of an Aboriginal Hallucination: *Banisteriopsis Caapi*. In *Flesh of the Gods: The Ritual Use of Hallucinogens*, edited by P. T. Furst, 84–113. London: Allen and Unwin.

———. 1978. *Beyond the Milky Way: Hallucinatory Imagery of the Tukano Indians*. Los Angeles: UCLA Latin American Center.

———. 1979a. Some Source Materials on Desana Shamanistic Initiation. *Antropológica* 51:27–61.

———. 1979b. Desana Shaman's Rock Crystals and the Hexagonal Universe. *Journal of Latin American Lore* 5:117–28.

———. 1987. *Shamanism and the Art of the Eastern Tukanoan Indians, Colombian Northwest Amazon*. Leiden: Institute of Religious Iconography, State University of Groningen.

Reinhard, J. 1975. Shamanism and Spirit Possession. In *Spirit Possession in the Nepal Himalayas*, edited by J. Hitchcock and R. Jones, 12–18. Warminster, England: Aris and Phillips.

Renfrew, C. 1989. Comments on "Archaeology into the 1990s" by M. Shanks and C. Tilley. *Norwegian Archaeological Review* 22:33–41.

———. 1994. Towards a Cognitive Archaeology. In *The Ancient Mind: Elements of Cognitive Archaeology*, edited by C. Renfrew and E. B. W. Zubrow, 3–12. Cambridge: Cambridge University Press.

Richards, W. 1971. The Fortification Illusions of Migraines. *Scientific American* 224:89–94.

Ricks, M. 1996. *A Survey and Analysis of Prehistoric Rock Art of the Warner Valley Region, Lake County, Oregon*. Department of Anthropology Technical Report, 91–96. Reno: University of Nevada.

Ripinsky, M. 1975. Cultural Idiom as an Ecologic Factor: Two Studies. *Anthropos* 70 (4–5): 449–60.

Ripinsky-Naxon, M. 1989. Hallucinogens, Shamanism, and the Cultural Process: Symbolic Archaeology and Dialectics. *Anthropos* 84:219–224.

———. 1993. *The Nature of Shamanism: Substance and Function of a Religious Metaphor*. Albany: State University of New York Press.

Ritter, D. W., and E. W. Ritter. 1977. The Influence of the Religious Formulator in Rock Art of North America. In *American Indian Rock Art*, vol. 3, edited by A. J. Bock, F. Bock, and J. Cawley, 63–79. El Toro, Calif.: American Rock Art Research Association.

Ritter, E. W., R. Brook, and N. Farrell. 1982. The Rock Art of Panamint City, Inyo County, California. In *Pictographs of the Coso Region: Analysis and Interpretation of the Coso Painted Style*, edited by R. A. Schiffman, D. S. Whitley, A. P. Garfinkel, and S. B. Andrews, 5–21. Bakersfield, Calif.: Bakersfield College Publications in Archaeology 2.

Roark, P. R. 1965. From Monumental to Proliferous in Nazca Pottery. *Nawpa Pacha* 3:1–92.

Roth, W. E. 1901. *Food: Its Search, Capture and Preparation*. North Queensland Ethnography Bulletin 3. Brisbane.

Rowe, J. H. 1961. La Arqueología de Ica. *Revista del Museo Regional de Ica* 12:29–48.

Sabloff, J. A., T. W. Beale, and A. M. Kurland. 1973. Recent Developments in Archaeology. *American Academy of Political and Social Sciences* 408:103–18.

Sacks, O. W. 1970. *Migraine: The Evolution of a Common Disorder*. London: Faber.

Safford, W. E. 1916. Narcotic Plants and Stimulants of the Ancient Americas. *Annual Report*. Washington, D.C.: Smithsonian Institution.

Salmon, M. H. 1975. Confirmation and Explanation in Archaeology. *American Antiquity* 40:459–64.

———. 1976. "Deductive" versus "Inductive" Archaeology. *American Antiquity* 44:376–380.

———. 1982. *Philosophy and Archaeology*. New York: Academic Press.

Samorini, G. 1992. The Oldest Representations of Hallucinogenic Mushrooms in the World (Sahara Desert 9000–7000 B.P.). *Integration* (2–3):69–78.

Sanders, W. T. 1994. Chiefdom to State: Political Evolution at Kaminaljuyu, Guatemala. In *Reconstructing Complex Societies: An Archaeological Colloquium*, edited by C. B. Moore, Supplement to the Bulletin of the American Schools of Oriental Research 20:97–121.

Sanders, W. T., and B. J. Price. 1968. *Mesoamerica: The Evolution of Civilization*. New York: Random House.

Schele, L., and D. Freidel. 1990. *A Forest of Kings: The Untold Story of the Ancient Maya*. New York: William Morrow.

Schiffer, M. B. 1976. *Behavioral Archaeology*. New York: Academic Press.

Schultes, R. E. 1972. An Overview of Hallucinogens in the Western Hemisphere. In *Flesh of the Gods: The Ritual Use of Hallucinogens*, edited by P. T. Furst, vii–xvi. London: Allen and Unwin.

Schultes, R. E., and A. Hofmann. 1972. *The Botany and Chemistry of Hallucinogens*. Springfield, Ill.: Charles C. Thompson.

———. 1980. *Plants of the Gods: Origins of Hallucinogenic Use*. New York: McGraw-Hill.

Selim, J. 2000. Chinatown, 1000 B.C. *Discover*, February.

Shafer, H. J. 1986. *Ancient Texans: Rock Art and Lifeways along the Lower Pecos*. Austin: Texas Monthly Press.

Shanks, M., and I. Hodder. 1995. Processual, Postprocessual and Interpretive Archaeologies. In *Interpreting Archaeology: Finding Meaning in the Past*, edited by I. Hodder, M. Shanks, A. Alexandri, V. Buchli, J. Carman, J. Last, and G. Lucas, 3–28. London: Routledge.

Shanks, M., and C. Tilley. 1987. *Re-Constructing Archaeology: Theory and Practice*. Cambridge, England: Cambridge University Press.

———. 1989. Archaeology into the 1990s. *Norwegian Archaeological Review* 22:1–14.

Sharon, D. 1972. San Pedro Cactus in Peruvian Folk Healing. In *Flesh of the Gods: The Ritual Use of Hallucinogens*, edited by P. T. Furst, 114–35. London: Allen and Unwin.

Siegel, R. K. 1973. An Ethnological Search for Self-Administration of Hallucinogens. *International Journal of the Addictions* 8:373–93.

———. 1977. Hallucinations. *Scientific American* 237(4):132–40.

———. 1978. Cocaine Hallucinations. *American Journal of Psychiatry* 135:309–14.

———. 1989. *Intoxication: Life in Pursuit of Artificial Paradise*. New York: Dutton.

Siegel, R. K., and M. E. Jarvik. 1975. Drug-Induced Hallucinations in Animals and Man. In *Hallucinations: Behaviour, Experience, and Theory*, edited by R. K. Seigel and L. J. West, 81–161. New York: Dutton.

Siskin, E. E. 1983. *Washoe Shamans and Peyotists: Religious Conflicts in an American Indian Tribe*. Salt Lake City: University of Utah Press.

Smith, V. 1944. Sheep Hunting Artists of Black Canyon Walls. *Desert Magazine* 7(5).

Solecki, R. S. 1989. On the Evidence for Neanderthal Burial. *Current Anthropology* 30:324.

Statnekov, D. K. 1987. *Animated Earth*. Berkeley: North Atlantic Book.

Steward, J. H. 1929. Petroglyphs of California and Adjoining States. *University of California Papers in American Archaeology and Ethnology* 24(2). Berkeley: University of California.

———. 1938. *Basin-Plateau Aboriginal Socio-political Groups*. Bureau of American Ethnology Bulletin, no. 120. Washington, D.C.: Smithsonian Institution.

———. 1941. Cultural Elements Distributions: XIII, Nevada Shoshoni. *Anthropological Records*, 4(2):209–359.

———. 1943. Cultural Elements Distribution: XIII, Northern Gosiute Shoshoni. *Anthropological Records* (Berkeley) 8:263–392.

———. 1955. *Theory of Culture Change*. Urbana: University of Illinois Press.

———. 1963. Review of "Prehistoric Rock Art of Nevada and Eastern California" by R. F. Heizer and M. A. Baumhoff. *American Anthropologist* 65:976–77.

———. 1968. Foreword. In *Rock Drawings of the Coso Range* by C. Grant, J. W. Baird, and J. K. Pringle. Maturango Museum Publication 4. Ridgecrest, Calif.: Maturango Museum Press.

Stringer, C., and C. Gamble. 1993. *In Search of the Neanderthals*. New York: Thames and Hudson.

Strong, W. D. 1936. Anthropological Theory and Archaeological Fact. In *Essays in Anthropology Presented to A. L. Kroeber*, edited by R. H. Lowie, 359–70. Berkeley: University of California Press.

Sullivan, L. 1988. *Icanchu's Drum.* New York: Free Press.

Tart, C. 1975. *Transpersonal Psychologies.* New York: Harper and Row.

Taylor, N. 1966. *Narcotics: Nature's Dangerous Gifts.* New York: Dell.

Taylor, W. W. 1967. Reprint. *A Study of Archaeology.* Memoir 69. Carbondale, Ill.: American Anthropological Association. Original edition: 1948.

Toulmin, S. 1977. From Form to Function: Philosophy and History of Science in the 1950s and Now. *Daedalus* 106(3):143–62.

Trigger, B. G. 1981. Archaeology and the Ethnographic Present. *Anthropologica* 23:3–17.

———. 1984. Archaeology at the Crossroads: What's New? *Annual Review of Anthropology* 13:275–300.

———. 1989. *A History of Archaeological Thought.* Cambridge: Cambridge University Press.

———. 1995. Expanding Middle-Range Theory. *Antiquity* 69:449–58.

Trinkaus, E. 1983. *The Shanidar Neanderthals.* New York: Academic Press.

———. 1986. The Neanderthals and the Origins of Modern Humans. *Annual Review of Anthropology* 15:193–218.

Turner, C., and G. E. Hannon. 1988. Vegetational Evidence for Late Quaternary Climatic Changes in Southwest Europe in Relation to the Influence of the North Atlantic Ocean. *Philosophical Transactions of the Royal Society of London* 318:451–85.

Vastokas, J. M., and R. K. Vastokas. 1973. *Sacred Art of the Algonkians: A Study of the Petersborough Petroglyphs.* Petersborough, Ont.: Mansard Press.

Villavicencio, M. 1858. *Geografía de la República del Ecuador.* New York: Robert Craighead.

Voegelin, E. W. 1938. Tubatulabal Ethnography. *Anthropological Research* (Berkeley) 2(1):1–90.

Von Winning, H. 1969. A Toad Effigy Vessel from Nayarít. *The Masterkey* 43:29–32.

Wadley, L. 1987. *Later Stone Age Hunters and Gatherers of the Southern Transvaal: Social and Ecological Interpretation.* Cambridge Monographs in African Archaeology, no. 25. British Archaeological Reports International Series, no. 380, Oxford.

Waring, A. J. Jr., and P. Holder. 1945. A Prehistoric Ceremonial Complex in the Southeastern United States. *American Anthropologist* 47:1–34.

Wasson, R. G. 1957. The Magic Mushroom. *Life Magazine,* 13 May.

———. 1968. *Soma: Divine Mushroom of Immortality.* New York: Harcourt Brace Jovanovich.

Wasson, R. G., and V. P. Wasson. 1957. *Russia, Mushrooms and History,* 2 vols. New York: Pantheon.

Watson, P. J. 1995. Archaeology, Anthropology, and the Culture Concept. *American Anthropologist* 97:683–94.

Weber, M. 1975. *Roscher and Kries: The Logical Problems of Historical Economies.* Translated by G. Oakes. New York: Free Press.

Wedel, W. R. 1941. *Environment and Native Subsistence Economies in the Central Great Plains.* Smithsonian Miscellaneous Collections, no. 101(3). Washington, D.C.: Smithsonian Institution.

Weil, A. T. 1972. *The Natural Mind: An Investigation of Drugs and the Higher Consciousness.* Boston, Mass.: Houghton Mifflin.

Wellman, K. F. 1978. North American Indian Rock Art and Hallucinogenic Drugs. *Journal of the American Medical Association* 239:1524–27.

———. 1979. *A Survey of North American Indian Rock Art.* Graz, Austria: Akademische Druck-und-Verlagsanstalt.

White, L. A. 1949. The *Science of Culture.* New York: Farrar, Straus.

———. 1959. *The Evolution of Culture*. New York: McGraw-Hill.

Whiting, B. B. 1950. *Paiute Sorcery*. Viking Fund Publications in Anthropology, no. 15. New York: Viking Fund.

Whitley, D. S. 1982a. Note on the Coso Petroglyphs, the Etiological Mythology of the Western Shoshone, and the Interpretation of Rock Art. *Journal of California and Great Basin Anthropology* 4:210–22.

———. 1982b. The Study of North American Rock Art: A Case Study from South-Central California. Ph.D. diss. Department of Anthropology, University of California, Los Angeles.

———. 1987. Socioreligious Context and Rock Art in East-Central California. *Journal of Anthropological Archaeology* 6:159–88.

———. 1988. Reply. "The Signs of All Times." *Current Anthropology* 29:238.

———. 1992a. Prehistory and the Post-positive Science: A Prolegomenon to Cognitive Archaeology. In *Archaeological Method and Theory* vol. 4, edited by M. B. Schiffer, 57–100. Tucson: University of Arizona Press.

———. 1992b. Shamanism and Rock Art in Far Western North America. *Cambridge Archaeological Journal* 2:89–113.

———. 1992c. Cation-Ratio Dating of Rock Engravings from Klipfontein, Northern Cape Province, South Africa. Paper presented at the XIth Biannual Meeting of the Society of Africanist Archaeologists, University of California, Los Angeles.

———. 1994a. By the Hunter, for the Gatherer: Art, Social Relations and Subsistence in the Prehistoric Great Basin. *World Archaeology* 25:356–72.

———. 1994b. Ethnography and Rock Art in the Far West: Some Archaeological Implications. In *New Light on Old Art: Recent Advances in Hunter-Gatherer Rock Art Research*, edited by D. S. Whitley and L. L. Loendorf, 81–93. Los Angeles: Institute of Archaeology, University of California.

———. 1994c. Shamanism, Natural Modeling and the Rock Art of Far Western North America. In *Shamanism and Rock Art in North America*, edited by S. Turpin, 1–43. Special Publication 1. San Antonio, Tex.: Rock Art Foundation.

———. 1996. *A Guide to Rock Art Sites*. Missoula, Mont.: Mountain Press.

———. 1998a. Finding Rain in the Desert: Landscape, Gender and Far Western North American Rock Art. In *The Archaeology of Rock-Art*, edited by C. Chippindale and P. S. C. Taçon, 11–29. Cambridge: Cambridge University Press.

———. 1998b. Meaning and Metaphor in the Coso Petroglyphs: Understanding Great Basin Rock Art. In *Coso Rock Art: A New Perspective*, edited by E. Younkin, 109–74. Ridgecrest, Calif.: Maturango Museum Press.

———. 1998c. New Approaches to Old Problems: Archaeology in Search of an Ever Elusive Past. In *Reader in Archaeological Theory: Postprocessual and Cognitive Approaches*, edited by D. S. Whitley, 1–28. London: Routledge.

———. 1998d. Science and the Concept of Sacredness: Interpretative Theory in U.S. Rock Art Research. Paper presented at the Second Alta Conference on Rock Art. Alta, Norway.

———. 1999. Shamanism and Rock Art Interpretation. Manuscript in possession of the author.

———. 2000. *The Art of the Shaman: The Rock Art of California*. Salt Lake City: University of Utah Press.

Whitley, D. S., and R. I. Dorn. 1987. Rock Art Chronology in Eastern California. *World Archaeology* 19:150–64.

———. 1988. Cation-Ratio Dating of Petroglyphs using PIXE. *Nuclear Instruments and Methods in Physics Research* B35:410–14.

———. 1993 New Perspectives on the Clovis vs. Pre-Clovis Controversy. *American Antiquity* 58:626–47.

Whitley, D. S., R. I. Dorn, J. M. Simon, R. Rechtman, and T. K. Whitley. 1999. Sally's Rockshelter and the Archaeology of the Vision Quest. *Cambridge Archaeological Journal* 9(2):221–47.

Whitley, D. S., and L. L. Loendorf. 1994. Introduction: Off of the Cover and into the Book. In *New Light on Old Art: Recent Advances in Hunter-Gatherer Rock Art Research*, edited by D. S. Whitley and L. L. Loendorf, xi–xx. Los Angeles: Institute of Archaeology, University of California.

Wilbert, J. 1972. Tobacco and Shamanistic Ecstasy among the Warao Indians of Venezuela. In *Flesh of the Gods: The Ritual Use of Hallucinogens*, edited by P. T. Furst, 55–83. London: Allen and Unwin.

———. 1977. The Calabash of the Ruffled Feathers. In *Stones, Bones, and Skin: Ritual and Shamanic Art*. Edited by Artscanada, 58–61. Toronto: Arts Canada.

Wilke, P. J., and C. Rector. 1984. A Reconsideration of the Prehistoric Rock Art of the Coso Range, Inyo County, California. Paper presented at the 19th Great Basin Anthropological Conference, Boise, Idaho.

Willey, G. R. 1953. *Prehistoric Settlement Patterns in the Virú Valley, Peru*. Bureau of American Ethnology Bulletin no. 155. Washington, D.C.: U.S. Government Printing Office.

———. 1974. The Virú Valley Settlement Pattern Study. In *Archaeological Researches in Retrospect*, edited by G. R. Willey, 147–76. Cambridge, Mass.: Winthrop.

———. 1977. The Rise of Classic Maya Civilization: A Pasion Valley Perspective. In *The Origins of Maya Civilization*, edited by R. E. W. Adams, 133–57. Albuquerque: University of New Mexico Press.

Willey, G. R., and J. A. Sabloff. 1980. *A History of American Archaeology*. 2nd ed. San Francisco: Freeman.

Winkelman, M. 1989. Shamans and Other "Magico-Religious" Healers: A Cross-Cultural Study of Their Origins, Nature, and Social Transformations. *Ethos* X:308–52.

Wobst, H. M. 1978. The Archaeo-Ethnology of Hunter-Gatherers or the Tyranny of the Ethnographic Record in Archaeology. *American Antiquity* 43:303–9.

Wrangham, R. W., and J. Goodall. 1989. Chimpanzee Use of Medicinal Leaves. In *Understanding Chimpanzees*, edited by P. G. Heltne and L. A. Marquardt, 22–37. Cambridge: Harvard University Press.

Wylie, A. 1982. Epistemological Issues Raised by a Structuralist Archaeology. In *Symbolic and Structural Archaeology*, edited by I. Hodder, 39–42. Cambridge: Cambridge University Press.

———. 1985. The Reaction Against Analogy. In *Advances in Archaeological Method and Theory*, vol. 8, edited by M. B. Schiffer, 63–111. New York: Academic Press.

———. 1988. Comment on "The Signs of the Times." *Current Anthropology* 29:231–32.

———. 1993. A Proliferation of New Archaeologies: "Beyond Objectivism and Relativism." In *Archaeological Theory: Who Sets the Agenda?* edited by N. Yoffee and A. Sherratt, 20–26. Cambridge, England: Cambridge University Press.

Yoffee, N., and A. Sherratt. 1993. Introduction: The Sources of Archaeological Theory. In *Archaeological Theory: Who Sets the Agenda?* edited by N. Yoffee and A. Sherratt, 1–9. Cambridge, England: Cambridge University Press.

Zigmond, M. 1977. The Supernatural World of the Kawaiisu. In *Flowers of the Wind: Papers on Ritual, Myth and Symbolism in California and the Southwest,* edited by T. C. Blackburn, 59–95. Socorro, N.Mex.: Ballena Press.

Index

About the Author

JAMES L. PEARSON received a B.A. in economics from Loyola University of Los Angeles in 1960 and spent the next three decades as an executive in the business world. Pursuing a lifelong fascination with archaeology, he returned to academia as a graduate student in 1993 and received his M.A. in anthropology from California State University, Long Beach, in 1995. He entered the University of California at Santa Barbara in 1995 and received a Ph.D. in anthropology in 2000.

Pearson has served as field director for archaeological excavations in the western Great Basin. Although trained as a hands-on "dirt" archaeologist, his current focus is on the archaeology of the mind. He has traveled extensively and lectured to grammar school students, university seminars, museum groups, and business organizations, as he is particularly interested in bringing archaeology to the general public.